Integration in Psychotherapy

Integration in Psychotherapy
Models and Methods

Edited by

Jeremy Holmes

Consultant Psychotherapist,
North Devon;
Senior Lecturer in Psychotherapy,
University of Exeter

and

Anthony Bateman

Consultant Psychotherapist,
Barnet, Enfield and
Haringey Mental Health Trust; and
Honorary Senior Lecturer,
Royal Free and
University College Medical School

OXFORD
UNIVERSITY PRESS

This book has been printed digitally and produced in a standard specification
in order to ensure its continuing availability

OXFORD
UNIVERSITY PRESS

Great Clarendon Street, Oxford OX2 6DP

Oxford University Press is a department of the University of Oxford.
It furthers the University's objective of excellence in research, scholarship,
and education by publishing worldwide in

Oxford New York

Auckland   Cape Town Dar es Salaam Hong Kong Karachi
Kuala Lumpur Madrid Melbourne Mexico City Nairobi
New Delhi Shanghai Taipei Toronto
With offices in
Argentina Austria Brazil Chile Czech Republic France Greece
Guatemala Hungary Italy Japan South Korea Poland Portugal
Singapore Switzerland Thailand Turkey Ukraine Vietnam

Oxford is a registered trade mark of Oxford University Press
in the UK and in certain other countries

Published in the United States
by Oxford University Press Inc., New York

ISBN 978-0-19-263237-1

Printed and bound by CPI Antony Rowe, Eastbourne

Contents

Contributors

Eia Asen
Consultant Psychotherapist,
Maudsley Hospital,
Denmark Hill,
London SE5.

Anthony W. Bateman
Consultant Psychotherapist, Barnet,
Enfield, and Haringey Mental Health
Trust, and Royal Free and University
College Medical Schools, London, UK.

Chess Denman
Consultant Psychotherapist,
Department of Psychotherapy,
Addenbrooke's Hospital,
Cambridge CB2 2QQ, UK.

Jeremy Holmes
Consultant Psychotherapist,
North and East Devon Partnership NHS
Trust, and University of Exeter, UK.

Laurie Gillies
209 Howland Avenue,
Toronto,
Ontario M5R 3B7,
Canada.

Rex Haigh
Consultant Psychotherapist,
Winterbourne Unit,
Reading, Berkshire.

Heidi L. Heard
Director of British Isles DBT Training,
St Louis, MO, USA

Chris Mace
Consultant Psychotherapist,
South Warwickshire Combined Care
NHS Trust, Yew Tree House,

Frank Margison
Consultant Psychotherapist,
Department of Psychotherapy,
Gaskell House, Swinton Grove,
Manchester M13 0EU, UK.

Kingsley Norton
Consultant Psychotherapist,
The Henderson Hospital,
2 Homeland Drive, Brighton Road,
Sutton SN2 5LT, UK.

M. J. Power
Professor of Psychology,
Department of Psychiatry,
Royal Edinburgh Hospital,
Morningside Terrace, Edinburgh EH9
1RJ, UK.

Suzie Van Marle
Consultant Psychotherapist,
Uffculme Psychotherapy Service,
Mindelsohn Way, Edgbaston,
Birmingham B15 2QR.

Chapter 1

Introduction

Jeremy Holmes and Anthony W. Bateman

Why this book?

'Glory be to God for dappled things', said Gerard Manley Hopkins, marvelling at the beauty of pattern and variety in nature. Integrative therapies are 'dappled' in the sense that they bring together elements from single traditional therapeutic modalities in an organized and systematic way, in order to enhance therapeutic efficiency. Alloys are often lighter and more durable than their component metals, while the 'tempering' of steel increases its strength.

To change the metaphor again, a well-known botanical phenomenon is the so-called 'alternation of generations'. Here simple plants vary between periods of asexual repro- duction when environmental conditions are stable and plentiful, and sexual reproduc- tion when conditions become changeable or adverse. Similarly, psychotherapies tend to breed true for periods of time, but when conditions change or ideas become repetitive or etiolated, cross-fertilization is needed, often leading to new vigour. There is a dialectic between integration and differentiation which we see played out through the theme of this book. In this introductory chapter we review the scope of integration in psychother- apy and review some historical, political, and research aspects of the subject, while offer- ing signposts to the main text as we go along.

Psychotherapy is currently in a phase of rapid change. The contribution of psycholog- ical therapies to the treatment of people suffering from mental illness is increasingly rec- ognized (Department of Health 2000), and training in psychotherapy is becoming more widespread and systematized (Bateman and Holmes 2001). Evidence-based practice is replacing methods based on tradition and authority (Department of Health 2001), and new methods of psychological therapy are being pioneered (Aveline 2001).

Much of this new growth is integrative, in both a theoretical and practical sense. At a theoretical level there is an attempt to move beyond traditional 'brand name' therapies and a focus on the fundamental mechanisms of psychological change. Overlaps and clear differences between different therapeutic approaches are being defined. In the real world of the clinic, a number of new therapies have appeared: dialectical behaviour therapy (DBT), cognitive analytic therapy (CAT), interpersonal therapy (IPT), psychodynamic interpersonal therapy (PIT), each with its own acronym, training methods, efficacy claims, and relevance to mental health work. As we shall see, all are to a greater or lesser degree integrative. CAT is eponymously so; DBT blends cognitive therapy with Zen Buddhism; IPT brings together psychodynamic and systemic approaches; while PIT springs from Jungian, literary, and existential roots. It seems that dynamic, cognitive, and systemic approaches to psychotherapy can be thought of as the 'primary colours' of integration – all hues and shades of integrative therapy can be derived from a combination of these three basic elements in varying proportions – even when the end result is strikingly different from the primary colour. From a theoretical perspective they can be thought of as operating at different levels: cognitive–behaviour therapy (CBT) at the intrapsychic level (see Chapter 2), dynamic approaches at both intrapsychic and interpersonal levels, and systemic at the social. At a practical level their fundamental contributions might be seen as follows: CBT brings the techniques of goal setting, collaboration, homework and time-limitation; dynamic therapy provides the holding and reticence that enable emergent and often unconscious meanings to surface, and to understand the difficult feelings that patients often engender in therapists; systemic therapy widens the field so that practitioners learn how to interact with more than one patient, to use paradox, and to be sensitive to the social and political aspects of therapy.

The purpose of this volume is to explore and expound these integrative currents as they impact on the spectrum of contemporary psychological therapy. In Part I leading practitioners within traditional models self-critically look outwards towards the limits and links between their own approaches and others. Part II is mainly a showcase for the cutting-edge new modalities in psychological therapy, all of which are, at this stage of their evolution, integrative. At what point a variant of therapy becomes sufficiently established (or 'speciated') to be seen as a 'pure' modality is a point for debate. Part II also includes chapters on two traditional approaches, milieu therapy and supportive therapy, which are inherently integrative.

The approach adopted here is distinct from Norcross and Goldfried's (1992) classic compilation in that we are not advocating integrative therapy as a modality of therapy in its own right, nor do we see it as inherently valuable (or indeed as something to be avoided). Rather, we are attempting to capture a particular moment in the history of psychological therapies in which flux, crossover, and recombination (to return to bio-logical metaphors) are in the air.

The idea of integration is predicated on a valid method of classification of psychologi-cal therapies. A recent UK attempt was made in the government-sponsored review *Psy-chotherapy services in England* (Department of Health 1996), which distinguished three types of psychotherapy. Type A is practised as part of a package that might include med-ication and social rehabilitation as well as a psychological intervention. Type B attempts to adapt a therapeutic strategy to the particular needs of the patient and his or her prob-lem, while Type C refers to the traditional models of therapy, such as psychoanalytic, cognitive–behavioural, or systemic. One aim of the review was to suggest ways in which psychological treatments in psychiatry could be better organized, targeted, and tailored to the needs of patients presenting to mental health services. It seems likely that, within publicly funded psychotherapy practice, integrative therapies – and Types A and B are inherently integrative – are much more widely used, and arguably more appropriate to the needs of mentally ill patients, than are more traditional 'pure' models.

Meanings of integration

Integration in therapy needs to be distinguished from eclecticism, although the terms are sometimes used interchangeably, and a clear distinction between theoretical and technical integration also needs to be considered. Integration implies the welding together of different strands into a new and coherent whole; new therapies such as CAT (Chapter 6) or DBT (Chapter 9) are integrative in this way. By contrast, the eclectic philosophers 'selected such doctrines as pleased them in every school' (*Oxford English Dictionary*), thereby implying a pick-and-mix approach that draws on the best aspects of a variety of approaches and applies them piecemeal to patients, without worrying about theoretical unity of approach.

We distinguish three main types of integration (cf. Albeniz and Holmes 1996), **organizational**, **theoretical**, and **practical**. First, therapy may be organized so that different types of treatment are offered simultaneously or sequentially to a patient suffering from an illness such as schizophrenia – here integration is a variant of eclecticism. Thus there may be a need for both family therapy to help reduce the levels of 'expressed emotion' and therefore decrease the risk of relapse, and cognitive therapy to help cope with delusions, and reduce the need for, or enhance compliance with, psychotropic drugs. This corresponds with Type A therapy as defined above.

A second meaning – 'integration in theory' – refers to hybrid therapies such as CAT or IPT, which explicitly bring together elements from other known therapies into new free-standing psychological treatments with their own methods and evolving traditions. CAT, which was originally devised as a brief therapy suitable for NHS practice and accessible to inexperienced therapists, explicitly combines cognitive elements such as diary-keeping and self-rating scales with an analytic attention to transference and counter-transference. IPT was devised as a brief, manualized, and therefore researchable therapy for depression.

Mace (Chapter 5) makes an interesting distinction between integrative therapies such as IPT (Chapter 8) and PIT (Chapter 7) which, he suggests, draw mainly on common therapeutic factors such as secure attachment, attunement, and remoralization, and more complex integrative therapies such as CAT (Chapter 6) and DBT (Chapter 10). The latter group have an integrative theoretical structure that goes beyond common factors. Thus CAT is critical of the patient passivity which it sees as implicit in psychoanalytic therapy (see Chapter 2), and draws on Vygotskian ideas about active learning to justify its more 'cognitive' elements. Conversely, DBT starts from the limitations of CBT (Chapter 3) when faced with very disturbed patients for whom the very idea of change is intensely threatening, and balances this with ideas drawn from Zen Buddhism (also relevant to supportive therapy, see Chapter 11), which upholds the patient's need and right to live as best they can within the limitations of their disability.

Thus at a theoretical level integrative therapies may be those that emphasize common factors in psychotherapy or those that attempt a synthesis of ideas under an innovative theoretical rubric. The latter can also be viewed from a meta-theoretical perspective – that is, a theory of change which can encompass the range of therapeutic modalities. Two examples here are Ryle's procedural sequence model (see Chapter 6; Ryle 1990, and Stiles' assimilation model (see Chapter 7; Stiles 1990).

A third facet of integration in psychotherapy – which might be referred to as 'integration in practice' – refers to the flexibility which is to be found in the practice of mature clinicians, whatever their basic training, in which they will often consciously or unconsciously bring in elements of technique or theory borrowed from other disciplines. Thus analysts present cognitive challenges to their patients, or make behavioural suggestions, while therapists with a cognitive–behavioural background, as their therapies extend in time, may well work with transferential aspects of their patients' behaviour, such as non-compliance with homework tasks or persistent lateness. Psychologists are often explicitly trained to work in this way, which corresponds with 'Type B' in the NHSE (National Health Service Executive) classification. Here integration takes on a developmental aspect as clinicians move, often over many years, from initial naivety and natural helpfulness, through mastery of a therapeutic modality, and finally to the mature stages of their clinical practice. Integration tends to be most popular at the first and third phases of this process.

Forces of change

There are many interwoven and competing pressures forcing change in psychotherapy theory and practice. In true dynamic fashion we see this change as resulting from both present circumstances and past experience. As in therapy, history informs the present and the present is used to reappraise history.

History of integration

Attempts to weld together the diverse approaches to psychotherapy are not new. As Bateman points out (Chapter 2), even Freud recommended sequential treatment using different psychological techniques for particular patients. A number of his followers experimented with varied techniques (Ferenczi 1922), but the competitive 'cold war' between behaviour therapy and psychoanalytic therapy, so prominent in their early years, meant that practitioners had little choice but to maintain ideological faith since training institutes and professional organizations demanded allegiance. Loyalty was expected and practitioners were often unaware of different theories and clinical methods.

Paradoxically this tense interaction of tenaciously held theoretical and clinical views might, in part, have contributed to the recent rapprochement. Returning to our earlier metaphor, environmental conditions have ushered in sexual reproduction. Propagation of pure forms of therapies has threatened their survival since clinicians find them inadequate for the complexity of contemporary clinical work. Practitioners and academics are reappraising their firmly held views, adapting them according to new findings of research and clinical practice, and training organizations are insisting that students gain experience in other therapies as well as their main discipline. Weaving together different psychotherapeutic techniques has gained pace, driven by political, clinical, social, educational, research, and financial forces – and disillusionment.

Disillusionment

New drugs are habitually greeted with enthusiasm and hope; similarly, emerging psychotherapies are often embraced as a new cure. But just as the side effects of a drug may jeopardize its extensive use and further development, the limitations of a therapy can lead to disillusionment before it finds its rightful place as an appropriate treatment for particular individuals in specific circumstances. The early excitement about psychoanalysis as an effective 'talking cure' for neurosis, or the hope of behaviour therapy as a potent modifier of maladaptive behaviour, have been tempered by a more balanced view. But not always before a sense of disillusionment has set in for many of their practitioners. Dissatisfaction with both psychoanalysis and behaviour therapy led to the development of cognitive–behaviour therapy, which itself was greeted with much the same enthusiasm as psychoanalysis had been half a century earlier. But these early hopes have not been fully realized. Symptom relief in complex cases is proving more difficult than predicted. Treatments are becoming longer. Pure theories and pure techniques are inadequate to explain and to treat complex psychological problems. Narrow conceptual positions and simplistic answers to major problems are inadequate. The contemporary zeitgeist demands a reassessment of theory and clinical practice, and integration has become the vehicle in which this review is taking place. (See Kay 2001 for a discussion of these topics.)

Emergent therapies

The phenomenal growth of psychotherapies is largely a manifestation of these integrative tendencies at their most promiscuous. In the 1960s there were about 60 different forms of psychotherapy, by 1975 there were over 125, 5 years later there were 200, and by the mid-eighties there were over 400 variants (Bergin 1994). Few, if any of these new psychotherapies have received the systematic appraisal that is required in the present climate of evidence-based practice. Indeed such a task is impossible. Many use techniques from more than one theoretical orientation and are commonly described as eclectic rather than integrative. Eclecticism seems to divide along professional lines, with psychologists more likely to describe themselves as practising an eclectic approach than other professional groups (Jensen 1990). Whilst eclecticism has its uses it can become an individual, idiosyncratic, pragmatic clinical approach without a coherent theory and, as such, defies definition. However, as suggested. eclectic approaches may consolidate into free-standing therapies with a coherent theory, fulfilling our second meaning of the term integrative (see p. 00). It has been interesting to observe CAT (see Chapter 6), which began life as an eclectic approach, gradually metamorphose into a therapy with its own theory and practice, and eventually become mature enough to be tested as an integrative treatment.

Eclecticism may have helped drive a further change, namely an attempt by therapists to tailor treatment interventions to specific problems. IPT was designed to treat depression (Chapter 8) and dialectical behaviour therapy to treat borderline personality disorder (Chapter 9), but both have moved away from an initially problem-orientated and pragmatic approach towards coherent conceptual and theoretical positions in which higher-order constructs inform intervention and explain change.

Socio-economic factors

Health services around the world have become increasingly subject to financial constraints. 'Third party' payers (i.e. bodies involved in the therapy that are neither the patient nor the therapist) – usually governments or insurance companies – want treatments with measurable outcomes and clear costs. At worst, quantity ('throughput') and symptom relief take precedence over quality and personality change. There is increasing emphasis on treatments which fit with a 'drug metaphor' (see below) and are cheap and quick to implement. Psychotherapists have perforce been influenced by this trend, and have developed short-term cost-effective treatments, many of which are integrative. This has inevitably meant a bias against long-term treatments. But there are signs that this short-term tendency may be changing. Realizing that some patients, particularly those with co-morbid disorders and personality disorder, need long-term therapy, therapists are once again placing an emphasis on the need for prolonged therapy and character change (Bateman and Fonagy 2000; Perry 1999). But rather than returning to pure forms of therapy, both psychoanalytic and behavioural models have begun to integrate different aspects of psychological understanding (see Chapters 2 and 3) as they attempt to find more effective methods. Nonetheless, the political emphasis remains on short-term, focused treatments, particularly due to the difficulty of subjecting long-term treatments to outcome research (Fonagy *et al.* 1999).

The 'drug metaphor' and medical model

In the 1970s, increasing anxiety about the cost of health care resulted in psychotherapy coming under the spotlight. In clinical trials, drug therapies were shown to be effective for a number of specific disorders and the National Institute of Mental Health (NIMH), a leading source of funds for psychotherapy research, decided that the same rigorous clinical trials should apply to psychotherapy (Goldfried and Wolfe 1998). Psychological treatments had to be standardized and evaluated in terms of their efficacy in reducing the symptoms of a specific DSM-defined mental disorder. Any serious doubts about the validity and current state of our knowledge of nosology, which 'resembles that of medicine a century ago' (Millon 1991) were put aside. Therapies were designed to be pure, polished, and packaged, and in being so became increasingly divorced both from everyday clinical practice and process research, which may have given a chance of defining underlying principles of integration. Efficacy of pure treatments in randomized controlled trials took precedence over effectiveness of treatments given within everyday practice. The result of this climate change is that our third facet of integration in psychotherapy – 'integration in practice', in which mature clinicians, whatever their basic training, practise flexibly – has become too 'impure' to subject to research, even though it is likely that therapist skill in integrating different techniques of psychotherapy into a coherent whole is as important for outcome as the purity of therapy (Garfield 1998).

Not surprisingly, then, research into integrative aspects of psychotherapy is sparse. Although we have tried throughout this book to ensure that each chapter addresses relevant research, the astute reader will notice that the evidence base is lacking in a number of areas and, where it is present, that there are many problems with the evidence itself. In particular, the lack of defining characteristics of integrated therapies, or their impurity, makes research difficult and leads to a danger that there is no consistency between studies even of the same named integrative therapy. A de-emphasis on process research means that if a particular integrative therapy is shown to be effective we still do not know what its 'active ingredients' are. Are they factors common to all therapies, are they unique aspects of the therapy itself, or are they the way in which the therapy is delivered? Similarly we do not know why a therapy may fail to show a positive outcome. Studies failing to show a positive outcome for DBT (Chapter 9) have been criticized for not applying DBT adequately (Linehan 2000), and the application of CBT in the NIMH trial has been questioned simply because there was equivalence between the potency of psychotherapeutic treatments (for a detailed discussion of this, see Chapter 3; Elkin *et al.* 1989). We are tempted to suggest that this might not have happened had CBT been shown to be more effective than IPT (Jacobson 2000)!

In contrast to these rather negative effects of the medical model on psychotherapy, it has ensured that therapies are properly packaged and assessed. Practitioners and researchers have been required to formalize exactly what they do and show that they are delivering it in an effective form. Nonetheless, it continues to constrain our understanding of the process of therapy by focusing on symptom reduction and remission of 'disease'. Failure to understand the way in which therapists intervene responsively according to their own and their clients interpersonal styles disadvantages the development of integration of effective therapeutic process on which overall outcome may be dependent.

Integration, common factors of therapy, and the therapeutic alliance

Whilst all therapies maintain that the quality of relationship between patient and therapist is pivotal, integrative therapies tend to place generic aspects of therapy at their centre and to foster a strong collaboration within a therapeutic alliance (Norcross 1992). The alliance is thus a key area for integration. It consists of four components (Gaston 1990):

◆ the ability of the patient to work purposefully in therapy;
◆ the capacity of the patient to form a strong affective bond to the therapist;
◆ the therapist's skill at providing empathic understanding;
◆ patient–therapist agreement on goals and tasks.

IPT (Chapter 8) actively encourages the therapeutic alliance. Similarly PIT (Chapter 7) pays careful attention to the emotional relationship between patient and therapist. Some have argued that the considerable overlap between psychotherapies compromises the possibility of reaching conclusions concerning relative effectiveness (Goldfried 1995).

The consistent finding that therapy outcome correlates reliably with patient–therapist alliance implies that stronger alliances should be associated with better outcomes, and indeed this seems to be the case (Stiles *et al.* 1998). The alliance is formed through the creation of a facilitative atmosphere between patient and therapist and is independent of the type of therapy. It may be strengthened or weakened by therapy-specific interventions and is probably dependent more on their style, timing, and affective content than on their type (Lambert and Bergin 1994). Overall the alliance has become the 'quintessential integrative variable' (Wolfe 1988).

Common factors such as the therapeutic relationship, the creation of hope, explanations, a pathway to recovery, and opportunity for emotional release remain important explanatory variables accounting for the similar outcomes for different therapies in the same conditions. Perhaps this constant finding has fuelled integration of therapies more than anything else. To give but two examples: Burns and Nolen-Hoeksema (1992) found that in cognitive therapy for depression, therapeutic empathy was highly positively correlated with decreases in measures of depression; Castonguay *et al.* (1996a) found that the therapeutic alliance and the client's emotional involvement in therapy were positively correlated with outcome, whereas the therapist's focus on distorted cognitions was not. Such findings have led practitioners to go beyond their training, to broaden their views, and to combine both common factors and specific techniques from a number of therapies, identifying themselves as integrationists (Garfield 1994). Lambert and Bergin (1994) concluded that this 'reflects a healthy response to empirical evidence and a rejection of previous trends toward rigid allegiances to schools of treatment'.

Conclusions

As will already be apparent, those looking in this book for a manifesto for psychotherapy integration will be disappointed. We try throughout to maintain a balanced approach, looking at the strengths and weaknesses of the integrative stance. Integration in its most general sense is both necessary and inescapable in that any therapeutic technique has to be adapted to the particular needs of each client and the context of therapy is as important as the training of the therapist. Context here refers to the particular nature and background of therapist and client, and to the setting in which they meet. Context literally means to 'weave together'. Therapist and client create the warp and woof of their joint work; or to use modernist jargon, they co-create a new integrative 'text' which is their unique therapeutic dialogue. Both Asen (Chapter 4) and Mace (Chapter 5) imply that there is an inherent tension between the therapist and her model pushing for focus and adherence, and the influence of the patient which widens the therapy process towards a broader more inclusive set of responses. Similarly the enterprise of psychotherapy is inherently integrative in that it aims to help the client recover and weave together disparate aspects of the self which, due to developmental difficulties and/or defensive strategies, are dis-integrated at the start of therapy (see Chapter 5).

To be interested in integration implies a questioning of established 'brand name' therapies. A given therapeutic modality is often more than a therapeutic technique – it can be a belief system, rallying call, or even a flag of convenience. At their best, integrative approaches move beyond the politics of psychotherapy to common factors and underlying mechanisms of human psychological change. But there is also a negative aspect to integration that also needs to be held in mind. There are real distinctions between the techniques and philosophies of the different therapeutic modalities, and glossing over difference or over-emphasizing commonalities can be a form of unconscious attack leading to a destructive mishmash rather than the emergence of valuable new paradigms.

Similarly, at the level of practice there are real difficulties in working integratively. Successful therapy requires a firm frame that cannot be disrupted by sudden lurches from one modality to another, however justified under the rubric of integration or eclecticism. Even within a particular discipline integrative training can be testing for students if they are expected to assimilate, say, Freudian, Kleinian, and Jungian approaches, or even individual and group approaches. To return to analogies and metaphors, multilingualism is admirable, but the attempt to create an 'integrative' European language, Esperanto, has never really caught on. It may be better to be able to play one musical instrument well and in all keys than to have a superficial acquaintance with a variety of instruments (see Chapter 3). The research evidence is helpful here in that it suggests that psychotherapy outcomes are better where practitioners stick within one therapeutic frame (which can of course be an integrative model such as CAT); but also, in treating difficult patients, therapists who are able to apply their models flexibly (i.e., perhaps integratively) get the best results (Luborsky *et al.* 1997). In short, we invite the reader to share our stance of enthusiasm and interest in integration, tempered with benign scepticism, seeing it as an essential 'moment' (both in the temporal and dynamic sense) in the evolution of psychological therapies, and to enjoy its exponents as they argue their case through the course of this book. As for the future of psychotherapy integration, we predict that there will simultaneously be attempts to deepen understanding of common factors and fundamental mechanisms of change in psychotherapy that cut across traditional boundaries, and the emergence of further integrative therapies tailored to particular social, administrative, and psychiatric contexts. We shall remain keen participant observers of both trends.

Part 1

Theory

Chapter 2

Integrative therapy from an analytic perspective

Anthony W. Bateman

Introduction

Freud (1919) recommended the integration of behavioural and analytic techniques for agoraphobic patients, suggesting that the analyst has to 'induce them by the influence of the analysis to go out alone' and that 'only when that has been achieved at the physician's demand will the associations and memories come into the patient's mind which enable the phobia to be resolved'. But nearly a century later, Freud's suggestion of clinical integration using various therapeutic techniques for different aspects of a disorder remains unrealized even though most patients with co-morbidity need combined approaches to their problems. Practitioners and their therapies, including psychoanalysts and psychoanalysis, continue to 'stand apart' both theoretically and clinically, stubbornly refusing to adapt and develop through each other. They argue that their therapy is distinct and 'brand' it to make it theirs and to maintain difference. But, as we shall see, this difference through 'brand-naming' is, to some extent, illusory.

Historically psychoanalysis itself has been the prototypical therapy on which other therapies have either based or differentiated themselves. Given their common heritage, some integration of both theory and clinical practice might be expected. Yet it is apparently rare. It seems that the children and grandchildren of the father of all therapies have been so keen to develop their own identities during their adolescence that links have been severed, history denied, similarity ignored, and difference emphasized. In typical parental fashion, psychoanalysis has become defensive and not acquitted itself well, failing to learn from its offspring, ignoring new ideas, resisting change, and seeing other therapies at best as a dilution of the 'pure gold' of psychoanalysis, and at worst as misguided. It has become a parent who forgets his own past. Ferenczi's (1922) experiments with active techniques and relaxation, with the analyst adopting definite roles and attitudes, were forerunners of many present-day therapies, and one of the first attempts to speed up the process of analysis and make it more widely available. Freud anticipated that 'the large scale application of our therapy will compel us to alloy the pure gold of analysis freely with the copper of direct suggestion'; he went on, 'whatever form this psychotherapy for the people may take, whatever the elements out of which it is compounded, its most effective and most important ingredients will assuredly remain those borrowed from strict and untendentious psychoanalysis' (Freud 1919).

Unable to consider new findings and fresh ideas, particularly from cognitive theory and cognitive–behaviour therapy, psychoanalysis is in danger not only of becoming intellectually isolated but also of becoming a body of knowledge uninfluenced by and unable to influence other disciplines. In the end this weakens its own development, impoverishes that of others and is likely to discourage the cross-fertilization that would benefit both parent and offspring.

I will argue in this chapter that, despite the schisms, the climate is changing and integration is taking place both at a theoretical level and in clinical practice. Many practitioners, including psychoanalysts, are applying their 'brand-named' psychotherapies in a flexible manner, using different techniques at the level of clinical application, and all are working within the domain of interpersonal process. Psychoanalysts may give cognitive challenges to their patients, or even on occasions make judicious behavioural suggestions as Freud recommended, while cognitive–behavioural practitioners pay increasing attention to transference, especially in longer-term work with patients with personality disorder. Brand name of a therapy no longer indicates what happens in practice. Mature clinicians, consciously and unconsciously, bring in elements of technique or theory borrowed from other models. Because psychoanalysis and cognitive approaches are commonly set against each other, I will use them in this chapter to make a case that integration from a psychoanalytic viewpoint is neither a threat to psychoanalysis itself nor a danger to the further development of cognitive approaches. On the contrary, increasing the interchange between the two is likely to increase the strength of both. The drive for this process is coming from the foot soldiers rather than the generals. A groundswell of opinion, particularly within the small army of empirical researchers, is forcing practitioners to consider and reconsider their practice and to make fewer theoretically derived assumptions. This bottom-up approach in which clinical practice informs theoretical development has arisen from findings of psychotherapy process research, which has begun to pay increasing attention to psychotherapy as applied within clinical situations rather than in experimental conditions. Under these circumstances it has become clear that psychoanalysts and psychoanalytic therapists are interested in cognitive processes as well as affective drives and interpersonal dynamics, and that cognitive practitioners are paying greater attention to emotions and relational aspects of a patient's problems.

In view of this I shall reverse the traditional order of discussion and start with practice before moving on to theoretical considerations.

Practice

At first sight the practice of psychoanalysis and psychoanalytic therapy seems at variance to cognitive–behaviour therapy (CBT), with even the frame of treatment appearing markedly different. In the former the patient may lie on the couch, attend frequently, talk associatively, and explore the past, whilst in the latter the patient sits up, focuses on problems, engages in homework, and explores the present. Similarly, the activities of the therapists may look different and yet, as we shall discuss below, some of the differences are more apparent than real, implying that integration takes place within clinical practice and competent practitioners usually disregard theoretical and political polemic. They have good reason. Firstly, practitioners are aware that all therapy requires the development of an alliance between patient and therapist. Secondly, stylized, formulaic interventions are unlikely to be effective and therapists have to tailor their responses to patients according to their assessment of the therapeutic problem of the moment. Whilst this will be done within a particular framework, theory will be only one aspect of how a therapist decides to intervene. Common humanity, personal experience, empathy, therapeutic sensitivity, and other factors will all play a part. Under these circumstances it is not surprising that in everyday clinical practice different therapies look remarkably similar in some respects. Of course, therapies can be distinguished according to some types of intervention, such as the use of homework or other activity, but when actual verbal interventions of the therapists are studied the situation is less clear.

Alliance

All therapies rely on a purposeful collaboration between patient and therapist. This process of 'collaboration in tasks of therapy' (Frieswyk 1986) forms the core of the therapeutic alliance. To this extent the therapeutic alliance is a central integrational element uniting all therapies. An emotional bond and reciprocal involvement between patient and therapist needs to develop for therapy to proceed, although different therapies develop this process using contrasting techniques. Gaston (1990) has proposed that the alliance can be differentiated into four independent aspects: (1) the patient's *affective relationship* to the therapist; (2) the patient's *capacity to work* purposefully in the therapy; (3) the therapist's *understanding* and *involvement*; and (4) the patient and therapist agreement in the *goals and tasks* of treatment. All are necessary for a therapeutic alliance. Inevitably, distinct therapies place greater emphasis on some of these than others: psychoanalysis stresses the affective understanding whilst cognitive–behaviour therapy harnesses goals and tasks of treatment as an active ingredient of therapy. But whatever the route to a positive therapeutic process, there is little doubt that the alliance has an important effect on the outcome of all treatments.

In a meta-analytic study, Horvath and Symonds (1991) concluded that there was a 26% difference in level of therapeutic success dependent on the therapeutic alliance. In a more recent meta-analysis (Martin 2000) this finding was confirmed with a correlation of therapeutic alliance with outcome being persistent, even when many of the variables that have been suggested to influence the relationship of process with outcome were taken into account. Thus, although most studies show little if any difference in outcome between therapies, when there is a difference this may simply be a reflection of the alliance between patient and therapist and not a differential effect of a therapy. In general the early alliance between patient and therapist is a better predictor of success than the strength of the alliance later in therapy, although this pattern is less evident in more recent studies. There seems little doubt that the alliance, when positive, makes a substantial contribution to the outcome of all forms of therapy. Of course this could be a self-fulfilling prophecy with patients reporting a positive alliance if their treatment is going well. But studies that have looked at this possibility suggest that this is not the case. There is no evidence that patients with a good outcomes view their therapy in a more positive frame than individuals whose treatment goes less well (Roth and Fonagy 1996).

Two major hypotheses of the role of the alliance have been proposed. First, the alliance may be an active ingredient of therapy effecting change through a positive emotional relationship between patient and therapist. But just because a patient works well with a therapist is no guarantee that improvement will result and so it has been suggested that the alliance is a necessary but not sufficient condition for change, but that it activates other interventions. Different aspects of an alliance may be necessary for specific interventions and alliance characteristics may vary over the course of therapy.

Theoretically the alliance is likely to be of most importance in psychoanalytic therapies since psychoanalytic therapy uses the emotional relationship between patient and therapist as a mediator of change. However, the alliance seems equally important in other therapies. Castonguay et al. (1996b) reported significant associations between the alliance and outcome measures at mid- and post-treatment for patients receiving CBT and CBT plus an antidepressant. Gaston et al. (1998) reported that working and therapeutic alliances, as measured by the Patient Working Capacity and the Patient Commitment scales, were predictive of outcome for behaviour therapy, cognitive therapy and brief dynamic therapy. Intriguingly, separate analyses suggested that the sub-scales of the alliance held more for cognitive therapy than the other therapies, implying the alliance was mostly predictive of outcome in this therapy. This result has been previously found by others (Marmar et al. 1989). However a study by DeRubeis and Feeley (1990) concluded that the alliance is less predictive in more highly structured interventions.

The impact of the alliance on outcome has been reported both for the National Institute of Mental Health (NIMH) (Elkin et al. 1989) and the Sheffield studies (Shapiro et al. 1995). Krupnick et al. (1996) reported that the alliance level averaged over all the treatment sessions accounted for 21% of the variance in outcome in the NIMH trial. Interestingly this factor showed importance across all the treatments, including pharmacotherapy. But this group was also given clinical management, which may itself be another name for therapeutic alliance. Detailed work suggested that the alliance was greater for the most improved cases, particularly in interpersonal therapy. In the Sheffield study the results are more complex but Stiles *et al.* (1998) also found a statistically significant association between a number of outcome measures and the alliance. Overall, the results confirm the hypothesis that the alliance may act differentially across treatment modalities with effective therapeutic interventions requiring different forms of alliance for them to be successful. However, we are not yet able to differentiate which types of intervention require which element of the alliance; for example, does a transference interpretation require either an affective bond or a working collaboration, or both.

Although the alliance is a potential area of integration between therapies and was originally a psychoanalytic concept, it has been neglected by psychoanalysts over the past few decades, commonly being considered as a woolly concept used to cover idealization of the therapist (Hamilton 1996). Others have considered it as a resistance in which a patient sets up a mutually admiring and seductive transference and countertransference interplay with his or her analyst – something to which training analysts and candidates may be susceptible! It has become something that should almost be avoided and interpreted if it develops. Freud himself held ambiguous views about the topic, noting that some idealization and erotic attraction on the one hand were possible resistances but on the other were also necessary to provide the active ingredients to keep the patient in treatment. Indeed, the high drop-out rate of patients from psychoanalytic treatments (Gunderson *et al.* 1989) may be related to inadequate attention being paid over recent years to the development of a therapeutic alliance.

The therapeutic alliance has been embraced by all therapies to a greater or lesser extent. It is recognized that patients are more likely to remain in treatment if the process on which they are embarked is understandable to them and they feel that the therapist is able to explain it to them. In the Sheffield study clients' endorsement of the treatment principles of psychodynamic interpersonal therapy after the initial session predicted improvement (Hardy 1995). A positive regard on the part of the patient for the therapist, and engendering a feeling that the therapist is on your side, are encouraged in many therapies, for example interpersonal therapy (IPT) (Chapter 8). Whilst this inevitably has its dangers, psychoanalysis has the tools with which to explore both the positive and negative aspects of the alliance. If it does so methodically it can provide a more balanced view, clarifying when it is a resistance, as surely it can be, and helping to decide when it should not be encouraged, and when it is an essential aspect of treatment.

Therapist intervention

At any moment in therapy, practitioners are faced with choices about how to respond to the content or form of a patient's talk. These choices are often guided by an underlying theory about what facilitates change, although it seems that experience about what works for whom may override theoretical views and training (Goldfried and Wolfe 1998). Nevertheless, there is evidence that therapists of different orientations use different interventions (see Blagys 2000 for review). This may seem obvious but the situation is more confused than may be expected from theory. *A silent, unspoken integration of different models may be occurring within clinical practice.*

In early work in this field, Stiles (1979) found distinct differences in intervention between client-centred, gestalt, and psychoanalytic therapists. Client-centred therapists relied heavily on reflecting and acknowledgement, gestalt therapists on advisement, questions, and interpretations, and psychoanalytic therapists on interpretation, acknowledgement, questions, and reflections. These results have been replicated in various ways. For example Stiles, Shapiro, and Firth-Cozens (1988) found significantly more instructions, advisements, and questions in CBT and reflections in psychodynamic therapy. Overall, the data from research trials suggest that whilst there is equivalence in outcome of different therapies in most conditions, there is non-equivalence of process.

But it is more informative to consider not just the types of intervention that therapists use in research trials but also to focus more on those interventions that are associated with change and to look at what practitioners do in clinical practice. Overlap between therapies seems to be more apparent in these two areas. Gaston *et al.* (1998) observed that in both brief dynamic therapy and CBT, therapists gave less supportive interventions towards the end of therapy than they did in early and middle phases of treatment. Presumably they were less necessary as patients improved. Therapists were not doing the same thing throughout treatment. In the same study the authors found that CBT therapists delivered exploratory interventions, although less than dynamic therapists, but that these exploratory interventions, when considered across sessions, contributed to outcome only in CBT. These results are consistent with results reported by Jones and Pulos (1993). They found that outcome in cognitive therapy was not predicted by cognitive techniques but was significantly associated with psychodynamic exploratory interventions, even though such techniques were not part of the manualized treatment. The possibility that an interpersonal/exploratory focus in cognitive therapy would be beneficial is also suggested by Ablon and Jones (1998), who found that interventions which addressed the interpersonal and developmental domains were associated with improvement in cognitive therapy.

Wiser and Goldfried (1996) found that, in sessions identified as important for change, CBT practitioners commonly used interpretations, questions, and reflections, all of which are normally identified as psychodynamic techniques. Relatively few between-orientation differences were noted by Goldfried *et al.* (1998b) in those sessions that master therapists identified as significant. Those sessions characterized as significant focussed on clients ability to observe themselves in an objective way, their evaluation of their self-worth, their expectations about their future, their thoughts in general, and their emotions, irrespective of theoretical orientation. Crits-Christoph *et al.* (1999) found that CBT therapists allowed patients to talk about interpersonal topics if patients seemed interested in doing so, but did not do so when patients seemed uninterested. In summary, theory does not neatly translate into practice, especially in everyday clinical work.

It seems that the literature has moved over the past few years from a position of non-equivalence of process to one of greater equivalence. There are a number of reasons for this. First, both psychoanalytic therapy and cognitive treatments have moved to an interpersonal focus. Second, more research is being done with master practitioners implementing treatments (Goldfried *et al.* 1998). Third, more information is becoming available about therapy as practised within naturalistic settings compared with therapy given in clinical trials. Could it be that practitioners, expert in their own field, are practising flexibly even when a treatment is manualized? In effect they are doing what they should be doing: judging the moment-to-moment clinical situation and intervening in a manner responsive to patient need. They are all working in the interpersonal domain. This implies that all therapies are orientated and structured around a core of specific techniques but that this core is a necessary but not sufficient ingredient for change. Change can only take place if an interpersonal process between patient and therapist is created, establishing a climate of seeing things differently, of recognizing personal limitations, of understanding what is ours and what is not. Ablon and Jones (1999) argue that the patient's experience of therapy and the therapist is the key feature. Patients who form an idealized view of the therapist and establish a positive sense of self achieve a better outcome. But why should this be? Blatt *et al.* (1996, 1997) suggest that patients construct in the therapists those aspects of themselves that they feel they lack within themselves. Through internalization and identification they create themselves anew within the therapeutic relationship. Impaired or distorted interpersonal schemas and object relations are transformed into more realistic cognitive and affective representations of self and others. This process may be mediated through many different types of intervention, ranging from a focus on cognitive processes to an exploration of the interpersonal world. More controversially, could it be that if there is a cognitive focus it is the 'surprise' of interpretation that leads to change and if there is a transference focus it is the surprise of the cognitive intervention? The active ingredients are the tripping up of the unconscious, being faced with the unexpected, and seeing things in a new light. Research on attachment styles and social competencies in therapy process support this view. Mallinckrodt (2000), in a review of his own research, suggests that therapists need to manage attachment proximity in the psychotherapeutic relationship by responding to the client 'against type' using 'counter-complimentary attachment proximity strategies', which are interventions that break with the clients' expectations and past maladaptive patterns.

The present evidence suggests that practitioners of CBT are moving towards an interpersonal model, especially for more complex problems (Safran and Segal 1991). But what about the practice of psychoanalysis and psychodynamic therapy? Interpretation of unconscious phantasy, the mobilization of affect, the identification of repetitive patterns of relationships, and the interpretation of transference remain central, even though there is only modest correlation between these processes and outcome. A focus by dynamic therapists on transference issues has not consistently been linked to good outcome (Piper *et al.* 1986, 1991), although interpretation overall has emerged as a rather effective mode of intervention in a number of studies (see Bergin and Garfield 1994 for review). However, psychoanalysts have moved to a focus on the interpersonal process within sessions, and psychoanalytic theory and practice has been adapted in psychoanalytically oriented programmes for complex patients, such as those with personality disorder. This will be discussed next.

Integration and personality disorder

It is becoming increasingly evident that few models of psychotherapy are applied in a pure form, particularly in the treatment of personality disorder. Therapists are combining techniques from different orientations, devising strategies of treatment, and creating packages for patients. Outcome evaluation is hampered by the lack of specificity (Roth and Fonagy 1996). In the treatment of personality disorder practitioners make complex choices in selecting interventions that take account of both behavioural and dynamic factors. In order to enhance specificity researchers have 'manualized' treatments and developed measures to assess the extent to which therapists are able to follow protocols outlined in these. Three approaches to therapy with borderline personality disorder have so far been manualized. These include psychoanalytic psychotherapy (Kernberg *et al.* 1989), dialectical behaviour therapy (Linehan 1987), and object relations/interpersonal approaches (Dawson 1988; Marziali *et al.* 1989). The manual for cognitive analytic therapy (Chapter 6) is as yet untested (Ryle 1997).

The modified individual psychoanalytic approach adopted by Kernberg *et al.* (1989) is based on clarification, confrontation, and interpretation within a developing transference relationship between patient and therapist. Initially there is a focus and clarification of self-destructive behaviours both within and without therapy sessions. Gradually aspects of the self that are split off from the patient's core identity are challenged, especially as they impinge on chaotic impulsive behaviour, fluctuating affects, and identity conflict which itself leads to dissociation. Understanding and resolving their impact on the transference relationship becomes central. Considerable work on elaborating and validating this therapeutic approach has been performed as part of an NIMH-funded treatment development project, demonstrating that it is possible to train clinicians to use this method (Clarkin, in press).

In contrast Linehan's strategy in dialectical behaviour therapy (DBT) uses support, social skills, education, contingency management, and alternative problem-solving strategies to manage impulsive behaviour and affect dysregulation. A mix of both individual and group psychotherapy is used. However, the relationship between the patient and therapist is pivotal in helping the patient replace maladaptive actions such as self-destructive acts with adaptive responses during crises. Linehan suggests that a number of aspects 'set if off from "usual" cognitive and behavioural therapy' and that 'the emphasis in DBT on therapy-interfering behaviours is more similar to the psychodynamic emphasis on "transference" behaviours than it is to any aspect of standard cognitive-behavioural therapies'(Linehan 1993a, pp. 20–1).

The treatment strategy developed by Dawson (1988) and colleagues is named 'relationship management psychotherapy' (RMP). In essence this approach conceptualizes the borderline patient as struggling with conflicting aspects of the self, leading to instability. Interpersonal relationships, including the therapeutic relationship, become the context in which the patient tries to resolve conflicts through externalization. For example, if a therapist is optimistic and active the patient becomes pessimistic and compliant. In some ways such polarities are similar to the reciprocal roles identified in cognitive analytic therapy (Chapter 6). The task of the therapist is to alter the rigidity of the dialogue and to disconfirm the patient's distorted experience through attention to the process of sessions rather than the content of the interaction. The format is exclusively through time-limited group psychotherapy.

At first sight these three methods may sound distinctly different, ranging from individual therapy to a mix of individual and group therapy to solely group psychotherapy. But beyond that there are some striking similarities. Both Kernberg and Linehan focus initial sessions on the establishment and negotiation of a treatment contract within the framework of their approach. A particular emphasis is placed on self-destructive behaviour, especially therapy-interfering behaviour, and appropriate limits are set and renewable contracts made. Both methods carefully define the responsibilities of the therapist on how self-destructive behaviour will be handled, regular appointments are arranged, acceptance of difficulties of remaining in treatment are recognized, and explicit statements made about the possibility of failure of treatment. Identity issues are central from a psychoanalytic viewpoint and therapists are constantly on the alert for split-off aspects of patients and how these are played out in the patient–therapist relationship. In DBT there is less emphasis on identity issues, but nevertheless a 'black-and-white' cognitive style is targeted using dialectical techniques to help the patient overcome the all-or-none thinking and polarized approach to life. Both treatments prescribe the level of contact allowable between patient and therapist. In DBT, emergency sessions are allowed to enable the therapist and patient to develop alternative ways of crisis resolution other than hospital admission or self-destructive behaviour. In psychoanalytic therapy contact between sessions is not permitted, although discussion of alternative routes to support between sessions may be a focus of a consultation. Implementation of the two treatments is consistent with theoretical views. Linehan provides information about cognitive–behavioural conceptualization of self-destructive behaviour, whilst Kernberg uses exploratory interpretations using idiographic hypotheses; that is, formulations specific to that individual, relating self-destructive behaviours to feelings about treatment. Both discuss alternative pathways to resolution of conflict and distress.

In contrast to these overlaps, RMP takes a more neutral stance. No formal contract is made, no attempt is made to interpret or to explain the patient's anger or self-destructive behaviour, and no emphasis is given to education or understanding about actions or threats that may disrupt therapy. Instead the primary therapeutic task is to identify 'core messages' that reflect the polarities of conflict with which the patient is struggling. Therapists generate hypotheses about these as they are played out in the group setting whilst avoiding enacting any of the externalized, polarized selves. On theoretical grounds it may be supposed that this is the least supportive therapy for borderline patients and likely to lead to early dropout or failure to take up the offer of treatment, whilst DBT is the most supportive, given its methods and the availability of the therapist. Whilst there is no data on the dropout rate for RMP, Linehan has shown that the dropout rate is 16% in DBT, whilst that for psychoanalytic therapy is 42% (Clarkin and Kendall 1992). But the dropout rate for psychoanalytically orientated treatment may be altered. Bateman and Fonagy (1999) had an attrition rate of only 12% by focusing on engagement of the patient in treatment and assertive follow-up of non-attendance.

The marked overlap between therapies for long-term treatment of personality disorder has significant implications for research since randomized controlled trials are increasingly seen as the 'gold standard' in evaluating treatments. Not only may this control for many processes independent of the treatment and common to all psychological treatments, it also may include tests between specific competing mechanisms. But 'horse-race' comparative studies in long-term treatment are unlikely to be helpful in identifying better methods of treatment since there is so much variance within each treatment and overlap between them that differential treatment effects are likely to be masked. In effect they are all integrated treatments with a different balance of ingredients. For research purposes it is more important to isolate the effective aspects of each treatment (Waldinger and Gunderson 1984). For example the low dropout rate for DBT is of interest to all clinicians, whatever their approach, because engaging personality-disordered patients is one of the many initial challenges to overcome if constructive treatment is to follow.

The day hospital and outpatient programme described by Bateman (1997) for borderline personality disorder has been developed with 'dismantling' in mind. The effectiveness of the day hospital programme has been shown (Bateman and Fonagy 1999), but its effective ingredients remain unknown. So, using theoretical understanding and clinical experience, core aspects of the day hospital programme have been identified and packaged as an outpatient programme. In effect the complex day hospital programme had been dismantled into three specific components. Firstly, there is a psychoanalytically based exploration within the transference and counter-transference relationship of the patient's internal object relational system within a weekly individual psychoanalytic session. Secondly, a group-analytic session takes place once a week to explore relationships with others in the here and now. Thirdly, there is a weekly supportive group in which the therapists target current problems faced by the borderline patient. In this group some cognitive techniques are used but there remains a focus on learning through the group. For example, a focus on reflective capacity helps the individual to think about others within the group and to understand the mental states of others. This is based on the psychoanalytic view that borderline patients fail to fully develop a mentalizing capacity (Fonagy 1991). Thus the programme is inherently integrative in that it is based on identified problems specific to a group of patients and then combines therapeutic techniques to help with those problems.

In a recent review of psychotherapeutic treatment of personality disorder, Bateman and Fonagy (2000) conclude that treatments shown to be moderately effective have certain common features. They tend

♦ to be well-structured;

♦ to devote considerable effort to enhancing compliance;

♦ to have a clear focus, whether that focus is a problem behaviour such as self-harm or an aspect of interpersonal relationship patterns;

♦ to be theoretically highly coherent to both therapist and patient, sometimes deliberately omitting information incompatible with the theory;

♦ to be relatively long term;

♦ to encourage a powerful attachment relationship between therapist and patient, enabling the therapist to adopt a relatively active rather than passive stance;

♦ to be well integrated with other services available to the patient. In short it is the level of integration that is crucial.

One way of interpreting these observations might be that part of the benefit which personality-disordered individuals derive from psychotherapeutic treatment comes through the experience of being involved in an integrated, carefully considered, well-structured, and coherent interpersonal endeavour. Social and personal experiences such as these are *not specific to any treatment modality* but rather are a correlate of the level of seriousness and the degree of commitment with which teams of professionals approach the problem. Informed by these aspects of clinical practice, both psychoanalytic therapy and cognitive–behaviour therapy have begun to frame a theoretical understanding of personality disorder within an interpersonal domain leading to a further area for future integration.

Theory

Psychoanalysis

Wallerstein (1992) suggests that, despite the theoretical plurality of psychoanalysis, there is common ground within 'clinical theory', which can be unified in a meaningful way. In clinical psychoanalysis there has been a move away from the monolithic hegemony of one-person psychology to a two-person psychology. Psychoanalysis is no longer focused on a model of veridical interpretation of defence and impulse from a position of neutrality of the analyst. It is more concerned with relational and interactional perspectives, particularly as mediators of change. There is a focus on the affectively charged transference–counter-transference matrix. At its extreme this becomes a defining feature of analysis, for example in the intersubjective approach of Stolorow *et al.* (1987), in which the therapeutic dialogue is viewed as an interplay between two participating subjectivities. In intersubjective psychoanalysis there is no place for an objective observer, either in the patient or the analyst. The analysand's history is created by the analyst–analysand interaction. Transference has become not a displacement of the past onto the present but a way of organizing the present according to developmental models. But, in the more moderate view, the transference–counter-transference focus is viewed as an actualization within the analytic relationship of internal object relationships (Sandler 1976). The analyst is neither subjective nor objective but moves between them both as he is pulled into an enactment of an unconscious relationship fantasy. He has to extricate himself in order to interpret. The focus of treatment is on the relationship, especially in its detail, its development, its history, and in how it is actualized in the session. This psychoanalytic approach to personality is effectively an idiographic perspective looking at the individual as unique and complex, and as a product of his singular experience. He is neither subject to universal laws nor measurable on dimensions of difference. He is his own person. The personality is the personal history. The person is biographical and contextual, emerging within an almost infinite environmental milieu from a constitutional base. Questions are asked about how this individual became like this at this time and why he has reacted in this way. Individual truths become generalized and descriptions become explanations.

Surrounding this clinical theory is a metapsychology – a superstructure so complex and overwhelming that most practitioners are both dwarfed and daunted by it. But in particular it is a theory that has the flexibility to address the complexity of personality and its disorders. Personality is viewed developmentally. Object relational systems are established through internalization and identification, and modified by fantasy. Most importantly, a relationship constellation is formed which is imbued with affect. External relationships arouse these affects and with them the relational fantasy. Conversely the relational fantasy and affect require enactment within an interpersonal context and it is this that is explored within therapy through the transference– counter-transference interaction.

Cognitive therapy

CBT fits alongside the nomothetic approach to personality, which is concerned with personality in a generalized sense. It emphasizes similarities between people. It is construct-centred, looking at phenomena subordinate to personality such as needs, mechanisms, traits, and schemas. Personality becomes an amalgam of units. Testability is preserved and universal propositions are promulgated.

Like psychoanalysis, CBT is an attempt both to understand and to treat the human mind and is a clinically derived theory. But in contrast to contemporary psychoanalysis, clinical cognitive theory remains a one-person psychology. The focus is on intrapsychic process within the cognitive domain. Cognitive processes are considered to be motivational and aetiological, determining affective and behavioural responses across time and situations (Beck 1976). Changes to this basic model have occurred and there are now a number of radiating developmental theoretical lines, leading to a situation in which cognitive therapy finds itself in a similar position to psychoanalysis – a complex plurality with splits, schisms, and controversial discussions (Perris 1998).

In summary, clinical psychoanalysis has gradually been moving clinically from an individual intrapsychic exploration towards an interpersonal endeavour whilst cognitive therapy has continued to focus on internal cognitive processes and, from a theoretical viewpoint, to minimize the relationship. But CBT is now moving towards an interpersonal arena.

Cognitive developments

Until recently cognitive therapy did not have the theoretical base to conceptualize personality. This has begun to change. Schemas have been postulated as the basic building blocks of personality. A schema is an inferred 'meaning structure' in the same way as an object is within psychoanalytic theory. Schemas are essentially both conscious and non-conscious. They may change over time and be modified through experience but in personality disorders schemas cannot adapt rapidly to a changing environment. Patterns, which may have been appropriate for survival in earlier contexts, persist and become maladaptive. Affect and views of the self and others are included within schemas, along with cognition and belief, thereby bringing not only an interpersonal aspect to cognitive theory but also a developmental one (Pretzer 1996).

Young's schema-focused therapy (Young 1990) adds what he says is a deeper level of cognition, namely the early maladaptive schema (EMS). This is an enduring theme of the self and others that develops during childhood and is elaborated throughout life. In personality disorder, EMSs result from dysfunctional experiences. They disrupt affect and establish self-defeating patterns of relationships. Schemas are maintained, avoided, and compensated for. They both drive behaviour and are fuelled by the results, much like phantasied object relationships are 'actualized' in such a way that they affirm the underlying experience. Alternatively, avoidance may allow the individual to reduce unpleasant affects by developing a style that bypasses the schema and prevents its activation. A patient may withdraw and so avoid abusive relationships or take up a cognitive and behavioural style that is the opposite to a painful schema. A borderline patient whose schema of herself is as someone with unfulfilled need becomes an excellent nursery nurse. For psychoanalytic theory this is a projective identificatory system seen within the internal object system and within the interpersonal context. For CBT it is a compensatory schema.

The work of Safran and Segal (1991) shows convergence with psychoanalytic work. Influenced by Sullivan and Bowlby, Safran and Segal suggest that individuals develop internal working models of self–other interactions which are based on previous interactions with significant others. During infancy and childhood the developing interpersonal schemas enable the infant to maintain proximity to attachment figures and are repeated throughout life.

Even central concepts of psychodynamic theory such as the unconscious are being reformulated. In psychoanalytic theory the unconscious has become a metaphor for affective meanings of which the patient is unaware, and which emerge through the relationship with the analyst. Within cognitive psychology, Epstein (1994) amongst many others, has suggested a cognitive–experiential processing system in which people apprehend reality in two fundamentally different ways. One is intuitive, automatic, natural, and non-verbal whilst the other is rational, deliberate, and verbal. Neither is superior to the other. Whilst not quite having the surrounding mystique of the unconscious in analytic theory, there is agreement that many aspects of personal functioning taking place outside consciousness (Chapter 3).

This overlap with a psychoanalytic point of view results in a problem of establishing exactly what the theoretical differences are. There is a danger of denying difference in which case no true theoretical integration can take place. A strong marriage takes pleasure in difference. Procreation occurs because of difference. We are only likely to establish more potent 'offspring' therapies, especially for personality disorder, if we understand and respect difference. Thus far it seems clear that both conscious and unconscious function and cognitive and affective–experiential processing, need to be taken into account in formulating an individual's problem and in structuring treatment. Once such basic principles are established further integration cannot be far off. Psychoanalysis has the knowledge of unconscious function and of affective processing whilst cognitive approaches understand conscious function and cognitive processing. A judicious mix of the two is likely to be a potent brew for problems such as personality dysfunction. Purer forms of each may be left for other disorders or patients with particular characteristics which suit them to one therapy rather than another.

Conclusions

Further integration of psychotherapies will only come about if we identify more precisely the mechanisms of therapeutic change. It is not just a case of picking a bit of this and a bit of that. Once mediators of change are established we will need to rebuild our cherished theories, and decide on the sequencing of interventions and on whom the interventions are to be carried out. If psychoanalysis and cognitive–behaviour therapy are to remain vibrant and living disciplines they must open themselves up to each other and change according to new findings of process research. The resulting therapies will be truly integrative.

Chapter 3

Integrative therapy from a cognitive–behavioural perspective

M. J. Power

Introduction

In the A–Z guide to psychotherapies Herink (1980) documented over 250 varieties of therapy. This number had increased to about 400 by the early 1990s (Norcross 1992) and the latest estimates put the number at nearly 500. Indeed, somewhere in California there is probably another therapy being christened at this very moment. The question that must be asked of this diversity is whether 500 different therapies require 500 different mechanisms by which they operate, or whether, alternatively, there exist common factors that can offer some unification of the diverse theories and practices that occur under the label 'psychotherapy'. These common factors might apply irrespective of whether or not the therapies or therapists are effective, so the more specific question must also be asked: Does the *good* underwater massage therapist share anything in common with the *good* behaviour therapist or the *good* dynamic psychotherapist? There is in fact a growing belief that, whatever the brand name, good (i.e. effective, popular, and ethical) therapeutic practice cuts across the artificial boundaries that therapies place around themselves in order to appear distinct from their competitors. This chapter will examine some of the possibilities for the integration of theory and practice without denying the need for at least some of the existing technical diversity. A framework will be presented, therefore, from which the strengths and weaknesses of different therapies can be viewed, but beginning very much from a cognitive–behaviour therapy perspective.

A guiding analogy that may help us to understand the problem of therapeutic diversity can be taken from the field of linguistics; thus, there are several thousand languages either currently in use or that have existed in the past. Now, as any holidaymaker can attest, each language is more or less impenetrable to speakers of other languages. Nevertheless, despite the considerable diversity there may be certain underlying 'universal rules' that are shared by all languages (Chomsky 1968). Likewise, even though the language of psychoanalysis may seem impenetrable to the behaviour therapist – and vice versa – there may be an underlying level at which they share common principles, or there may be principles that are more apparent in one than in the other, but which nevertheless guide the practice of *good* therapists of either persuasion. Following the language analogy further, there is no argument that we should all speak the same therapeutic language; we should not ask the Inuit to give up a language that can distinguish between 20 different types of snow for a language that can describe only one type! A therapy in which the focus is on unconscious conflicts will require a different language and set of concepts to a therapy that focuses on social skills training. However, we should aim to have a working knowledge of, and respect for, languages other than our own!

Some of the impetus for the exploration of integrative approaches to psychotherapy has arisen from the failure of many studies of the effectiveness of different therapies to find significant differences in outcome. Stiles *et al.* (1986) have labelled this the paradox of 'outcome equivalence contrasted with content non-equivalence'. That is, it is clear from analyses of the content of therapy sessions that therapists of different persuasions do different things in therapy which are broadly consistent with the type of therapy to which they adhere (DeRubeis *et al.* 1982; Luborsky *et al.* 1985). Nevertheless, despite the difference in content, the results from a broad range of outcome studies are consistent with the proposal that no one therapy is ascendant over any other; thus, in the so-called meta-analytic studies in which the results from large numbers of different studies are combined statistically, the general conclusion has been that all therapies are more effective than no treatment whatsoever, but there is little to distinguish amongst the therapies themselves. To give one example, Robinson *et al.* (1990) combined the results from 58 studies of psychotherapy for depression in which, at minimum, one type of psychotherapy had been assessed against a waiting-list control group or a 'placebo' control group. The results showed that psychotherapies were substantially better than control groups both at immediate post-treatment assessment and at follow-up. Furthermore, the initial apparent superiority of cognitive–behavioural interventions over dynamic and interpersonal ones disappeared once the allegiance of the therapists taking part in the treatment was taken into account statistically.

Stiles *et al.* (1986) further argue that outcome equivalence applies not only to areas such as depression but also to areas where 'clinical wisdom' might suggest otherwise; for example, such wisdom would suggest that behavioural and cognitive–behavioural methods are more effective than other forms of therapies for the treatment of phobias. However, the evidence for this proposal arises from analogue studies with sub-clinical populations (primarily students), but, they argued, it is less clear-cut from clinical trials.

In order to illustrate the problems that have arisen from the general failure to find differential effectiveness of therapy outcome, the National Institute of Mental Health (NIMH) Collaborative Depression Study will be considered as a specific example (Elkin *et al.* 1989). This trial is the largest of its kind ever carried out. There were 28 therapists working at three sites; 8 therapists were cognitive–behavioural, 10 were interpersonal therapists, and a further 10 psychiatrists managed two pharmacotherapy conditions, one being imipramine plus 'clinical management', and the second placebo plus 'clinical management'. Two hundred and fifty patients meeting the criteria for major depressive disorder were randomly allocated between the four conditions. The therapies were manualized and considerable training and supervision occurred both before and throughout the trial by leading authorities for each therapy (see Shaw and Wilson-Smith 1988) for a graphic account of this process). To cut a long story short, Elkin *et al.* (1989) reported that all four groups improved approximately equally well on the main symptom outcome measures. Perhaps the most surprising result was the extent of the improvement in the placebo plus clinical management group which substantially out-performed control groups in most other studies, though a post hoc analysis showed that it was less effective for patients with more severe depressive disorders.

Imber *et al.* (1990) have further shown that by and large there were no specific effects of treatments on measures such as the Dysfunctional Attitude Scale on which, for exam-ple, the cognitive therapy condition would have been expected to make more impact than the other treatments.

In summary, there are a rapidly increasing number of therapies, which, by analogy with languages, it is suggested share a number of common factors or basic underlying principles. This proposal does not deny that therapists of different persuasions can be distinguished by what they say and do in therapy, though it will be argued later that *good* therapists of different persuasions may be more like each other than they are like 'text-book therapists' of the same persuasion. One of the puzzles that arises from the vast array of psychotherapy outcome research is the general lack of differential effectiveness of treatments despite their technical diversity. As discussed above, one of the most dra-matic examples of this effect is the multi-million dollar NIMH study in which the least 'active' of all the treatments, the placebo plus clinical management condition, overall performed as well as the other conditions. Results such as these point to the operation of powerful common factors and individual therapist effects that swamp whatever treat-ment effects might exist. In the remainder of this chapter I will consider how such fac-tors might be viewed, beginning, first, with a look at the prospects for *theoretical* integration from a cognitive–behaviour therapy perspective.

Cognitive–behaviour therapy: an integration story

The key point to make about integration from a cognitive–behaviour therapy perspec-tive is that cognitive–behaviour therapy is in itself a success story of the integration of behaviour therapy (BT) and cognitive therapy (CT). In the US, BT developed out of the radical behaviourism of Watson and Skinner and therefore rejected any possible causal role for internal mental states (see Power and Dalgleish 1997, for a summary). From the 1940s onwards, therefore, behaviour therapists in the US developed methods for working with the most extreme behavioural deficits seen, for example, in the long-stay institutionalized patient population.

In the UK, Skinnerian radical behaviourism had little influence and a more pragmatic approach to behaviourism and behaviour therapy was taken (e.g. Eysenck 1952). The focus for BT in the UK was not, therefore, the extreme behavioural deficits of long-stay patients, but the dysfunctional behaviour seen in the neurotic disorders. Given that much of this development occurred at the Maudsley Hospital, it perhaps was no coincidence that Henry Maudsley had originally founded a hospital where the maximum stay was meant to be 12 months.

The combined efforts of the US and UK behaviour therapists led to considerable successes, with the development of techniques such as the token economy, systematic desensitization, and graduated exposure. However, one of the less-than-praiseworthy features of the BT movement was its attack on psychoanalysis. Eysenck, as we know, held extreme positions on most things (whether psychotherapy, intelligence, or even the causes of smoking) and he in particular encouraged the unnecessary hostility between BT and psychoanalysis (Eysenck 1952). But from the 1950s onwards, *academic* psychology moved away from behaviourism and the dominant metaphor of the brain as a telephone exchange; it took on the new computer metaphor of brain as hardware and mind as software (Power and Champion 2000). Behaviourism had gone up a theoretical cul-de-sac, though it was some time before many of the BT practitioners realized this!

At the same time that academic psychology 'went cognitive', BT practitioners were also beginning to realize some of the limitations of their therapeutic approach. The successes for BT with many of the anxiety disorders were not matched in the area of depression. Simplistic behavioural models of depression, for example, as low rates of positive social reinforcement (Lewinsohn 1974) did not lead to successful interventions; depression could not be conceptualized in terms of the anxiety reduction and avoidance model that was successful with the anxiety disorders. Instead, depression needed to be conceptualized in terms of *internal* mental states such as guilt, shame, anhedonia, and self-criticism, states that might or might not lead to behavioural deficits (e.g. Champion 2000).

The developing cognitive therapies of Beck and Ellis offered a sanctuary for troubled behaviour therapists (cf. Rachman 1997). Although both Beck and Ellis had originally been in psychoanalytic training, and neither had come from academic cognitive psychology, they offered therapeutic approaches that incorporated and valued behavioural techniques, whilst offering an appearance of theoretical acceptability with their own cognitive models. Beck in particular made the role of behavioural techniques both explicit and crucial within CT, which may be one reason for the success of CT in attracting the BT practitioners. From the 1980s onwards, therefore, the BT and the CT approaches have been integrated and known as cognitive–behaviour therapy (CBT).

Whatever the pragmatic therapeutic advantages for the integration, there are a number of crucial theoretical issues that make this integration as problematic as the earlier attempts to integrate behavioural and psychoanalytic approaches (Dollard and Miller 1950; Wachtel 1977).

Problems of integration

To begin with the laws of learning, which provided one of the cornerstones of twentieth-century psychology, it is now well known that none of the basic ideas have withstood the test of time (e.g. see Dickinson 1987; Pearce 1997). As summarized in Table 3.1, phenomena such as long-delay conditioning (e.g. nausea some hours after food intake) show that temporal contiguity of the conditioned and unconditioned stimuli are not necessary, whereas phenomena such as the Kamin blocking effect show that learning does not necessarily take place even when there *is* temporal contiguity. The upshot of these problems is that modern learning theories have become cognitive with an emphasis on selective attention, prediction, and memory (Pearce 1997). As yet there is no dominant paradigm, though Power (1991) suggested that the so-called 'Inductive Learning within Rule-Based Default Hierarchies' approach of Holyoak, Koh, and Nisbett (1989) could be usefully applied to clinical problems, even if the name didn't slip off the tongue quite as easily as 'Pavlovian Conditioning'. The basic argument, therefore, is that modern learning theory has of necessity become cognitive, and that one of the reasons why previous attempts to integrate behaviourism and psychoanalysis failed was because both of these theories were wrong in the first place! A broad-based cognitive-science approach can supply the theoretical foundations for at least some versions of a possible integration of BT, CT, and even psychoanalysis. It is worth noting in passing that in a classic paper on depression, Bibring (1953) presented an ego psychology reformulation of Freud's account of mourning and melancholia that anticipated the subsequent cognitive models, even down to the use of terms such as 'helplessness' and 'hopelessness'.

One of the concepts that the CBT theories have struggled with is that of unconscious processes, even though modern cognitive science has a substantial focus on such processes. However, the CBT hostility to the concept is unwarranted given, first, the

Table 3.1 Some problematic examples for traditional learning theory

Procedure	Problem
Long-delay conditioning	Learning occurs without temporal contiguity of CS with UCS/UCR
Blocking Overshadowing Learned irrelevance	No learning occurs despite temporal contiguity between neutral stimulus and UCS/UCR
Reinforcer devaluation	Fast extinction of CR, not predicted by traditional theory

CR = conditioned response; CS = conditioned stimulus; UCR = unconditioned response; UCS = unconditioned stimulus.

traditional behavioural suspicion of (conscious) verbal reports (see Power and Brewin 1991), which seems to require something in the 'black box' that controls non-verbal behaviour and, second, the concept of 'underlying' dysfunctional schemata within the cognitive therapy approach which seems to imply something remarkably close to a cognitive dynamic unconscious (see Power 1989). Similarly, the hostility from behaviour therapists and cognitive therapists to the concept of 'transference' seems odd given, in the cognitive therapy approach for example, the importance of dysfunctional schemata arising in childhood which govern the patient's interactions with 'significant others' (which by definition should include the therapist). In fact it is heartening to see that the therapeutic relationship and the importance of transference have recently begun to enter cognitive–behavioural thinking (e.g. Safran and Segal 1991).

Theoretical integration

The starting point for an integrated cognitive model that could underpin the CBT approach can begin to be outlined. Table 3.2 shows some of the key features of this integration. First, following in the learning theory tradition, two main types of learning need to be considered, namely associative and rule-based. However, the category of 'automatic' or 'associative learning' covers both classical and operant conditioning, whereas the 'conscious' or 'rule learning' variety has received less attention in learning theory (see Holyoak *et al.* 1989 for details). To give an example, some of the learning that happens in therapy can be fast or immediate: fast learning can be seen when patients learn that panic attacks do not cause heart attacks or madness, or that they are not alone in feeling depressed. Nevertheless, patients suffering from panic may continue to experience symptoms in feared situations and the weakening of the association between the situation and the symptoms typically happens more slowly.

Table 3.2 The minimum elements for an integrative theory

Towards a unified cognitive theory		
Types of learning		
(1) conscious or rule learning	→	Fast-change processes in therapy
(2) Automatic or associative learning	→	Slow-change processes in therapy
Types of unconscious processes		
(1) Cognitive		Need to be integrated, e.g. to provide an
(2) Dynamic		account of emotion, goal conflicts, resistance to change in therapy
Types of knowledge representation		
(1) Modular connectionist (associationist) networks ('Low'-level propositional semantics)		
(2) Mental models ('High'-level semantics)		

Second, Table 3.2 shows that conscious and dynamic approaches to the unconscious need to be integrated into a single model (Power and Brewin 1991). The cognitive approach emphasizes, for example, the importance of pre-attentive processes in perception and attention; these cognitive accounts have been incorporated into recent approaches to anxiety disorders (e.g. Beck and Emery 1985). However, an acceptance of a dynamic unconscious within a broad cognitive model leads to some challenges to cherished cognitive–behavioural beliefs. For example, conscious and unconscious goals and aims may conflict with each other as when the patient and therapist in CBT both agree that doing such-and-such homework may be of much benefit, but the patient repeatedly fails the homework assignment. In such a situation, the therapist should explore the hypothesis that completion of the assignment would be contrary to an unconscious goal, as suggested by the following example.

Mr B. was a 24-year-old student unable to work for exams which he had previously failed. He had worked extremely hard for these exams and so believed that he now had to work even harder to have any chance of passing. After some discussion of the importance of leisure time and limits on powers of concentration, he agreed that time needed to be allocated each day for pleasurable activities. Furthermore, he agreed that once he was 'stuck' it was better to try something else rather than force himself to sit at his desk unproductively. Despite this agreement, he was repeatedly unable to put these ideas into practice, but could offer no explanation as to why. We therefore began exploring the background to his views about work. His father, whom he idolized, was a highly successful businessman who worked 7 days a week and resented even having to take Christmas Day off. His father's work ethic did not allow for pleasure. Only after substantial work on overcoming his fear of breaking his father's directives, and his fear of failing to be as successful as his father, was he able to experiment with time for pleasure in his daily activities. He passed all of his exams at the next attempt.

The third element outlined in Table 3.2 is the type of knowledge representation that needs to be incorporated into an integrative theory. We have argued elsewhere that the single semantic level that is incorporated into the notion of schemas in cognitive therapy is insufficient to capture high-level meaning and that it is too sluggish to capture fast-change processes in an elegant way (Power and Champion 1986; Power 1987). The alternative proposal is that an integrative model should have two levels of semantic representation that are parallel but not identical to the two types of learning considered above (see also Teasdale and Barnard 1993). The advantages of a two-level semantics can again be illustrated with a clinical example.

Ms G. was a 30-year-old deputy director of a small charitable organization. She came into therapy feeling extremely depressed, one of her complaints being that she thought that she was a failure both in her work and in her personal life. In one of our early sessions we therefore examined the 'evidence' for this belief; we considered how successful she was in being the first member of her family to go to university, how she had obtained a good degree, how rapidly she had gained promotions in her work, and so on. However, the greater the number of 'positive' things we examined in the session the worse rather than better her mood seemed to become. When we looked at why this was the case, she said that she felt 'out of control' of what was happening in the session and that I was working harder than she was, both of which made her feel worse rather than better.

As this example demonstrates, the advantage of a two-level semantics – one immediate and propositional, the other 'high level' and encapsulating more general meanings and attitudes – is that it allows the therapist not only to focus on the specific propositional meaning of the patient's individual utterances, but also at a high-level model of which those propositions are only a part and whose meaning may be very different. That is, at the propositional level of meaning Ms G. was presenting negative statements about herself that in traditional cognitive therapy might each be countered by evidence to the contrary. However, to remain at the propositional level of the meaning of each individual negative statement would be to ignore a higher level of meaning in which Ms G. felt increasingly out of control in the session. Only by taking account of the more general level of meaning could the therapist understand why the patient felt worse rather than better (see Power and Brewin 1991 for further discussion of levels of meaning).

To summarize, the claim is that no unified cognitive theory yet exists (*pace* Newell 1990) that can provide an integrative theoretical account. Certain features provide a number of pointers suggesting that a broad-based integrative cognitive model is possible. However, even as the preliminary discussion considered here demonstrates, the resultant integrative theory is not simply a replica of the cognitive theory that underlies cognitive therapy, but, rather, an integrative theory will have to be radically different because of the incorporation of phenomena both from traditional learning theory (e.g. different types of learning) and from psychoanalysis (e.g. a dynamic unconscious).

Recent models of cognition and emotion have incorporated in one form or another the characteristics outlined in Table 3.2. These so-called multi-level theories of emotion (e.g. Power and Dalgleish 1997; Teasdale and Barnard 1993) offer, we believe, a sufficiently complex theoretical base for cognitive–behavoural therapies. Although there is insufficient space to spell them out here (see Teasdale 1999 for a summary), an important point to make is that these models now offer scope for further integration between CBT and psychoanalytic approaches. That is, the inclusion of multiple levels of processing, two or more routes to emotion generation, and different types of learning processes, take these models into the domain of unconscious processes, self-deception, and intrapsychic conflict. If, as many psychoanalysts have argued (e.g. Wachtel and McKinnney 1992), these are at the core of the psychodynamic approach, then the possibility for future theoretical integration emerges.

An integrative therapeutic framework

At first sight, the proposal that there could be an integrative *therapeutic* as opposed to theoretical framework might seen ludicrous given both the diversity of therapeutic practice and the hostility that exists between different approaches. How, for example, could behavioural exposure be in any way similar to transference resolution? The argument to be pursued here is that this level is not the appropriate one at which to state the problem. Instead, by analogy with the discussion of 'low-level' and 'high-level' semantics above, a focus on specific techniques or on specific types of intervention may lead one to ignore a higher level of meaning in which these diverse techniques and types of intervention share common aims and purposes. Two things will be proposed. First, that there is a common context in which therapies occur, that is, the therapeutic relationship. Second, that there is a common mechanism of change, the transformation of meaning, through which all interventions proceed. Of course, there are a number of other stage theories of therapy (e.g. Beitman 1992; Prochaska and DiClemente 1992; Stiles *et al.* 1990); the present summary is consistent with the broad view of these previous theories, while differing in the details.

In the framework outlined in Table 3.3, it is proposed that any type of therapy can be viewed in terms of three phases (see Power 1989). In the first phase the primary task is the building of an alliance with the client or patient; thus, although there are also other subsidiary tasks such as assessment and formulation, unless a therapeutic alliance develops it may be pointless entering into the work of therapy because the work is likely to fail. The second phase is the work phase, and it is here that the differences between therapies are most dramatic. The third phase is that of termination of therapy. Again,

Table 3.3 An 'idealized' framework for psychotherapies with primary and secondary tasks outlined for each phase

	Phase 1	Phase 2	Phase 3
Primary task	Alliance	Work	Termination
Secondary tasks	Problem assessment	Tasks	Relapse prevention
	General assessment	Interpretation	Self-therapy
	Formulation	Challenge	Use of social network
	Sharing therapy rationale	Transference development	Transference resolution
		Problem reformulation	

therapies and therapists differ considerably in how termination is dealt with, but we would argue that the issues and problems remain the same whatever the type of therapy.

Before the details of these three phases are spelled out, however, there will be a short digression to consider more traditional approaches to common factors in psychotherapies. The traditional approach is best summarized in the series of hand-books that have been edited over the years by Garfield and Bergin (1986) and which have exhaustively detailed research into *therapist* factors, *client* factors, and *therapy* factors. Work on therapist factors was best exemplified by research into client-centred therapy (e.g. Rogers 1957) and the proposed trinity of non-possessive warmth, empathy, and genuineness (e.g. Truax and Carkhuff 1967) which every therapist was supposed to embody. However, the early optimism that characterized this work eventually gave way to the realization that even 'ideal' therapists had patients with whom they did not get on well and that the mere presence of such factors was not sufficient for therapeutic change. As Stiles *et al.* (1986, p. 175) concluded: 'The earlier hope of finding a common core in the therapist's personal qualities or behaviour appears to have faded.'

Work on client variables has in the past been characterized by the examination of atheoretical lists of sociodemographic and personality variables from which it has been possible to conclude little if anything. In a re-examination of the issue Beutler (1991) concluded that there still has been little development in our understanding of client variables. Following a summary of some of the major variables that might be examined, Beutler (1991, p. 229) also pointed out that: 'There are nearly one and one-half million potential combinations of therapy, therapist, phase, and patient types that must be studied in order to rule out relevant differences among treatment types.'

Fewer than one hundred methodologically sound studies have been carried out to test these possible interactions! There are, however, some promising leads from investigations of client attitudes and expectations which provide a more sophisticated view. For example, Caine and his colleagues (Caine *et al.* 1981) found that the type of model that clients had of their problems (e.g. 'medical' versus 'psychological') and the direction of their main interests ('inner-directed' versus 'outer-directed') predicted dropout rates and outcome in different therapeutic models.

Work on specific *therapy* factors has also run aground on the problems of finding any differential effects. Some of these problems were outlined earlier in the examination of the pattern of outcome equivalence of psychotherapies for a range of disorders. There may possibly be advances in this area in the future with the use of so-called 'dismantling', in which one or more of the putative 'active' ingredients of a therapy are dropped in some of the conditions, and the manualization of therapies combined with measures of treatment adherence, which ensure that something like the therapy in question is actually taking place. However, as the NIMH Collaborative Depression study illustrated, the fact that some therapists did extremely well and some not-so-well, irrespective of the type of therapy, demonstrates that therapy factors will only emerge in interaction with other therapist and client variables rather than as main effects. A specific example of this point comes from the Sheffield Psychotherapy project carried out by David Shapiro and his colleagues. The initial published analyses of this project showed an advantage for prescriptive (i.e. cognitive–behavioural) therapy over exploratory (i.e. psychodynamic) therapy in the treatment of stressed managers. However, a later re-analysis (Shapiro *et al.* 1989) found that this advantage was true for one of the principal therapists involved in the study, but the second therapist was equally effective with both types of therapy. In an interesting conclusion, Shapiro and colleagues turned the initial question of which brand of therapy is better than which other brand on its head, as follows: 'The present findings are broadly consistent with the clinical lore that each new therapist should try different approaches to find the one in which he or she is most effective.' (Shapiro *et al.* 1989, p. 385.)

Therefore, rather than examining these lists of separate therapist, therapy, and client factors any further, we will now return to the suggested framework (see Table 3.3) which encompasses the range of therapy models, and examine the factors in interaction with each other.

Alliance

The notion of the importance of the alliance between therapist and patient arose early in the psychoanalytic literature. Freud (1912) viewed it as the healthy part of the transference, a proposal that was later extended by other psychoanalytic writers. Carl Rogers (1957) also focused on the importance of the therapeutic relationship, though the client-centred view is different to the psychoanalytic. The diverse influences on the origins of the concept and the growing awareness of its importance in cognitive–behaviour therapies (Safran and Segal 1991) make it a cosmopolitan concept with the advantage that therapists of different orientations can begin to talk to each other because of a shared language, but with the disadvantage that they might mistakenly think they are talking about the same thing! Fortunately, this problem is not insurmountable; as Wolfe and Goldfried (1988, p. 449) stated: 'The therapeutic alliance is probably the quintessential integrative variable because its importance does not lie within the specifications of one school of thought.'

In order to understand the concept, the three factors proposed by Bordin (1979) provide a reasonable starting point; namely, that there should be a bond between the therapist and the patient, that there should be an agreement on goals, and that there should be an agreement on tasks. In addition, the work of Jerome Frank (1973, 1982) provides a more general framework from which to view both the therapeutic relationship and the whole question of common factors in psychotherapy. To quote: 'The efficacy of all procedures . . . depends on the establishment of a good therapeutic relationship between the patient and the therapist. No method works in the absence of this relationship.' (Frank 1982, p. 15.)

Frank goes on to describe a number of shared components that help to strengthen the relationship with the patient and which help the patient to have more positive expectations. To highlight a couple of these components:

A confiding relationship

The patient should be able to trust and talk to the therapist about painful issues without feeling judged. These issues may be ones that the patient is 'confessing' for the first time. This feature of confiding is not of course unique to therapeutic relationships (e.g. Power *et al.* 1988). One of the problems that has been identified in poor therapeutic relationships is that the confiding and expression of negative feelings by the patient is responded to with hostility by the therapist; unsurprisingly, the outcome of such therapy is often unsuccessful (e.g. Henry *et al.* 1986).

Ms H. was a 28-year-old single woman who within minutes of the beginning of the first session began shouting and banging her fists on the arms of her chair and the wall next to her. This behaviour did in fact occur spasmodically over several sessions and only gradually declined. My initial reaction was both shock and fear and the thought that I needed to run for cover. Fortunately I didn't run but weathered the onslaught, though the embarrassed stares after sessions of my colleagues in adjoining offices was somewhat harder to cope with! Amongst other things, Ms H. was angry because she had been given a male therapist when she had wanted a female therapist. It turned out that she had previously had a female therapist who was so frightened of her that Ms H. had no respect for her and so made no progress whatsoever. The alliance subsequently developed because I was able to accept her hostility without either becoming hostile in return or becoming paralysed with fear.

The development of an alliance with Ms H. was of course a key part of the effectiveness of the therapy, because the patient comes to experience a relationship that is not dominated by one or other partner, and in which impulses and emotion often experienced as overwhelming or damaging by the patient are contained in a safe manner by the therapist. The patient thereby can learn to experience such affect as safe and containable (Power and Dalgleish 1997).

A rationale

Patients need both a framework within which to understand their distress, and an outline of the principles behind the therapy and what treatment might involve from a practical point of view. Failure to provide such a rationale may leave the patient mystified or anxious, with misconceptions about what might or might not happen and, as a consequence, at risk of dropping out of therapy prematurely. The cognitive– behaviour therapies are particularly strong on providing such rationales; for example, the *Coping with depression* and *Coping with anxiety* booklets are typically handed to patients after one or two sessions of cognitive therapy as a homework assignment. Indeed, Fennell and Teasdale (1987) reported that a positive response to the *Coping with depression* booklet was a good indicator of positive outcome in cognitive therapy. Similar findings apply to dynamic therapies, in which preparation and explanation of methods of treatment – even to the extent of predicting resistance and reluctance to attend – have been shown to result in fewer dropouts, although here a balance needs to be struck between such explanation and the fostering of emergent meaning.

Misalliance

One of the points that must also be dealt with in therapy is the likelihood, as in real life, of the development of 'misalliances'. Some of these may be temporary and resolvable, whereas others may, for example, require referral on to another agency or other drastic action. As a starting point from which to consider misalliances, we can consider again Bordin's (1979) three components of the therapeutic alliance, that is, the bond, the goals, and the tasks, all or any of which can be implicated in a misalliance. It is well recognized that some patients are more difficult to develop an alliance with than others; thus, the extension of cognitive therapy into work with personality disorder individuals has helped to heighten awareness of the therapeutic relationship amongst cognitive therapists, together with a re-examination of a number of related psychodynamic issues (Beck and Freeman 1990; Linehan 1993a). Less intractable misalliances occur when, for example, the patient attends therapy in order to appease someone else such as a spouse, partner, or professional such as a GP, or the patient expects drug treatment rather than psychotherapy, or is attending because of a court order, and so on. Through careful discussion of the relevant issues the therapist should be able to identify these types of misalliances.

Even when a satisfactory alliance has been established the painful work of therapy can lead to 'ruptures' (e.g. Gaston 1998); for example, a behavioural exposure session that goes wrong and becomes too anxiety-provoking can lead to a setback in the relationship that needs to be addressed before the therapeutic work is continued.

Mr J. was a 32-year-old man with a variety of problems that included a lift phobia. This phobia was especially inopportune because the psychology department was located several floors up in a tower block! After some weeks of preparation, the establishment of a hierarchy, and some work in imagination, Mr J. agreed to travel one floor by lift accompanied by myself. As we stepped out, momentarily feeling successful, a hospital trolley pulling a considerable amount of dirty laundry cornered too fast and fell over onto both of us. Fortunately, neither of us were physically injured, but it was several weeks before Mr J. accompanied me again in a lift!

Other factors, such as breaks in therapy for holidays, or an approaching therapy termination, can also lead to problems in the alliance that need to be dealt with sensitively.

Of course, psychoanalytic therapists reading this account are likely to respond 'so what – we've known this all along'. The point is that until recently cognitive–behavioural therapists have simply concentrated on phase 2, the work phase (see Table 3.3) and ignored phase 1, the alliance. Clinical reality and the extension of the CBT approach into work with more intractable problems have led to a re-evaluation of this piece of short-sightedness.

The work phase

It is in this phase that the differences between schools of therapy are at their most dramatic, yet it is possible that there may be unexpected common factors that link this diversity. Perhaps the most dramatic difference is that claimed by Carl Rogers for his client-centred psychotherapy (e.g. Rogers 1957) for which he claimed that there was no work phase because the mechanism of change was through the unconditional positive regard from the therapist (i.e. all phase 1). However, this claim ignores the fact that work occurs even when the therapist is non-directive. As stated earlier, there is doubt that the textbook differences between different types of therapy are reflected in practice in therapy itself, and, furthermore, that the same therapist acts differently with different patients, or even with the same patient at different points in therapy (e.g. Luborsky *et al.* 1982). To consider an example, the typical sequence in cognitive therapy for depression might consist of something like that shown in Fig. 3.1.

Behavioural tasks are set initially both to increase the activity level and the day-to-day experience of success of the depressed individual. The second stage consists of the identification of negative automatic thoughts and the construction of rational responses to

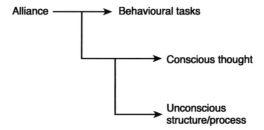

Fig. 3.1   The typical sequence of stages in cognitive therapy.

obviate their mood-worsening consequences. And the third stage consists of the identification of underlying dysfunctional assumptions which are challenged through a variety of techniques such as *in vivo* experiments that test out faulty assumptions. However,
although this apparently neat sequence may be very useful for teaching purposes and
may even be useful once in a while clinically, it is inconceivable, as was argued earlier,
that a coherent psychological model could work with independent processing systems
of this variety (Power and Dalgleish 1997). It seems likely that the mechanism of change
may be the same for all three 'steps' in this sequence; thus, in order for the individual to
perform behavioural tasks successfully, change may be necessary at both a conscious
and unconscious level. The crucial factor is the overcoming of inhibition of positive
thought and action, that is, counteracting the 'loss of the positive' that is typical in
depression. The gist of this argument is the viewpoint that behavioural change cannot
occur without underlying cognitive change and, especially if the person is unable to
report the behavioural change, this implies that the change has occurred at an underlying automatic or unconscious cognitive level.

In a similar manner, at a more clinical level, the cognitive therapist may feel unaware
of where negative thoughts end and dysfunctional beliefs begin, because there is no simple relationship between a 'thought' and a 'belief'; thus, a statement such as 'I am a failure' could represent a thought that is not a belief, a belief that is also a thought, a thought
that is part of a belief, or a belief that is believed partly or sometimes but not at other
times. The point is that however one might try to slice up the cake, we cannot have a slice
of one 'active ingredient' without also having the other ingredients.

Perhaps a more dramatic attempt to analyse the similarities rather than the differences in the work phase is portrayed in Table 3.4. This table takes each of the corner-
stone techniques from behaviour therapy, psychoanalysis, and cognitive therapy,
namely, behavioural exposure, transference resolution, and the challenging of dysfunctional assumptions, and then asks similar questions of each. To take the first point
shown in the table: although the three approaches differ in the extent to which they
focus on childhood, nevertheless, it is commonplace to identify the original source of
the problem in childhood, whether it is the learning of phobic reactions from primary
caretakers, the repression of forbidden wishes and impulses, or the development of
self-critical attitudes. The procedures by which these issues are explored are astonishing
in their similarity given the traditional hostility and rivalry between the approaches. In
each case, the patient is encouraged to a heightened emotional response in the presence
of the particular object, person or situation (cf. similar analyses by Bertram; see Lewin
1973; Frank 1982). In psychoanalysis, the therapist encourages this reaction to develop
to the therapist him or herself, but in principle the mechanism seems similar. Cognitive
therapists might aver that it is the cognitive *belief* rather than the emotional reaction that
is being accessed, but more recent views of the relationship between cognition and emotion reject such a simplistic, linear causal view in that cognition and emotion are viewed

Table 3.4 An analysis of the key therapeutic techniques from behaviour therapy (exposure), psychoanalysis (transference resolution), and cognitive therapy (challenging dysfunctional assumptions).

Therapeutic technique	Problem origin	Procedure	Putative mechanism of change
Exposure	Learning typically in childhood (traumatic, observational, information transmission)	Heighten emotion with relevant object/situation in therapist's presence	Extinction/relearning coping
Transference	Childhood experience in relation to significant others	Heighten emotional reaction to thearapist as object	Working through to realistic perception of therapist, etc.
Challenging dysfunctional assumptions	Childhood experience in relation to significant others	Heighten emotion to person/situation object	Reinterpret Reconstruct

as mutually interdependent (Power and Dalgleish 1997). More correctly, therefore, the argument is that therapy heightens access to cognitive–emotional structures and processes that relate to past and present significant objects, and significant others including the therapist. In the context of this heightened access there is the common therapeutic goal that patients will re-learn, cope more successfully with, view more realistically, re-interpret or reconstruct, that is, in some way view more constructively, the object, person, or situation that has been the source of their distress or conflict. *The transformation of meaning provides, therefore, a mechanism of change that, we suggest, is common to all therapies* (see Power and Brewin 1997).

An interesting addendum to this proposal comes from a study reported by Goldsamt *et al* (1992), which consisted of a content analysis of a video produced to illustrate the therapeutic approaches of Beck (i.e. Beckian cognitive therapy), Meichenbaum (i.e. Meichenbaum's form of cognitive–behaviour therapy), and Strupp (psychodynamic therapy). In this video, these three well-known therapists each interview the same patient, named 'Richard', in order to illustrate their therapeutic approaches. The results of the content analyses showed unexpectedly that Meichenbaum and Strupp were more similar to each other than they were to Beck, rather than finding the predicted similarity between Beck and Meichenbaum; thus, whereas Meichenbaum and Strupp both tended to focus on the patient's impact on other people, Beck focused more on the impact that other people had on the patient. The moral, in re-emphasis of what has long been well-known in the therapy literature, is that purported differences in therapy should not be based on what therapists say they do, but rather, what they actually do; and that the contrast can be considerable (Sloane *et al.* 1975).

The termination phase

The termination phase can often be the most avoided and most difficult phase of therapy, especially for trainee therapists. It may, for example, be the phase when the therapist's fantasies of omnipotent healing face the reality of mere minor therapeutic gain; when guilt about premature termination is avoided by therapist and patient alike to the detriment of therapy; or when the sadness and anger at the loss of a productive relationship are avoided because they are too painful. For whatever reason, therefore, this phase requires a healthy honesty which is often not dealt with adequately in the CBT literature because of the traditional focus on technical skill rather than the therapeutic relationship.

The termination phase in short-term therapies may be more difficult to manage than in longer-term therapies. One reason for this difficulty is that in longer-term therapies there may have been numerous breaks in therapy which provide important information about how the patient will cope with termination; for example, whether the patient avoids discussing an upcoming break, and the extent to which the alliance is disrupted following a break. In short-term therapies, there may never have been any breaks, and the therapist may mistakenly believe that there is insufficient time to deal with termination issues. In fact, given that cognitive therapy was designed as a short-term therapy for depression (Beck *et al.* 1979), the central depressive concerns about dependency and loss imply that an approaching termination will reawaken these areas of conflict and should therefore be actively and explicitly dealt with by the therapist.

There are of course a range of assessment measures which the cognitive–behavioural therapist in particular will be likely to use if information is needed to help decide whether or not the patient is ready to finish therapy. Most of these measures are well known and include self-report indices of symptom levels, dysfunctional attitudes, automatic thoughts, activity levels, and achievement of therapeutic aims. However, in view of the traditional behavioural ambivalence about self-report noted earlier, it is surprising that cognitive–behavioural therapists rely so heavily on measures that are reactive to factors such as self-report biases, the need to please the therapist, etc. It is surprising that there has not been greater development of behavioural performance measures and psychophysiological indices such as heart rate and galvanic skin response (Power 1991). In addition to the self-report, behavioural, and psychophysiological measures, there are a number of other ways in which therapists can gauge the readiness of patients for the termination of therapy. One of these is when the patient has internalized a positive model of the therapist (cf. Casement 1985); evidence for such models comes, for example, from reports of imaginary dialogues that the patient holds with the therapist between sessions: 'I was just about to leap over the checkout in the supermarket in absolute panic, when I stopped and wondered what you would say to me in such a situation'. Such imaginary dialogues are a sign that the therapeutic work is actively continuing outside of sessions; they also provide the therapist with clues about the type of therapist model that the patient has internalized. This process of internalization can be encouraged in sessions when, in response to questions from the patient such as 'what do you think I should do about such-and-such?', the therapist can encourage the patient to construct a reply 'Well, what do you think my answer would be?'

A second interpersonal measure concerns the patient's way of relating to significant others in his or her social network. It is well-known that the majority of neurotic and psychotic problems remain untreated in the community, as shown for example in the various papers from the large Epidemiologic Catchment Area Study (e.g. (Bourdon *et al.* 1988; Myers *et al.* 1984). A reasonable hypothesis is that a key difference between referred and non-referred cases lies in the quality of support available in the individual's network (e.g. Frank 1973), a factor, for example, that might also explain the originally unexpected finding that the outcome of schizophrenia was better in the developing rather than the developed countries. Thus, one of the largely unexplored areas of therapy outcome may be whether, following progress in therapy, patients make better use of their social networks, whether they relate in healthier ways to key individuals in their networks, and, particularly if significant role relationships are missing, whether they have the capacity to establish new healthy relationships. This type of assessment can either be made using established measures of the quality of social support (e.g. Power *et al.* 1988) or can be undertaken informally with the patient. Hence, a key question is whether the patient has a 'therapeutic' significant other, or, if not, has the capacity and motivation to establish new healthier relationships that will replace the relationship with the therapist. The following is an example of a change in a relationship with a significant other and the subsequent effects on how the patient related to others in her network.

Ms H., who was also referred to earlier, was in a permanent state of anger with everybody, or so it seemed. This anger was expressed with everyone apart from her mother with whom, she stated categorically, she had never been angry. It transpired that her mother had a heart condition and a range of other symptoms with which she had manipulated and blackmailed her family for many years. Ms H. firmly believed that if she got angry with her mother, her mother would die. Ms H.'s belief in this murderous anger was first put to the test in the therapeutic relationship in which I had managed to contain her anger and survive. After about 6 months of therapy, and with great trepidation, she eventually got angry with her mother for the first time. As the considerable backlog eventually came out, so she felt less angry with other people. One of the first people she became close to was her younger sister who, she found, had similar views and difficulties to herself. It also turned out that her mother's 'heart condition' had not been diagnosed by any specialist, though her mother had failed to mention this fact to her family.

One final health warning should be issued for therapists who find themselves unable to finish therapy with patients. Stieper and Weiner (1959) reported a study of so-called 'interminable patients' who had been seen in therapy for a long time in a particular clinic. They found that these patients tended to be restricted to a few therapists, and that the therapists involved tended to have unrealistic aims for what the patients might achieve, and also had excessive needs to be appreciated both in their role as therapists and in their private lives. In a dramatic intervention in this study, the administrators of the clinic discharged the patients concerned against the wishes of the therapists! Follow-up showed that they subsequently did no worse than any of the other patients.

The accidental nature of theory and practice

There are a number of reasons why therapies and therapists need to over-emphasize the differences between therapies whilst under-emphasizing or even denying the similarities. The first reason was considered earlier in the discussion of Eysenck and behaviour therapy. It was proposed that, in order to establish a niche for the new behaviour therapy, Eysenck argued for political reasons as much as anything else that behaviour therapy was good and scientific, and that psychoanalysis was bad and unscientific. Each new therapy faces the same problem, that is, the need to promote itself while denigrating other competing therapies. A second reason is the imperative in an evidence-based culture for randomized control trials in which research therapists are studiously kept 'on-model' for the therapy in which they are participating and 'off-model' for other therapies in the study. Therapies in such studies are kept artificially as distinct as possible so that, for example, a 'pure' version of cognitive therapy is compared to a 'pure' version of interpersonal therapy. Unfortunately, this is not the way that therapy is practised in routine clinical practice, and the increasing recognition of the need for so-called 'effectiveness' studies of therapy as it is normally practised should eventually provide some answers. There is, however, still a failure to recognize a more fundamental problem: the links between theory and practice are often *accidental* rather than essential, which hopefully the following examples will illustrate.

Table 3.5 shows examples of three major types of theory – psychoanalysis, cognitive science, and behaviourism – together with three key aspects of therapeutic practice associated, respectively, with each type of therapy. The table is designed to demonstrate that although, for example, the technique of 'free association' is considered to be uniquely linked with psychoanalysis, there is no inherent *theoretical* reason why this should be the case. In other words, free association could equally have been developed by cognitive therapists or behaviour therapists if psychoanalysis had not got there first! Similarly, the technique of desensitization in imagination developed by the ardent behaviourist, Joseph Wolpe, could have been even more readily linked to cognitive or psychoanalytic theory than to behaviourism. Indeed, if one works through a list of the key elements of practice, most of them could have been generated equally effectively from theories other

Table 3.5 Examples of actual and possible theory–practice links

Theory	Practice		
	Free association	Diary-keeping	Desensitization in imagination
Psychoanalysis	Actual	Possible	Possible
Cognitive science/ cognitive therapy	Possible	Actual	Possible
Behaviourism/ behaviour therapy	Possible	Possible	Actual

than the one from which they are supposedly derived. As we have argued elsewhere (Power and Dalgleish 1997), there is no necessary one-to-one correspondence between theory and practice in the psychotherapies. Many theories could generate many practices, and many practices could be based on many theories. The differences between the therapies are in many ways more accidental than deliberate and get over-emphasized for both political and research-driven reasons. Good practice on the ground does not honour these artificial barriers and is not based on 'textbook' simplifications of therapy.

Final comments and conclusions

To conclude that there are no significant differences between the various types of therapy is a conclusion that attempts to prove the null hypothesis, which, as any statistically minded individual will tell you, is not the way to proceed in research. In fact, the appearance of such a conclusion as a consequence of meta-analytic studies or large outcome studies such as the NIMH Collaborative Depression Study, necessitates a number of important qualifications to the 'all have won' and therefore 'anybody can do anything' conclusion. One of the most crucial qualifications relates to the therapist's skill in establishing a therapeutic alliance. What little evidence there is suggests that therapists of all persuasions have particular difficulty with patients who are negative and who express hostility in therapy; the failure to establish an alliance may be the most important factor that contributes to negative outcome in therapy, that is, the fact that a proportion of patients get worse rather than better. However, it may only be when a therapeutic alliance is established that additional effects of specific techniques for specific problems can emerge. Even outcome studies which manualize treatments and assess therapist adherence to these treatments do not generally assess factors such as the quality of the alliance or other factors common to all therapies.

At a more general level, the Grand Unified Theory of psychological therapies, is, as in physics, a long way off. Nevertheless, there are positive signs: a broad-based cognitive model seems capable of incorporating the strengths of both traditional learning approaches and psychoanalysis while overcoming some of their limitations. Any such cognitive model is substantially different to the current models that underpin CBT approaches, because of the need to incorporate, for example, both modern learning theory and a cognitive version of the dynamic unconscious. The theory also needs to provide a framework in which to view the great diversity and ever-increasing number of psychotherapies. Only then will we understand what distinguishes the *good* underwater massage therapist from the *bad* behaviour therapist – and vice versa – and understand why each may be useful in the right place.

Finally, it should be noted that in terms of the history of the psychotherapy integration movement, the approach taken here is an example of the common factors and theoretical integration viewpoint (Norcross 1992). Although many therapists now adopt a so-called 'technical eclecticism' in that they may use techniques and procedures from different approaches without adopting a particular theory, our approach has been to argue strongly for the possibility of theoretical integration (e.g. Power and Dalgleish 1997). As agreed throughout this chapter, the CBT approach already represents an integration of behavioural and cognitive viewpoints which have at times in the past been at war with each other. Part of this integration has occurred because practitioners came to ignore some of the earlier theoretical arguments. Hopefully, the more recent integrative theories will equal clinical experience in their richness, and offer further hope of progress.

Chapter 4

Integrative therapy from a systemic perspective

Eia Asen

Introduction

The term 'systemic perspective' requires some explanation. A system is any unit structured by and around feedback (Bateson 1972). It is made up of interacting parts which mutually influence one another, forming patterns of behaviour and communication. When two or more people interact, they are involved in a joint construction of actions and meanings. This relationship is an evolving one, with each person influencing the other and being in turn influenced by the other's responses and actions. Any action is viewed as a response and any response can be conceptualized as an action. In that sense there is, like in a circle, no identifiable beginning or end to any interaction: it really is impossible to say whether chicken or egg came first. Such circularities are characteristic of relationship patterns and these are governed by explicit and implicit rules, established over time through the process of constant feedback (Watzlawick *et al.* 1967). The *context* within which such feedback takes places is of importance: this refers not only to the family, but also the social and cultural context within which families live. The notion of a 'systemic perspective' entails the idea that there is a whole multi-verse of different perspectives from which to view a person's specific problems: individual, couple, family, extended family, social setting, cultural and religious context, economic and political larger system. This multi-level view of a person's predicament is what can be summarized as a 'systemic perspective'. In terms of psychotherapeutic practice, systemic therapists will consider interventions that take into account context and the different levels of the system.

The development of systemic therapies

One of the major influences for the development of the systemic therapies came from a group of researchers and clinicians in Palo Alto (Bateson *et al.* 1956). They examined communication patterns in families containing a schizophrenic member and related these to the complex communication requirements seemingly imposed on the 'identified' or 'designated' patients by their families. Bateson's group also postulated that some of these families 'needed' a symptomatic person so that they could maintain equilibrium within the family. At that time the patient was seen as the victim of the family and the resulting practices often resulted in scapegoating mothers – note the term 'schizophrenogenic mother' – and subsequently the whole concept of the family (Cooper 1970). A provocative psychiatric view in the 1960s and 1970s was that confusing and mystified communication patterns inside the family were the causes of the ill person's distorted perceptions (Laing and Esterson 1964). Not surprisingly, in those days parents in particular did not seem at all keen to be at the receiving end of this new treatment, called 'family therapy', since they felt blamed for their offspring's ill-health.

Influential and inspiring though these ideas were at the time, they did not deserve to be described as 'systemic', given that the practitioners seemed to side with one part of the system, the patient, against another part, the parents. Moreover, as is so often the case when new ideas are introduced, systemic family therapists behaved rather arrogantly, claiming miraculous cures of their patients after a few dramatic interventions. This tended to alienate colleagues with different orientations, even more so because, during its rather stormy adolescence, family therapists enjoyed breaking many traditional therapeutic taboos. The confidential, intimate setting of traditional individual psychotherapy was displaced by teams of four, with therapists behind one-way screens, making use of cameras and video recorders. Disturbing though this may all have been to families when first faced with such an approach, family therapists certainly benefited. The new technologies allowed them to videotape sessions and to analyse these afterwards. It permitted the study of interaction sequences as well as pinpointing ways of 'pausing' these and providing different endings to familiar recursive processes. For example, viewing a segment of videotaped family interaction and freeze-framing it at a specific point allows time for reflection: thinking back about how the interaction started; looking in some detail at how it evolved; and speculating as to what different future (inter-)actions might result in a different outcome. Pausing a videotape and thereby disrupting the predictable unfolding of familiar patterns not only helps therapists to have new ideas, but – if done with clients – also helps these to identify new ways of communicating and interacting.

It has to be remembered that at the outset the vast majority of systemic therapists had been trained psychodynamically and that some of the pioneers attempted to combine psychoanalytic and family systems ideas and practices (Ackerman 1966; Skynner 1976). Soon, however, psychoanalytic ideas were discredited, if not 'banned', within systemic circles. Looking back, it seems that cutting itself off from its origins, above all psychoanalysis, may have been a necessary developmental phase through which the family therapy movement had to go. It allowed family therapists to experiment with new and at times quite irreverent ideas and practices – without feeling restricted by traditional concepts. Thus anti-integrationism is often an essential component of differentiation.

A review of systemic approaches

Over the decades many different systemic approaches have emerged in a whole range of different working contexts, both private and public. Whilst some of these have remained rather precious if not esoteric, most systemic therapists working in public contexts now match their approach to the perceived needs of the clients, families, and organizations.

The subsequent section summarizes some of the major systemic ideas and practices on which integrative systemic practices are based.

The **structural approach** (Minuchin 1974) postulates that families function particularly well when certain family structures prevail, such as hierarchies between the generations within a family, with semipermeable boundaries permitting a sufficient flow of information up and down, for example between parents and their children. The approach also maintains that it is more functional if there are boundaries around the nuclear family so that it can preserve its identity and rules whilst at the same time being receptive to the outside world. The structural therapist has the task of intervening with the aim of making the family structure approximate this normative model. Techniques include challenging directly absent or rigid boundaries, 'unbalancing' the family equilibrium by temporarily joining with one member of the family against others, or setting 'homework' tasks designed to restore hierarchies. The structural approach is very active, with the therapist encouraging family members to 'enact' problems in the consulting room so that the stuck or pathological communications and interactions can be observed and challenged. In this way therapeutic crises are induced deliberately, with the aim of the family discovering new resources and solutions to old problems and dilemmas.

Strategic family therapy (Haley 1963; Watzlawick *et al.* 1974) aims to deliver interventions or 'strategies' to fit the presenting problems. The underlying assumption is that the symptom is being maintained by the apparent 'solution', namely the very behaviours that seek to suppress the presenting problem. For example, the depressed woman with low self-esteem may elicit her partner's over-protectiveness, a 'solution' which may well perpetuate the problem. Once some changes are achieved in relation to the presenting symptom a domino effect sets in, affecting other interactions and behaviours in the whole family. Strategic therapists use 'reframing' as a major technique: the family's or patient's perceived problem(s) are put into a different meaning-frame, which provides new perspectives and therefore potentially makes new behaviours possible. In fact, it could be argued that psychoanalytic transference interpretations are no different in that they attempt to reframe the patient's communications in terms of the 'here and now' relationship with the analyst.

The Milan systemic approach (Selvini Palazzoli *et al.* 1978) focuses on multi-generational family patterns, describing the interactions and struggles of family members over several generations. There is considerable emphasis on the making of elaborate hypotheses – for example of how mutual disqualification between the parents, connected with the expectations from their own families of origin, traps their own child. A disqualification is a communication affirmed at one level whilst being disconfirmed at another: 'of course, you must do what you think is right', said in a very angry tone of voice, can be a first step of an interaction of mutual disqualification. If a family member is disqualifying her own and others' messages, it will be very difficult for everybody else not to reciprocate. The only response to messages that conflict on different levels is more messages that conflict on different levels (Haley 1963). Thus a vicious circle of mutual disqualification evolves which, once established, is hard to stop.

The making of hypotheses leads to designing interventions which take into account the anticipated attempts of the family to disqualify the therapy. The resulting 'counter-paradoxes' prescribed by the Milan team are aimed at recommending 'no change' in the hope that the family would resist this command and do the opposite, namely change – if only to defeat the therapist(s)! Paradoxical prescriptions were fashionable in the 1980s but are rarely used nowadays. What the original Milan team is now remembered for is above all its introduction of a particular style of interviewing: circular and reflexive questioning (Selvini Palazzoli *et al.* 1980). This technique enables systemic therapists to become curious inquirers who solicit information about the various family members' beliefs and perceptions regarding relationships. Eliciting such information in the presence of family members and asking these to comment and reflect on the answers given by the various family members, creates an infinite set of feedback loops which themselves change the fabric of family interactions. The therapist conducts the family session mostly by asking questions, seeking information about people, their differences and the various relationships, and their specific characteristics. By responding to feedback from the individual family members the therapist enacts the systemic notion of the circularity of interaction.

In the early 1980s the original Milan team divided into two groups, with Selvini Palazzoli (Selvini Palazzoli *et al.* 1989) and her team pursuing their interests in unravelling the 'games' of psychotic and anorectic families. The team became preoccupied with designing an 'invariate' prescription, which included secret pacts with the therapist and mysterious parental disappearance acts. The aim was to disrupt chronic family organization and the dramatic techniques seemed to work for some families but not for others.

Interestingly, the other half of the original Milan team (Boscolo *et al.* 1987), now called Milan Associates, went in the opposite direction, away from any prescriptiveness. Their commitment to positive connotation produced a non-blaming approach: the actions of all family members are in no way seen as negative but always as the best everyone could do under the circumstances, with the intentions being positive even if the outcome was not (ideas that have been taken up by those interested in supportive psychotherapy: see Chapter 11). Inspired by the writings of physicists, neuro-scientists and philosophers (Maturana and Varela 1980; Von Foerster and Zopf 1962), the Milan Associates and their followers challenged the position of the therapist as an apparent objective outside observer of the family system. They now focused on how the observer actually constructs that which is being observed. The term 'co-construction' entered the field, acknowledging how therapists themselves contribute their own perceptions and prejudices to the therapeutic process. In therapy as much as in family life meanings are co-constructed over time, and the shared histories of relationships provide the context within which current behaviours are interpreted (Pearce and Cronen 1980).

The most recent phase of systemic therapy has been influenced by the **social construc-tionist approach**, based on the awareness that the 'reality' therapists observe is 'in-vented', with perceptions being shaped by the therapists' own cultures and their implicit assumptions and beliefs. Foucault's assertion that each culture has dominant narratives and discourses (Foucault 1975) is influencing many systemic practitioners and has led to an examination of how language shapes problem perceptions and definitions. The notion of the 'problem-determined' system (Anderson and Goolishian 1986) refers to how interactions between clinicians and clients or families are programmed by the built-in assumptions inherent in the traditional clinical discourses employed to discuss experiences and relationships. If therapeutic encounters focus exclusively on clients' experiences as evidence of illness or pathology, then clients and their families remain trapped in pathology frames, only being able to make sense of their experiences within that framework. If the narratives in which clients story their experience – or have their experience storied by others – do not fit these experiences, then significant aspects of their lived experience will contradict the dominant narrative (White and Epston 1990) and be experienced as problematic. Systemic **narrative therapy** attempts to enable cli-ents and families to generate and evolve new stories and ways of interpreting events to make sense of their experiences. Therapy is seen as a mutually validating conversation from which change can occur. Family and therapist 'co-evolve' or 'co-construct' new ways of describing the family system so that it no longer needs to be viewed or experi-enced as problematic. Therapists practising in this way would describe themselves as being even-handed and realistic about the possibility of change, with no wish to impose their own ideas, being alert to openings and curious about their own position in the observed system, taking non-judgemental and multi-positional stances (Jones 1993). Central to this work is the stimulation of a process of reflection. The 'reflecting team' (Andersen 1987) is one of the major innovations in recent years. No longer are there 'se-cret' discussions between therapist and team members behind the one-way screen, but these now take place openly in front of the family. The implied sharing of the therapists' thinking with clients involves the latter in a process of reflection rather than imposing interventions on them. Members of the reflecting team may at times take quite different positions and even loudly disagree with one another. This can be helpful to families at times who can then see re-enacted in the team issues that they themselves are struggling with. This allows them to look at themselves from a different perspective.

'Externalization of problems' is both an orientation and a technique used by narrative therapists (White 1997). It is based on the view that problems are derived through the internalization of 'problem saturated' ways of thinking about the world at large and relationships in particular (Lang and McAdam 1997). 'Externalizing' encourages families to personify the problem they experience as oppressive so that the problem becomes a separate entity external to the person (White 1997). One such example is the work with encopretic children. The child is asked to think of the soiling as his enemy, who is given the name 'sneaky pooh'. This enemy needs to be defeated at all costs (White 1989). The help of the family is enlisted to devise strategies to trick this imaginary monster. Soon everyone joins forces to outwit sneaky pooh – the symptom – which now becomes the enemy number one of the whole family. A number of ingenious steps are employed to defeat 'sneaky pooh', involving all family members in playful interactions. This approach has been applied to a whole range of symptoms and conditions, from anorexia to depression and schizophrenia.

Brief 'solution focused' therapy (De Shazer 1982) emphasizes the competencies of families and individuals. It deliberately ignores 'problem saturated' ways of talking and instead focuses on the patterns of previously attempted solutions. The approach is based on the observation that symptoms and problems have a tendency to fluctuate. A depressed person, for example, is sometimes more and sometimes less depressed. Focusing on the times when she is less depressed are the exceptions on which therapeutic strategies are built. These exceptions form the basis of the solution. If clients are encouraged to amplify the 'solution' patterns of behaviours, then the problem patterns can be driven into the background. Many claims are made as to the effectiveness of this approach but, as so often with psychological therapies, there is no systematic research backing them up.

Another family therapy model that has been influential over the years, particularly since it does have a strong evidence base, is the **psycho-educational approach** (Anderson and Sawin 1983; Leff *et al.* 1982). It contains behavioural elements but also draws on structural techniques. The model is based on the findings that people suffering from schizophrenia who return to live with a family whose attitudes towards the ill person are critical or emotionally over-involved (high EE) are significantly more likely to relapse in the 9 months following discharge from hospital than those patients who return to low EE families. Consequently the aim of therapy is to reduce the emotional intensity as well as the degree of physical proximity. This is achieved by essentially using three separate therapeutic ingredients: (a) educational sessions for the family – about schizophrenia and the part the family can play in keeping the patient well; (b) a fortnightly relatives' groups – to share experiences and solutions; and (c) family sessions (Kuipers *et al.* 1992).

Integrating and re-integrating systemic approaches

The emergence of different systemic approaches has, as in other fields of psychotherapy, produced diverse schools and institutes, some of which are highly critical of one another. Thankfully, most practitioners working in the public domain can simply not afford to remain married to one particular school or dogma and thus have to adapt their delivery of systemic work to the various contexts within which they work. For example, when working with multi-problem families, a structurally based approach may be indicated at the outset, with time for a more reflective narrative or post-Milan approach at a later stage. Conversely, with very rigid families it may be more useful not to face them with too-structured work as it is likely to increase their own familiar structures and defences. Instead, exposure to Milan-style questions is more likely to indirectly challenge their beliefs. Different phases of therapy require different techniques, styles, and positions of the therapist. In practice one can in most sessions combine the more direct '*in vivo*' structural approach with the more reflective Milan, post-Milan, and narrative approaches. The result is an integrated approach which I have provocatively termed the 'structural Milan approach' (Asen 1997). Integration here is a function of the external context in which the work takes place.

Working in a number of different public health contexts has led to an integrated approach. One place of work is the Marlborough Family Service, a child and adolescent mental health service which is integrated with an adult psychotherapy service, serving a defined catchment area in central London. Another work setting is the Psychotherapy Department of the Maudsley Hospital, a prestigious institution with a strong research bias. A third work context is the Mother-and-Baby Unit of the Maudsley Hospital, an inpatient unit with a brief of carrying out parenting assessments. Working in different settings faces clinicians continuously with having to re-examine and adapt their practices. It is a common experience that certain approaches seem to work in one setting but do not fit another. Different working contexts clearly require different responses to presenting patients and problems. This experience fits with examining the origins of the different systemic approaches outlined in the first part of this chapter. Each of these approaches has been developed within specific contexts, some public and some private, some child focused, others based on working with adult mentally ill inpatients.

In the past – and perhaps still at present – quite a number of clinicians and institutions have developed their own brand of psychotherapy and prescribed this without evaluating the benefits to a particular patient. Here patients have to fit the treatment and if they do not respond, they risk the 'diagnosis' of 'treatment resistance'. The alternative 'diagnosis', namely that the treatment was 'patient resistant', not fitting the patient's individual needs and requirements, is hardly ever made. One of the more positive aspects of the new fetish of evidence-based medicine (Sackett *et al.* 1996) is the implied emphasis on matching appropriate treatments to patients (and their conditions) and not the other way round! In my own practice, if a patient or family does not respond to the therapy offered, I blame my technique and model. Non-systemic though this stance may be, it nevertheless induces curiosity rather than despair, so much so that I wish to discover why my therapeutic efforts have come to nothing! It is continuous curiosity that leads to a search for creating a different context for the therapeutic encounter. Cecchin *et al.* (1992) make the point that a healthy irreverence towards one's own methods and assumptions is a necessity for any therapist to ensure continuing flexibility and creativity. Once therapists fall in love with their models and believe these to be true and universal, complexity risks being reduced to some banal principles, with 'invariate' prescriptions or other stale interventions churned out with frightening consistency.

Such practices may be reassuring to the therapist, though a stance of 'committed safe uncertainty' is more likely, especially if co-evolved with users, to produce a mutually informed therapeutic encounter (Asen 1999). Uncertainty permits openness, invites curiosity, allows mutual exploration. However, uncertainty may also generate anxieties in both clients and therapist. The distinctions between safe and unsafe certainty and uncertainty (Mason 1993) may be useful in describing the various possible positions of therapists. Clients who seek out therapy are usually in a state of *unsafe uncertainty*: they are full of doubt about relationships, their own identities, their feelings and actions. They hope or believe that the therapist, as an expert in mental health, will change their situation by offering explanations or solutions, or in other words, some *safe certainty*. The therapist who 'knows all' about what goes on in the client risks reducing the wealth of feelings and thoughts to predictable patterns, irrespective of feedback. This is likely to produce a context of unsafe certainty. The preferred position of systemic therapists is that of *safe uncertainty*: it is one which is always in a state of flow, consistent with an exploration which allows new explanations being placed *alongside* rather than *instead of*, or in competition with, the clients' ideas (Mason 1993). Being committed to such safe uncertainty allows therapists to fall out of love with their ideas and prejudices and not to impose these on their clients.

Systemic practitioners working in public contexts will borrow from the various different approaches and find their own idiosyncratic ways of integrating ideas, dependent on their own training as well as on the specifics of the work setting (Asen and Tomson 1992). Integration is a dynamic process, based on continuously evaluating one's working model in the light of feedback. Changing political climates and economic realities, and changing clinical priorities and media attention all affect which aspects of what model may be more relevant and which of the various integrated approaches provide a better fit with the developments in the larger social system. For example, it could be argued that the emergence of 'solution focused therapy' in the 1980s fitted with Thatcher's and Reagan's ideologies, which did not wish to examine the causes of dis-order, but rather to provide quick solutions. A whole cohort of quickly trained solution-focused therapists emerged literally overnight and seemed to apply their purist method to whoever seemed to come their way. Whilst there are aspects of this approach which are clearly useful when combined and integrated with other systemic ideas, it is the prescription of just one medicine, or an 'invariate' intervention, irrespective of context and presentation, that seems limited.

Using and inventing contexts for change

The systemic model, with its emphasis on circularity, permits to conceptualize the relationship between the users (formerly known as patients) and the service providers in interactional terms. This is not a static but dynamic relationship, with the needs and requirements of users changing the services, and with services creating or changing the needs of users. For example, the provision of a family therapy service signals that families can be 'therap-ed', a revolutionary concept some 40 years ago. Creating a new context for potential change thus generates an apparently new need and it takes time for referrers and families to make sense of that new context within which to look for change. Accessibility is a related issue that lends itself to systemic reflection. It is well known that specific potential users from certain backgrounds, notably minority ethnic groups, often do not access psychotherapy services. Much of this has to do with the perceived non-relevance of Western-inspired psychotherapy models and practices for these groups and communities. Their cultural beliefs and presentations require different contexts so that change can be promoted. Culture-sensitive services have to be put in place to provide an appropriate fit.

In the following section some aspects of the work of the Marlborough Family Service will be described. This serves as an illustration of how clinicians design and redesign services continuously in the light of feedback, so that these are more relevant for the users. In so doing clinicians have to invent a whole series of integrative approaches, based on the different models and techniques of the various systemic approaches described above.

The Marlborough Family Service

The overall approach is systemic

Each week some 10–20 new referrals are received from GPs, social workers, schools, courts, psychiatrists, psychologists, and health visitors. There are also many self-referrals. The whole team meets at the beginning of each week and considers how to respond to these different requests. The guiding principle is embodied in the question:

'What is the most relevant context to respond to this specific request?' Responses to this question can range through providing individual, couple, family, or group sessions. Looking at context further, one can consider the most relevant site for such interventions – be that the consulting room in a clinic, a school, an inpatient ward, the home, or elsewhere. Moreover, further consideration is given to the most appropriate persons present at the outset of therapy – the users alone, users plus professionals, professionals only for consultation – and so on. When clinicians think contextually then there is a whole range of different responses to each individual request for help or consultation, with not just one but a number of options possible.

There was a time when many systemic practitioners, including my team, believed that it would be best to deal with all clients and their individual problems by reframing these as soon as possible into family issues. Logically we prescribed family therapy, which was conducted by one therapist and supervised by invisible colleagues behind a one-way screen, preferably in teams of four, with sessions lasting for 60–90 minutes. From time to time there were breaks, with the therapist consulting with the team and, on returning to the consulting room, facing the family with some well-designed intervention. Whilst this therapeutic context may be relevant for some users, it is insufficient or inappropriate for others.

It was the encounter with apparently 'disorganized' families (Minuchin *et al.* 1967) that made our team at the Marlborough first pose the question: 'What is the context that we need to use or *invent* to address the issues these families want or need to address?' At the time we knew that once-weekly family therapy was insufficient to address the many issues in multi-problem families, which almost always tended to include violence, drug or alcohol abuse, adult mental illness, social exclusion, and other 'heartsink' presentations. We therefore had the idea of creating a day unit where families could attend every day of the week, for 6–8 hours, for weeks or months. We also thought that having quite a number of families attending at the same time might deal with their social exclusion and isolation. Problems such as physical and sexual abuse, alcoholism, and domestic violence have a tendency to isolate families from neighbours and friends. Moreover, the stigma attached to these problems further enhances the sense of being different or feeling marginalized. Bringing families together and encouraging them to make contact with one another counteracts such isolation. Multiple family work is geared towards families becoming curious about one another and considering helping one another (Asen *et al.*, in press; Laqueur *et al.* 1964). The stigma of mental illness, abuse, or violence is addressed when different families presenting with similar problems of living exchange their experiences and can feel that they are 'all in the same boat'.

The design of the Marlborough Family Day Unit programme very much addressed the issue of chaos – a tightly constructed timetable requiring families to constantly adapt to the ever-changing contexts and requirements (Asen *et al.* 1981). Designed as 'an institution for change' (Cooklin *et al.* 1983) the family day unit has itself gone through many different transitions and phases over the past two decades. It aims to create and replicate familiar crises rather than providing a sanctuary from everyday stresses. Having a number of families present at the same time intensifies living. Providing a therapeutic context that deliberately enacts crises (Minuchin and Fishman 1981) that are familiar in that they revolve around everyday issues, allows planning and a proactive approach. This is a very different experience to that of the apparently random production of crises that multi-problem families tend to be so good at, forcing professionals continuously to react. Instead the family day unit is an intensive daily living context, which allows exploration of, and experimentation with, developing different behaviours, be that around issues of violence, inappropriate sexual behaviours, or drug and alcohol abuse.

Inventing a school for families

All systemic therapists will have had the experience of not making any progress in therapeutic work with some families. Instead of blaming the family and labelling them as being intractable, it may be worthwhile to reflect on why the therapeutic context provided seems irrelevant. One such problem area concerns children who cannot be contained by schools.

The Marlborough Family School was created to deal with pupils who had been excluded from their schools because of serious learning difficulties, violence, or disruptive behaviours. The schools seemed to put all the blame at the family's door whilst the family tended to blame the school entirely for the educational failure of the children. The more the family blamed the school, the more the school blamed the family. Soon an impasse was reached, with the child caught between the warring parties. The family refused to seek psychiatric or psychological help and the teachers no longer wanted these difficult children in their classes. To overcome this deadlock we decided to open a family school, where parents could witness their children's educational problems and where teachers could witness the family issues that are often transferred into school (Dawson and McHugh 1994).

Rather than considering a pupil's behaviour in isolation, the systemic approach focuses on relationships between pupil, school, and family (Dowling 1985). Whatever the presenting problem, the ability to use a systemic perspective can help to make sense of a child's difficulties that are being played out in the school context (Dawson and McHugh 1986, 1994). Seeing connections between a child's presentation at school and their relational experience and learning at home has been crucial in the attempt to create an integrated intervention approach that reflects the true dimensions of the child's world.

In the early years it seemed that going to the families' homes was the best way of engaging people to attempt to allay their fears and to persuade them to accept the referral. Over recent years we have largely stopped doing home visits and have come to rely on the multi-family group to engage new families thinking about taking up a place at our family school (Asen *et al.*, in press). The new family is invited to visit our school just to look at what goes on there. It is explicitly stated that there is no expectation of a commitment to take up a place at this stage. The prospective families always come during the morning when other children and their parents are there. After a brief discussion with the child and their parents, they are introduced to one or more of the parents who are already attending our family school with their own child. They are left alone together by the teacher after the new family has been advised to find out as much as they can about what actually happens and whether the place is any use or not. There is no doubt that, in the vast majority of cases, this is the single most effective element of the process of engaging new families into the family school.

However, working systemically does not mean just working with families. In the family school individual psychodynamic orientation work with children often complements the family work. It is an acknowledgement that children have their own issues, which are at times best addressed in an individual context. Similarly, it is possible to provide psychotherapy for some of the adults. Moreover, group work takes place, with a weekly children and adults' group. Occasionally psychotropic medication may be prescribed if the acute symptoms require this. Whilst the overall approach is systemic, this does not exclude the use of other treatment models and modalities. The resulting work is a good example of an integrated approach – bringing together systemic, psychodynamic, and more traditional psychiatric practices.

Creating dedicated psychotherapy services for minority ethnic users

Family therapists, perhaps more than any other group of mental health professionals, have in recent years become increasingly preoccupied with gender, race, and class issues and how these affect clinical practice. Gender assumptions, racism, and class prejudice are all-powerful determinants of behaviour. Many systemic therapists have started examining their own professional attitudes in relation to these issues, aiming to develop more sensitive and appropriate practices (Boyd-Franklin 1989; Goldner *et al.* 1990) when consulting with individual clients or families, as well as when dealing with the larger professional networks.

When looking at referral patterns more than a decade ago, the Marlborough team discovered that we had remarkably few clients and families from the different minority ethnic cultures that are so prevalent in the centre of London, with its huge first and second generation immigrant population. We had to question our practices and ask what it was that made it so difficult for families from other cultures to access our services. Posing the question: 'What is the context that we need to create to get these families to use our service?' proved yet again useful. The first step was to examine our own work context, including our own prejudices and non-conscious racist practices. Inviting an outside consultant experienced in anti-racist training led to (at times painful) organizational change, culminating in the development of a culture- and race-sensitive family therapy training course and subsequently a major training / service development: the Marlborough Asian Family Counselling Service (Krause and Miller 1995; Miller and Thomas 1994). This service was aimed at providing a culturally sensitive socio-psychological service to people of all ages from specified local minority ethnic groups who had, or were likely to develop, psychological or psychiatric problems. In order to deliver such services, a culturally sensitive training programme had to be created, to provide a sound foundation for the counselling of Chinese, Bangladeshi, and Pakistani–Punjabi families. Senior clinicians from the Marlborough eventually managed to convince local politicians and health managers to fund this project. Six workers from the relevant communities were appointed in 1995 and received systemic training. In the event the training became a two-way process, with the Asian trainees training the rest of the Marlborough team to understand culture-specific presentations, the meanings of symptoms, and illness patterns. The Asian counselling service, made up of seven part-time therapists, now provides systemic work for many individuals, families, and professionals from different cultures. At the outset most families, particularly from the Bangladeshi community, needed to be engaged in their homes. They seemed reluctant to come to the clinic, but over time the Bengali community has become more trusting of the service provided. Based on positive feedback from satisfied users, families started attending the clinic and the demand soon became overwhelming. This meant that non-Bangladeshi clinicians had to see some of the individuals and families. This did not prove a major issue as, by association, other staff had also become acceptable over time and the work could be done by any member of staff, with the help of interpreters. Chinese families turned out to be particularly difficult to engage and, again, the key question for us to get a direction was: 'What is the relevant context that we need to create or utilize to engage users from the Chinese community?' If Chinese users were not coming to see us, we would go and see them in their living contexts. This led us to consider to start an outreach project in Soho, London's Chinatown, where once a week, in a local health centre, our two colleagues from Hong Kong see people 'on-site'.

Multi-level systems interventions

Systemic therapists have to think about intervening simultaneously at different levels of the systems: the individual, family, social, and professional levels. The family lives in a social setting which is often an appropriate site for intervention – be that the neighbourhood, school, friends, work, or religious contexts. Multi-problem families often tend to be multi-agency families and change is impossible if the professional network is not included. Network meetings, involving professionals as well as the family's own network, are often the prerequisite for carrying out therapeutic work subsequently. The aim of a network meeting is to provide a map of the significant relationships within the family–professional network, to understand each person's concerns, and to design an action plan, clearly spelling out aims, duration, and focus of the work (Schuff and Asen 1996). A series of questions addressed to both family members and professionals provide the structure for the meeting. Professionals who are unable to attend the meeting are asked to address these questions prior to the meeting so that their views can be represented. The questions asked centre around the reasons and purpose of each professional's involvement, their views on problems and possible solutions, and their relationships with the family. Family members are asked to comment on the reasons for the professionals' involvement, their own views on the work carried out, and any goals for change they themselves have. This allows for a joint network action plan to be constructed, possibly in the form of a contract between the various agencies that specifies the tasks to be addressed and the frequency and purpose of therapeutic work, as well as agreeing on the consequences of change or no change. It has to be emphasized that network meetings usually take place within the context of childcare cases. Here the ability of families to change is being assessed and a trial of systemic therapy prescribed to see whether change can happen within a timescale compatible with the children's needs.

Working systemically with individuals

The term family no longer implies an intact, two-parent, heterosexual couple with children and pets. In our culture we have a co-existence of multiple forms of committed relationships and it is not necessary to have a family in order to work systemically – any relationship lends itself to receive systemic therapy. Some family therapists used to insist that the whole family had to attend for the first session and they would simply not start any therapeutic work until everyone was present. Not surprisingly, this meant that many therapies never took off. Nowadays many family therapists leave it to the referred person to decide who should attend. They then see it as the therapist's job to turn an individual into a family. It is not at all uncommon for the number of clients attending the actual therapy sessions to increase over time, from one person to as many as six or ten, including members of the extended family or friends. The guiding principle of this approach will no longer come as a surprise to the reader: 'What is the context that needs to be created for the work to start?' The answer must be obvious by now: any context that permits engagement. If the referred person chooses an individual context rather than bringing along the partner or whole family, then this does not mean that systemic work can not take place. Systemic work with individuals, or 'family therapy without the family', is another important context that can promote change (Jenkins and Asen 1992). In this approach the 'therapeutic system' is kept open, ready for anyone else to join if and when it seems right. Work within such a framework is very different from traditional psychotherapeutic work where the individual therapeutic space is protected.

Specific applications of systemic work

Research has shown that systemic work can produce good results. In this section two specific projects demonstrating the efficacy of systemic work will be mentioned.

Eating-disordered patients and their families

The value of systemic family therapy for the treatment of eating-disordered patients has been well established (Dare 1992; Russell *et al.* 1987). In practice, family therapy is at present used both as a sole form of treatment and in conjunction with other treatment methods. Once an appropriate target weight has been achieved on an inpatient unit, the patient is discharged home and continues to attend as a day- or outpatient, receiving individual and family therapy and, occasionally, medication. A frequent observation made is that, once discharged, patients tend to lose weight rapidly, particularly if the parents or other significant family members have not been involved in learning how to manage the eating routines of their teenagers, grown-up children, or partners. Successes achieved in a hospital setting are rarely generalized to the home and this raises the question as to what context would need to be invented to avoid immediate deterioration. Jointly with teams in Dresden (Scholz and Asen 2001) and London (Dare and Eisler 2000), we have experimented with a more intensive involvement of parents.

Systemic interventions with families containing an eating-disordered person aim to challenge diffuse or absent boundaries, parental hierarchies, and covert conflicts (Minuchin *et al.* 1978). Parents often report their own sense of trying to manage in isolation and being very reliant on doctors and therapists. To overcome their isolation they can be connected with other parents and thus contribute to a context of mutual support, with up to six families attending for the whole day over a period of a week and/or for a weekend. To see other parents struggling in similar ways creates a sense of solidarity and reduces some of the burden experienced by the carers. Being in the presence of other families highlights not only similarities but also differences between them. Families cannot help becoming curious about one another and this results in them viewing their predicaments from new and multiple perspectives. If therapists encourage feedback between families, this can lead to mutual learning, as peer support and peer criticism are often more effective than input by qualified therapists. Bringing a number of families together for intensive days or weeks creates a hothouse effect. Interactions are necessarily more intense in a group setting where children and parents are participating in different tasks and where they are required to examine not only their own but also other families' communications and behaviours. This increased intensity can lead to rapid growth – change is more likely to take place as familiar coping and defence mechanisms cannot be employed. Being part of a multi-family setting requires families and their individual members continuously to change context and adapt to new demands. Such intensity cannot easily be created in individual family sessions. The sheer energy released in the course of such a programme provides a new structure for adolescents and parents alike, and creates hope. Many of the families form friendships which often continue long after the therapeutic work has finished.

Not all the work in such a multi-family programme is exclusive family group therapy. Other forms of psychotherapeutic treatment are provided alongside: individual with both psychodynamic and cognitive elements, some behavioural work, and occasionally medication. Preliminary results are very encouraging, with significantly increased recovery rates and high reductions of relapse, weight loss, and hospital re-admission.

Systemic couple therapy for depression

This was another project in which a systemic approach for working with depressed patients and their partners was developed and proved effective. When compared with cognitive and drug therapy, systemic couple therapy seems to have significantly better results (Leff *et al.* 2000). A health economic analysis showed that antidepressant treatment is no cheaper than systemic couple therapy.

The development of a treatment manual for this form of therapy was a precondition for the funding of the study by the body providing the grant. It proved possible to do this, with two systemic therapists from different orientations being able to integrate their similar and different ideas into a coherent manual (Jones and Asen 2000). Embarking on the project of manualizing therapy seemed a daunting task. How could it be possible to pin down therapeutic practice in a technical and prescriptive format? Psychotherapy is to many not a science but an art. Moreover, it also meant integrating the practices of two therapists sitting at somewhat different ends of the systemic spectrum. One could be described as being placed somewhere in the 'post-Milan' group, strongly influenced by feminist and social constructionist ideas (Jones 1993), the other occupying a position which draws on a number of different approaches, from structural to strategic to post-Milan therapies (Asen 1997). In the introduction to this manual we wrote: 'each therapist is likely to use most of these techniques during the course of therapy with each couple'. Yet, when retrospectively evaluating our work, we noticed that some techniques were very unlikely to be used, at least in their pure form, by either therapist. This is not at all surprising since experienced therapists are unlikely to be working in a way that reflects a pure model. It is common that after a significant period as a practitioner one's style becomes personal and influenced by a continuous learning process, integrating experiences from colleagues, clients, and one's own life. This corresponds to the 'mature clinician' version of integration (see Chapter 1).

The treatment manual (Jones and Asen 2000) describes the different phases of systemic couple work. In the beginning stages the therapist signals, by overt, para-verbal, and non-verbal communication, by even-handedness, willingness to hear both points of view, a neutrality towards outcomes and multiple perspectives, that s/he is someone with whom a containing space can be created in which the couple's dilemmas can be explored.

At the outset the therapist explores the problem definitions of the couple and their reports of those of significant others, thus simultaneously obtaining a picture of the network of significant relationships within which the problem is contextualized. This may be done with the help of a genogram (family tree) or by using other relationship maps. Exploring the problem definition has behavioural and constructionist-associated elements; the therapist will seek information about how the problem has manifested itself over time, its effects on all concerned, and how others respond to it, as well as what meanings are attributed to it by the various participants in the couple's social network. Thus current patterns are linked to multi-generational patterns in the past. Sessions in this phase are likely to be spaced closely together (e.g. at weekly or fortnightly intervals).

In the middle stage of therapy the exploration is likely to be less tightly problem-focused. Instead there is an exploration of the wider patterns which are maintaining and are being maintained by the problem. This altered emphasis may represent an attempt to widen the focus of therapy in order to shift a still intractable problem, or to stimulate change in the couple's relationship with each other (and others) in order to prevent recurrence of the problem, or to begin to focus on 'quality-of-life' questions.

By this stage the clients are likely to be more active in setting the agenda for therapy, including making decisions about optimum spacing of sessions (which is likely to be at longer intervals now). The time frame of therapy will continuously be moving backwards and forwards from dilemmas in the present, to connections in the past of the couple and the 'luggage' they may be carrying from their families of origin, to the feared or desired future. Now therapy will predominantly focus on the detailed work of altering habitual patterns of behaviour and of belief which may, by now, have been identified as reinforcing and maintaining unwanted feeling states or actions, including the client's depression.

The formation, by now, of a working alliance between therapist and client means that the therapist in this phase can feel more confident about using techniques likely to trigger major perturbation and change for clients, such as feed-forward questions, challenging, enactment, reframing, amplified use of stories and metaphors, tasks and non-verbal techniques, and so on (Jones and Asen 2000). There is likely to be an ever-strengthening focus on client strengths and resources, on the amplification of whatever small changes may be present, and of a constant shifting of responsibility and 'ownership' of change from therapist to clients. It is also the phase in which therapist and clients may have the most frustrating experiences of being stuck, of wrestling with intractable difficulties, and of despair.

The last phase of therapy is characterized by a review of the work done, as well as by anticipation and prevention of relapse. This includes the identification of patterns which in the past have led up to a depressive episode, and rehearsing new strategies for dealing with it differently. This may include an unpacking, more explicitly than before, by the therapist of their own understandings and hypotheses about client dilemmas, which can act as a sort of 'take-home' message for the clients. Sessions in the later phases of therapy are likely to be more widely spaced than before (several weeks if not months), and may include booster sessions after completion of the therapy.

As part of the preparation for ending therapy it may be useful to discuss the role of the therapist in the couple's life. This might include a consideration of how the couple will, in the future, continue the work started in the therapy, and will therefore lead on to hypothetical explorations of future scenarios, hopes, fears, strategies for actions, and the development and maintenance of new narratives and beliefs.

The treatment manual also describes in considerable detail the specific techniques used. It could be argued that writing a treatment manual is one thing but adhering to it may be another. Manual adherence is important in research so that research can be replicated and results can be compared. Each session was videotaped and tapes were randomly selected by an independent rater to check for treatment adherence and treatment integrity. It was concluded (Schwarzenbach and Leff 1995) that it was possible to describe systemic therapy for couples in great detail and to adhere to the treatment manual during therapy.

The integration of systemic therapy

After a promising infancy and a rather stormy adolescence, the systemic approach has finally come of age. Systemic practitioners have attempted to integrate their work into the mainstream of psychiatry and psychology. Systemic work has been scientifically researched for a variety of illnesses and disorders, from schizophrenia to depression, from eating disorders in teenagers and adults to behavioural disorders in children. It has proved to be highly effective for these and other conditions. Family therapy has become an acceptable form of treatment, not only to colleagues but also to the public at large (Asen 1995).

Sadly the two disciplines of family therapy and psychoanalysis remain organizationally and conceptually dissociated from each other despite considerable overlap (Dare 1998). Both therapeutic approaches have come closer in the past two decades, agreeing that there is a joint preoccupation with telling stories and personal narratives. When it comes to the public sector, the dialogue between psychodynamic and systemic practitioners is in practice now flourishing in quite a few settings, driven by the need to provide appropriate treatments for clients.

Systemic work is no longer marginalized but has become increasingly central to much mental health and psychotherapeutic work. It is practised in many different settings, from primary care to specialist centres, with professionals from very different disciplines receiving training. Family therapist posts were first created in the UK in 1983 and have since mushroomed. When thinking about working systemically it may be helpful to be reminded of the difference between systemic therapy as one of a number of psychological treatment methods and systemic therapy as a way of conceptualizing psychological and psychosocial disturbance. The latter, namely 'thinking systems', is an indispensable tool for any clinician to view the patient, the family, the institution in context. The systemic approach provides different perspectives and thus informs the clinical management of most patients and their treatments. Whilst systemic work is well integrated in the field of child and adolescent psychiatry, its place in adult psychiatry is in no way established. It is easy – and unsystemic – to lay the blame for the failure to embrace the family systems approach entirely at the door of traditional psychiatry and psychiatrists. Systemic therapists also need to question their own beliefs and prejudices: what is it that systemic therapists do that makes their services so unattractive to psychiatry? Working alongside psychiatry, not in competition with it, is one way of helping integration. Humility about their own successes *and* failures might help systemic therapists to engage the curiosity of traditional psychiatry. After all, how can one hope to help a family – or an individual for that matter – to integrate if the services provided are themselves dis- or un-integrated?

Chapter 5

Groups and integration in psychotherapy

Chris Mace

Psychotherapeutic models in the group

After agreeing to write this chapter, I went to a symposium on the interface between psychoanalytic and cognitive psychotherapies. It was well attended by practitioners schooled in one or other tradition. The session began with illustrated presentations from two psychoanalysts and two cognitive therapists. The cognitive therapy speakers were clear, honest, and willing to exchange their perceptions and ideas. The psychoanalytic speakers likewise, but they also spiced the atmosphere with several references to the greater breadth, depth, and subtlety of their art, and an uninvited analysis of one of the cognitive speaker's actions. The clinical illustrations had been sufficiently transparent to indicate the severity of the patients the speakers were working with and shared considerable overlap.

With the set presentations over, discussion began. This developed well, exploring points of difference and commonality in what had just been said. Many of the overt themes from that discussion are raised in the present volume. An initial focus on the traumatic content of both narratives from the presentations led to questions on whether the most important divisions between therapies concerned theory or practice (cf. Chapter 2). Did apparently fundamental differences in aim reflect a difference between what it is bearable or unbearable to think about and what it is possible or impossible to live through? In any case, might the talk of opposing models conceal a more significant opposition – one separating reconstructive therapy from brief therapy of any persuasion? Whatever their labels, weren't all brief treatments, being fundamentally supportive as opposed to reconstructive, essentially similar in terms of underlying process and impact?

After testing tensions between the two models, the discussion looked at ways of living with them. How does one decide during assessment which form of therapy is most suitable? Who should decide this anyway? How important is it really to know this before you start? It was interesting that the cognitive–behavioural therapists expressed the greatest uncertainty about the usefulness or reliability of these predictions. One of them also observed that, rationales notwithstanding, hope was more important for patients than insight. Other participants lamented discrepancies between ideals and actual practice as an attrition of the analytic attitude in the face of service demands. The discussion had not flagged for a moment.

At this point, a member of the audience asked the panel to comment about whether doing psychotherapy in groups affected the models. No reply came. Instead, there were anxious glances across the podium. Speakers avoided the chair's eye. It seemed nobody had anything to say about groups. Silence. Finally, a waving hand was found in the audience into which a microphone could be placed. The new speaker, having a very different point to make, began by admitting he was really talking to fill an uncomfortable gap.

What was happening here? The exchanges of looks seemed to say, first, that the question was puzzling and perhaps irrelevant. As far as this chapter is concerned, of course, the question was central. I don't think this kind of response to it is uncommon when therapists are personally unfamiliar with group treatments. It is more paradoxical for it to occur at a meeting that began with observations on the reflexivity of the afternoon's task and on the need for psychotherapists to address their own assumptions in order to understand each other. The group question had prompted people to become aware of being there together, in an unexpected, unsettling, and quietening way.

While the above account does little justice to the texture of a discussion as it unfolds among a group of people, it is enough to indicate how different this is to a printed argument. The question about groups is genuinely difficult. Nobody there agreed or denied that being in, as well as thinking about, groups affect the models they were discussing, but there was an uneasy sense of recognition around the idea. It needs to be developed. Does the shift in therapeutic modality from individual to group make contrasts between one model and another more or less acute? And what might this mean for anybody working therapeutically in groups now and in the future?

Analysis in the group

The group is slow to start its session. Jackie has not appeared, but everybody else has arrived, including Kevin, the newest member, who is attending his third session. Larry asks if Jackie will be coming, and when he hears that she has sent no message to the group, he comments that she seemed very upset the previous session and may have been unable to face coming to the session. Larry admits he was upset himself by arguing in the last session. Mary says that she's annoyed because she felt she'd supported Jackie and it was selfish of her to stay away. Norman suggests that Mary should say more about her feelings of irritation, they sound important. At this point, Kevin, who has been growing increasingly restless, interjects. He asks if it's usual for people to be discussed in the group when they're not present. He is hostile, and the others murmur that they see nothing wrong in doing so. Kevin becomes more agitated, saying the others should not talk about people behind their backs. People need to be here to answer for themselves. The conductor, Dick, points out that it is important for members to discuss anything that feels important to them. For instance, he indicates Mary may need to explore her reactions to what has happened in order to work something out for herself. Dick notes that Kevin is clearly agitated by what has happened, and wonders why this might be so. Kevin says he never talks about people behind their backs and other people shouldn't do so either. He's fed up with back-stabbing and if that's what other people want to do, they can count him out of it. However, when Norman attempts to help Mary understand her irritation with Jackie, Kevin can't stay quiet. He asks them not to talk about Jackie. The others ask why it is, if Kevin wants people to get off his back, that he can't allow them to get on with what they need to do either. [A]

An interesting situation is developing. An event like the unexplained absence of a group member is likely to affect all members of a group. It can be expected to precipitate responses, such as Mary's protest, Norman's pairing with Mary, or Kevin's idealization of Jackie coupled with denial of his own and others' needs, that are characteristic of each member's style of coping with separation. In a psychodynamic working context, these can be construed in the languages of defensive styles, attachment dynamics, internal objects, and so forth. However, in this case there is a more immediate obstacle to progress, one likely to preclude an exploration on such lines. Kevin's behaviour is so disruptive to the work of the group it cannot be ignored.

Kevin responds to Norman and Mary where we left them by saying that they're now getting at him. He thinks that everyone in the group just wants him to push off. Dick suggests that Kevin feels attacked and Kevin says that he does. Dick refers back to Kevin's objections when the others started to talk about Jackie, and wonders whether Kevin felt that any talk about her would have to be an attack on her. Kevin agrees with this, but insists that the others do have it in for her. Perhaps Kevin assumes that anybody who is absent will be attacked here? It seems that if Kevin remains silent, he fears he will be attacked. Otto, who has shown a similar tendency in the past, suggests that Kevin's own aggression is really making people attack him. Kevin asserts that Otto's the one who's being aggressive, when Patsy, who has been silent up until now, looks hard at Kevin and asks if he thinks she's aggressive. He says maybe not, at least not yet. Patsy then sits up, juts her head forward, swings her arms back in a way that all the group recognize. She asks Kevin whether he'd say anyone who was doing what she was doing was aggressive. Kevin protests he doesn't really do what she's doing, anyway, he can't help how he walks because, because . . . . Patsy's point is made. Kevin stays silent. Later in the session he is able to listen to the others telling him how his aggressive behaviour makes them feel, and he admits for the first time to being vulnerable himself.

Episodes like this are not uncommon in outpatient groups. Beyond helping to hold Kevin in the group, it was probably not mutative in itself. Further repetitions with variations were necessary before small but real changes in Kevin's approach to others were felt by them. Our interest here is more in the kind of process that is going on. There is a plethora of elements. Ventilation and disclosure of reactions occur alongside visual and verbal feedback. 'Hot cognitions' in the form of Kevin's beliefs about attack and the dangers of being spoken about are recognized and drawn out. Interpretation highlighted self-maintaining aspects of Kevin's behaviour, in the relative absence of attention to early experiences, transference, or fantasy. Within individual psychotherapies, these elements would be seen as variously proper to behavioural, cognitive, or integrative treatments. Yet nothing here is actually incompatible with the range of activities acknowledged by Foulkes (1975) within group-analytic groups, or by Yalom (1995) in respect of groups in which interpersonal learning is seen as the agent of change. How can this be so?

These mixed events might be seen as an example of drift on the part of the group leader, failing to stick to his model or manual, rather than a necessary accommodation to the group setting. The principle that psychotherapists should be identified by what they do rather than what they say they do is certainly applicable to group leaders. After conducting blind independent assessment of 20 groups conducted by adherents of 10 distinct schools of group intervention, Yalom and colleagues had to conclude:

> *The ideological school to which a leader belonged told us little about the actual behaviour of that leader.* We found that the behaviour of the leader of one school – for example, gestalt therapy – resembled the behaviour of the other gestalt therapy leader no more closely than that of the other seventeen leaders. In other words, the behaviour of leaders is not predictable from their membership in a particular ideological school.
>
> (Yalom 1995, p.497; italics in original.)

In this instance, the flavour of the group owes a great deal to the leader's willingness to allow members of the group to find creative responses to the difficulties Kevin presents. Their striking variety owes everything to Kevin's fellow patients rather than to the calculation of the therapist. This reliance on the group members' potential to therapize is consistent with the stated philosophies of both group-analytic groups ('analysis in the group, by the group, for the group'; Foulkes 1946) and Yalom's emphasis on 'interpersonal learning' as the key to change. The importance of members' contributions to the climate of any group is likely to be a major factor in it seeming impervious to its leader's training.

It might still be true that ambiguity concerning a group's model is peculiar to groups within a psychodynamic spectrum, where there may be relatively fewer constraints on members' as well as therapists' behaviour. Not all authors would agree. Albert Ellis has taken this theme up in observations about cognitive–behavioural groups. It is worth summarizing his method first.

Patients join Ellis' groups after previous therapy and with a well-formulated agenda. The group's therapist takes responsibility for checking members' homework, while he actively encourages other group members to learn to give feedback as part of the process of overcoming their own cognitive inhibitions. The emphasis is as much on interpersonal teaching as learning. Ellis favours groups as a medium for cognitive change because of their emotionally arousing character and the opportunities they offer for flushing out otherwise dormant behaviours, feelings, and beliefs for therapeutic attention. Ellis is particularly keen to harness a group's potential to overcome emotional resistances due to shame.

Ellis' therapeutic targets tend to be enduring beliefs concerning self, others, and the world – themes that would correspond to 'deep cognitions' or schemas in cognitive theory. In contrast to work focusing on situation-specific, 'surface' cognitions, these are also closer to the kind of internal representations that preoccupy therapists working with psychodynamic and psychoanalytic models (cf. Chapter 3). Ellis' use of groups for a cognitive therapy also adopts a relatively dynamic approach to technique. He comments

> even, then, when a therapy group tries to follow a somewhat narrow theory of psychotherapy . . .
> it tends to be much wider ranging in its actions than it is in its theory, and often takes on a
> surprisingly eclectic approach.
>
> (Ellis 1993, p. 78.)

However desirable and frequent accommodations of therapeutic models to the group context may be, are they necessary? Is it possible to run a group in which a psychotherapeutic model will be adhered to strictly, with the group being little more than a means of sharing a treatment in order to make the most efficient use of therapists' time? A different scenario may help the discussion.

An experiment with group cognitive–behaviour therapy

Ed and Elsa are starting a group for young women referred to a specialist clinic. They intend to use it to introduce a cognitive–behavioural intervention in which they will first of all provide learning materials. They have a definite schedule of topics to take the group through, session by session. These introduce the members to the cognitive techniques they intend to use, as well as ideas about the thinking processes typically associated with their difficulties. Six women attended the initial meeting, but at the second there are only four.

They sit together in the group room, eyes averted, half listening. Two seem to be trembling slightly. Ed and Elsa come in and Elsa tells the group that in future weeks they'll review homework from the previous session at the beginning of the meeting. However, as there wasn't any last time, they ask the members how they've been getting on. Rosie asks Ed what has happened to Sue and Tracey who are missing. Elsa says they don't know and asks again how everyone has got on since the previous week. Una says she has been so bad she doesn't think anybody in the group will understand what she has done. Ed says of course they will, and starts to talk about how all women with her condition feel they are the only ones to have the problem. He gives examples of how people believe they have ruined themselves if they lose control. He suggests this is common if someone is too hard on themselves, and goes into reasons why this might be. Ed talks for some time, and when he pauses, nobody speaks. Elsa suggests that the women must know what Ed is talking about. Vera says she thinks she used to be something like this. Ed and Elsa then move into a prepared talk on the relationship between behaviour, thoughts, and mood. They ask the women to try and catch ways in which they have automatic thoughts, and to bring some examples of these back the following week.

Una did not return the following week, and the group collapsed beyond the point of recovery at the fourth session. Neither Ed nor Elsa turned up to take the group that day. Each assuming the other would be there to take charge, neither contacted the other before the session amid the various alternative calls on their attention. Instead, Eric, a senior colleague of Ed and Elsa's, confronted with three waiting patients, and hearing Ed and Elsa had not appeared, chose to meet with them himself. Eric had met all three before and was told they expected to work on straightening out thoughts that day. He said that should be easy, and started to comment on how miserable the women looked. Then he went round each one in turn, going over what he remembered about each of them and asking in great detail about their past as if the others were not there. He promised them he would see Ed and Elsa were there the following week and left. The next week, only Vera returned. It was decided she should be seen individually from that point.

This group had different patients and a different method. Of course, general conclusions cannot be drawn from this one rather disastrous instance. Plainly, the therapists were anxious, hasty, and inexperienced, and their attempts to follow recipes for treatment will not be representative of the actions of an expert in cognitive–behaviour therapy. The episode nevertheless illustrates a number of contrasts. Alongside efforts to keep the group to a preconceived task, expressed anxieties about the absence of other members were not responded to. Any attributions other members might have had about this went unheard. Una's belief that she was exceptional was explained away before it was understood. While these are questionable practices in any setting, there was evident unwillingness to make concessions to the group situation by Ed, Elsa, or Eric. Beyond treating it as a modified classroom or consulting room, they did not seem to wish to seek out positive ways in which opportunities unavailable in a one-to-one encounter could be realized.

At the same time, the fact that the group as well as the patients here suffered from the experience indicates the importance of identifying factors which are undermining for any group, irrespective of its model. Beyond individual treatment models, are there some common principles of hygiene that, while not guaranteeing a group's health, certainly promote it? Attempts to identify factors associated with a therapeutic group's capacity to survive and function should be fertile ground for integrative thinking. While having affinities to the so-called 'therapeutic factors' (concepts such as universality, altruism, or cohesiveness that have been used to explain how exploratory groups are beneficial for the individual), this kind of understanding needs to be closer to group events and less dependent on inference if it is to be very broadly applicable.

An ABC of group health

In psychotherapy, there are few normative concepts which manage to transcend specific models while maintaining a capacity to qualify as a requirement for different theoretical approaches. In one-to-one situations, the therapeutic (or working) alliance is one example of a parameter which can not only be experienced and thought about within therapeutic sessions, but also formally assessed outside of them (cf. Chapter 3). It can be an immediate object of therapeutic interventions. Respecting cognitive–behaviourists' preference for 'ABC' schemata, I shall outline three features of any group that seem to fulfil these requirements.

A is for affect. Among all the 'feeling' words (mood, emotion, etc.), 'affect' is the one that relates to reception of feeling. It is impossible to sit in a group without being affected by tides of feeling. These may fluctuate from moment to moment, and individuals vary in their sensitivity to them. Group affects reflect the subjective emotional states of individual members, but also attitudes and relationships in the room. Groups naturally differ in the extent to which they make exploration of feelings an explicit therapeutic task. Implicit in this is the view that nobody conducting a group can afford not to be open to and questioning of themselves, especially about the affect that they experience.

In the two groups discussed earlier, recognition of and response to affect were very different. Dick was not only attuned to the irritation of the other members with Kevin before arguments surfaced, but also sensed much of the fear that was driving Kevin's behaviour. These apprehensions were put to use when Dick spoke to Kevin in the group in a way that allowed its affects to come fully to the surface and be appreciated by everybody in a way that, at least temporarily, contained them. The interventions of Ed and

Elsa paid little attention to the affect in the second group. Recognition of the fear, and probable guilt, over the loss of Sue and Tracey might have allowed Ed and Elsa to help the group to get on with its tasks, even if these did not include detailed examination of how all the members were feeling. Careful reassurance based on accurate empathy might have left the members less paralysed and more trusting of the group and its leaders. Inattention to affect probably had further consequences here. Ed and Elsa's fixation on protocols was not responsive to members' concerns, but represented their means of coping with the group's affect. Their subsequent avoidance of the group, while still failing to recognize how it was literally affecting them, mirrored the retreat of its members in the face of an unbearable situation.

B is for boundaries. While open to broader interpretation, a group's boundaries will refer here to its membership, setting, and duration. These need not only to be clear, but also secure. Whether this is so or not will depend less on provision of information than the active efforts made by the group's leader(s) to maintain them. As in the case of affect, attention to boundaries may be a more or less prominent part of the conductor's work, according to the type of group concerned. However, there is no therapeutic group in which the need to establish, clarify, and maintain appropriate boundaries can be ignored. Most patients find it harder to trust, depend upon, and expose themselves to a group than to an individual, and consistency of boundaries needs to be actively maintained. At the same time, threats to these boundaries from within and beyond a group can take an astonishing variety of forms. In practice, continuing attention to the boundaries of membership, setting, and duration is necessary if they are not to be compromised and the work of the group to suffer. This may involve the group leader(s) working outside the group sessions to ensure that a group's structural needs are understood and respected within the institutions in which it meets.

Both of the groups described were not only having to cope with the unexpected absence of one or more members, but also they had not yet established secure membership. In Dick's group, Kevin had just arrived: it was far from certain whether he would stay. In directing his interventions towards Kevin, Dick can be seen as working to reduce immediate threats to the group's membership as well as to its functional integrity. The newness of Ed and Elsa's group meant that its membership was far from being consolidated, despite an understanding that, once started, no new members could join. Ed and Elsa allowed themselves to be preoccupied with other issues to the exclusion of membership. The manner in which their colleague could expect to simply act in their place, without any invitation or making any attempt to contact them, betrayed a much wider failure to establish boundaries for the group within the unit in which it met.

C is for communication. Whether a group sits in silence, or its members all speak at once, it is permeated by communications which have direction and meaning. Therapists work in the group through their communications with members, but the signals that members send to each other can have more impact. These can work to the advantage or disadvantage of a group. Some groups place a high premium on the therapeutic value of members' spontaneous communications: something that had remained isolated in silence becomes freed through the linking that verbal communication provides. However, silence within the group can be destructive when it fails to be followed by such linking. All kinds of pathogenic expectations of the consequences of speaking out are reinforced if the experiment is not made. At worst, unchallenged covert communications may precede gross attempts by group members to join up in wordless and group-destructive regression through sex or intoxication. Leaders of any group need to monitor the quality of communication, being vigilant as to whether it is congruent with affect and progressing in spontaneity and depth.

In Dick's group, there was not only consonance between the leaders' and members' communications, but the non-verbal communications were creatively used to develop and respond to the group's immediate dilemmas. In Ed and Elsa's group, the leaders' presentations of an explicit therapeutic agenda grew alongside silences in which the remaining patients continued to develop catastrophic and self-fulfilling expectations. Like their leaders, they communicated nothing of their wish to flee until it was too late.

These parameters of affect, boundary, and communication do seem to represent elements of therapeutic groups that are integrative in transcending particular models. They are also potentially critical to a group's soundness as a vehicle for treatment. Once considerations of each group's own integrity surfaced, the admittedly dramatic examples highlighted a different meaning to integrative practice than the purity of a group's working philosophy. Seen in relief against a background of possible disintegration, 'integration' emerges as a practical, even moral, concept as well as an academic one.

Anxieties about personal disintegration will inform almost all psychotherapies at some level, but the prospect of visible disintegration in the fabric of the group, sometimes remote, sometimes obscuring all else, lends a distinct edge to group practice (Nitsun 1996). Tendencies for experienced group leaders to integrate methods may reflect lessons learned in living with this threat. However, as Bion (1961) demonstrates, there are ways of addressing such a threat that, while they allow people to restore some sense of comfort, do not help a group establish an ability to work. Attention to affect, boundaries, and communication should also find justification in Bion's terms by their incompatibility with group functioning based on what he termed 'basic assumptions'.

Are some therapeutic groups more integrative than others?

By attending to key parameters of group process, this account suggests how groups might be more or less integrative, irrespective of the model they formally adopt. Should 'integrative' therefore designate a dimension against which any group might be rated, rather than a particular range of eclectic practice? It is time to ask whether there are groups whose first and only description should be 'integrative'.

A therapeutic group might claim to be 'integrative' on several counts. While not mutually exclusive, these might emphasize the integrative nature of a group's model, of its aims, of specific techniques it employs, or of a group's relationship to its setting. These will be briefly considered and illustrated in order to consider what an 'integrative' group could be like.

Group delivery of integrative treatments

Other chapters in this book provide descriptions of recently introduced individual therapies that are seen to be 'integrative' because of their hybrid theory and practice. Examples would include the interpersonal therapy (IPT) of Klerman and Weissman (Klerman *et al.* 1984; Chapter 8, this volume) and the cognitive analytic therapy (CAT) of Ryle (Ryle 1990; Chapter 6, this volume). An integrative group can therefore be a group in which an attempt is made to transpose one of these models to a group setting.

Although the adjective 'interpersonal' is rather frequently and indiscriminately applied to therapeutic groups (this is almost a default position), it has begun to be used to designate IPT conducted in a group setting (IPT-G) (Wilflety *et al.* 1998). Although the potential of groups to amplify active components of the treatment such as affective exploration and problem solving is recognized, the group setting was felt to compromise the phased course of IPT. Group sessions have been augmented by three individual sessions, one each at the beginning, middle, and end of treatment. These are directed, respectively, towards initial reconnaissance of interpersonal problems and contract setting; review of progress and refinement of interpersonal goals; and agreement of an individualized plan for continuing work. There has been a heavy emphasis on written materials that is not found in individual IPT, with patients provided not only with a summary of their interpersonal goals, but also with a four-page summary of the interactions and personal implications of each session before the next session starts.

CAT has been adapted to group formats by Maple and Simpson (1995). The methods described in Chapter 6 for individual treatments were modified in ways which, in the retention of some individual sessions, resemble the IPT approach. Group CAT began with reformulation over four preparatory individual sessions, prior to patients joining a group for the subsequent treatment phase. The group then lasts for 12 sessions, everybody starting and finishing together. The therapists have prior knowledge of everybody's formulation (ideally, having been the therapists who agreed these with each future group member). All formulations then become group property, shared between the members. Members collaborate on helping each other recognize and revise their procedures within their formulations.

In both IPT-G and group CAT, therefore, an agenda worked out individually with the therapist is worked through in the group situation. This parallels techniques found in the earliest days of psychoanalytic group psychotherapy – a phase in which it remained psychoanalysis in a group, rather than group analysis proper. This could suggest both IPT-G and group CAT have some way to travel before becoming true group therapies. Maple and Simpson do describe a further step on that path, in the shape of group reformulation of dynamic patterns which impede the work of the group as a whole. However, the use by integrative therapists of focused preparatory sessions is consistent with one of the more robust findings in the group-outcome research literature: the association of positive outcome with some prior experience of individual therapy (Malan 1976).

Groups with integrative aims

The question of whether some forms of practice are more integrative than others in their aims is a delicate one. Hinshelwood (1988) has upheld a 'principle of integration' as the ethic of all psychotherapeutic activity. His philosophically informed discussions also illustrate the difficulties of suggesting that some practices might be more likely to realize this aim than others. If one is agnostic on the question of success, and simply asks whether some approaches are more consciously concerned with integration as a goal, a paradox emerges – having integrative aims is not invariably associated with integrative methods. For instance, despite the emphasis on systemic thinking as a 'formal' model of therapy (i.e. one that can be set alongside psychoanalytic and cognitive behavioural paradigms), systemic practice in groups is potentially more 'integrative' than work informed by other models. The reason is not that systemic therapists are often adept at making implicit use of analytic and cognitive understandings in what they do. It is because 'integration' is a more explicit objective of the therapeutic work in a systemic group. Convergence between positive changes in the process of the group and in members' own adjustment has been recognized by non-systemic therapists as a marker of success. Malcolm Pines' (1998) account of coherence in groups is a masterly example of this in an analytic context. In the systemic group, personal integration is achieved neither through retrospective analysis nor cognitive restructuring. *It follows total individual participation in a process in which conflicts are identified using oppositions between subgroups within the group.* These are first highlighted, populated, and articulated before resolution is invited through a cathartic understanding of the partiality of both subgroups' perspectives. Intragroup and intrapsychic boundaries are simultaneously redrafted and realigned. A new equilibrium is achieved, until the flow of tensions in the group, inevitably, draws attention to subgrouping elsewhere. In all this, the conductor is a ringmaster rather than a co-ordinator of ceremonies, staging a series of set pieces in a way that can nevertheless feel surprisingly natural.

The fluidity of systemic work of this type can make it seem elusive. Its principles have been set out by Agazarian (1998). They might be best illustrated from familiar ground. An impasse was reached in Dick's group at point [A] (cf. page 00). To see how this might be addressed by a systemic group therapist, assume that the members of the group have some working familiarity with systemic ideas, and the group is now led by a systemic therapist, Diane.

Diane turns to Kevin, and suggests he feels intensely uncomfortable about being in the group. She asks if he has a strong urge to do anything. He says he does. He wants to leave the room. She turns to the other members, asking if anybody else is feeling this urge and inviting them to join Kevin's subsystem. Both Otto and Mary, sitting on either side of Kevin, say they are. Diane invites them each to describe their urge to leave. Otto says he's afraid of hitting someone. Mary says she feels everybody is about to turn on her and that she'd better leave to prevent this. Diane asks if anybody else would like to join this 'leaving' subsystem. When no one volunteers, she identifies everybody else as members of the staying subsystem, and asks what they are feeling. When Larry says he doesn't see why members of Kevin's subsystem should feel they have to go, Diane remarks that what he has said is not a feeling. Larry obliges by saying he wants everyone to calm down. When he is challenged again, he admits he is feeling frightened and actually he did want them to go but was afraid of saying so. Norman admits he felt the same and is ashamed now. From the leavers' subsystem, Mary says that she is now feeling less like leaving. Diane suggests Mary checks out with Kevin how he is feeling now. Kevin says he is less angry, and feeling sorry towards the others he has frightened.

In this way, after invited intensification and consolidation, the internal boundaries between subsystems can be attenuated through exchanges within the subsystems and between them. Had no one joined Kevin's subsystem, Diane would probably have joined him to ensure that the intense polarization of wishes and feelings in the group did not become identified with individuals alone.

This style of active group management, and direct access and ventilation of affect through the leader's facilitation, has much in common with gestalt and psychodrama groups. These use different external vehicles instead of Agazarian's focus on group subsystems in order to access and clarify conflictual material, but are similarly integrative in that they attempt to identify and unify unintegrated subsystems – of the group, personality, or role. These approaches are also dialectical (cf. Chapter 9) in that there is constant interplay and flux between integration and disintegration, as the therapeutic process evolves.

Group use of integrative techniques

Group leaders may adopt particular techniques, irrespective of theory or other aims, to help a group integrate its own experience more effectively. By analogy with use of 'reflecting teams' in family therapy, these often seek group reflection through adjustments to working arrangements that introduce and exploit within-therapy functions traditionally left to supervision. Within systemic practice, a reflecting team of therapists observes an encounter between a therapist and a family. At a signal from the team, the therapist will end his session and invite the family to join him in the viewing room while their places in front of the window are taken by the reflecting team. Their subsequent unedited reflections on what they have seen are observed by the family and therapist, who then return to the room to discuss them.

A similar strategy has been used in training contexts to help groups observe and discuss themselves. However, a therapeutic group can also act as its own reflecting team through the use of audio or video technology. One technique is to introduce a temporal split halfway through the session, when spontaneous interaction is brought to a close. Members of the group adjust their chairs to watch the videotaped recording of their previous 45 minutes' interaction. The tape runs continuously while the members, and their conductor, comment on the interaction. Each member may be invited to take a lead when he or she is the subject. The result is a kind of meta-session. Comments may be more analytic but also more frank. The members find out more about what lay behind the words, deeds, and silences they registered the first time around, and they can voice their wishes, fulfilled and unfulfilled. The conductor offers observations on the process that may well have been distracting or inhibiting were they to be made (or thought of !) the first time around. These may now help the group to see patterns lying undiscovered in the heat of the moment and explain any of the conductor's comments that had not been appreciated. The intent of this reiteration in improving communication is obvious. It has close parallels to Robert Hobson's (1985) use of audio tape playback during sessions of individual therapy to deepen therapeutic conversation (cf. Chapter 7).

As Yalom observes, some of video's impact is unique, providing personal visual feedback to each member in a form that needs little elaboration to work its effect; a brief exposure goes a long way. Berger (1993) also comments favourably on the value to interacting group members of extended video exposure as they integrate multiple self-presentations within a more unified self.

Groups that are integrated within their setting

If all groups are a social microcosm, some enjoy greater integration with their reference groups than others. Among therapeutic groups, those that work not only to improve members' well-being, but also directly affect the milieu in which members live can claim to be integrative in this distinctive sense.

Although most therapeutic groups are stranger groups, those in which members (and leaders) also live alongside each other – for instance, in hospitals, communities, or therapeutic prisons – are likely to value integration in this way. Special techniques may be called for, respecting circumstances such as forms of staff participation apart from formal therapeutic leadership, the throughput of the group, and the members' level of functioning. Ways in which these are flexibly accommodated can be illustrated by reference to a weekly group for inpatients on an admission ward of a psychiatric hospital.

The therapist, Frank, arrives on the ward well before the session is due to begin. The group is new and Frank and his co-therapist Freda build its membership by asking any patients and staff they encounter if they know who is coming to that day's session. Everybody who is available, including staff, is encouraged to come along – provided patients are in a clear majority. At the start of the session Frank introduces himself, and asks each member to give their name and to say how long they've been on the ward (whether as patient or staff member). Following this, there is an active, facilitated discussion in which everybody in the room is included in some way (even by acknowledging their wish to be silent). Whatever is discussed is used to draw connections between people. Thus, if someone asks Frank how long his antidepressant, Smilex, will take to work, Frank will ask if anybody in the group knows. A clinical member of staff is likely to give a factual answer, but other patients will give their own experience. This is rarely what is stated in the pharmacopoeia, but may lead to identification of a subgroup of people who've been helped by Smilex, and those who haven't. What was good about it? What was bad about it? Why did they stop taking it? All contributions are welcomed, and are positively framed. They are never criticized. The focus changes quickly and, in terms of content, can seem inconclusive. Once a further view is aired, the reactions of others to it are sought. If the matter is contentious, and the group slow to respond, the therapist and co-therapist may themselves act out a difference in views. They do not argue to score points. Indeed, it is important they model enthusiasm for the exchange. Once a contrast is established – for instance, the therapist thinks its too noisy outside, the co-therapist does not – then an invitation is extended to voice feelings of sympathy with one view or the other by asking 'Who agrees with Frank?', 'Who agrees with Freda?' Problems and difficulties inspire most of the topics and contributions. No resolution is actively sought. The group is not intended to be problem solving, nor to transfer problem-solving skills. Its focus, unannounced, but constant, is encouragement to reduce isolation and overcome the fear of articulating private experience. In most sessions, the therapist or a chosen member will prepare the group for ending by introducing a closing review or summing up as an invitation for everyone to reflect on what they have shared.

These sessions have closer parallels with an confessional TV talk show than more sedate therapeutic groups. For some, a single session has to be sufficient. It is quite far from being a casual conversation as, individually, patients not only overcome barriers in communicating experience directly, but also come to understand how this always links them to some and separates them from others. It is also different from exchanges between strangers at a talk show as it inevitably returns to matters of communal concern, and seeds further exchanges through the week until the next session.

The use of therapist and co-therapist to draw out opposing views and feelings in the group extends the systemic techniques described in the previous section. It is increasingly used in ward-based groups, Johnson (1997) describing how 'therapeutic divergence' is harnessed by members of a staff team taking up roles of 'lead' and 'co-lead' (as here), with the addition of a 'shepherd' to encourage those who remain reluctant to join the flock.

Conclusion: strengths and challenges of integrative groups

Where are integrative groups going?

In this author's opinion, there is a considerable gap between 'integrative' models such as IPT and PIT (see Chapter 7), which cut across theoretical divisions because they are primarily skilful attempts to exploit 'non-specific' therapeutic factors on the one hand, and, on the other, those like CAT, whose rationale is more complex and theoretically driven (see Chapter 1). This exploration of what it means for a group to be integrative sits more happily with the first of these approaches.

This chapter opened with some observations on what can happen when differences between therapeutic models are examined in the context of a group discussion. After noting that models are inevitably attenuated through any attempt to apply them in groups, the need to make groups work (and resist disintegration) prompted a search for practical principles that might be identified in relatively atheoretical language. This meant looking at factors which appeared critical to the outcome of the group, as well as for individuals using it, independently of the group's theoretical model. Understanding of 'non-specific factors' is possibly much less well-developed in group psychotherapy because of failure to differentiate between these two interdependent kinds of outcome. The selection here of three factors – namely affect, boundary, and communication – is capable of testing through subsequent research, and could well be modified in the light of this.

Each of these three parameters has been independently subject to far more sophisticated elaboration within established traditions of group psychotherapy: for instance, 'affect' in psychodynamic and gestalt work; 'boundary' in systemic and structural traditions; and 'communication' in behavioural and interpersonal models. Nevertheless, having sampled additional ways in which functional groups with a claim to be integrative have adapted to particular needs and situations in the previous section, it is possible to speculate what future groups aspiring to an integrative ideal might be like.

As in some other integrative therapies, acceptance of the primacy of affect is likely to be associated with active expression of feeling, and examination of members' ease with it, rather than analysis of its determinants. As recent work by Louis Ormont (1990, 1999) indicates, appreciation of how affect spontaneously links (and polarizes) members within a therapeutic group can be expected to lead to much more interest in emotional intersubjectivity. This is likely to demand more emotional transparency from a group's therapists, with a need for them to model affective responses to group members while remaining acutely sensitive to group affect. New ways of distributing these functions between more than one therapist may need to be developed.

Attention to traditional group boundaries should continue to promote the security and containment necessary for personal risk-taking on which good work depends. An integrative approach to other boundaries would permit greater experimentation with group format alongside this. Deliberate adjustment of temporal boundaries to delineate zones within group sessions could extend their range by safeguarding space for active reflection. At its simplest, this may involve no more than introduction of a review period at the close of each session. When successful, temporal zoning might be as effective in introducing this shift in perspective as special techniques (such as recording and playback) which have had this function in the past. It may also mitigate pressure to undermine an integrative group's primacy by mixing group and individual sessions. Deliberate attention to in-group spatial boundaries (exemplified in the concept of subgroups) facilitates learning about ubiquitous psychological dispositions (such as those of disowning and demonizing) that get expressed through the collusive erection of barriers. Once these are experienced as joint creations within a group, they become relatively clear and safe to work with. The challenge is to integrate the focused intensity of a gestalt exercise within the containment of a long-term group.

The overwhelming desirability of communicational freedom among group members suggests that, if pre-group preparation is to potentiate the work of a therapeutic group, this should be its focus. Stone and Klein (1999) report that participation in a 'waiting-list group' placing a high premium on self-disclosure improves subsequent group use. Recognition of conflicted communication, and use of active methods to uncover this, are already relatively familiar to psychoanalytic and systemic therapists, accounting for some of their ambivalence surrounding excessively simplistic formulations of 'cohesion' as a group goal. Techniques that facilitate constructive opposition through expression and resolution of implicit conflict within the group as well as within members seem fertile territory for further development.

Who are integrative groups good for?

Until changes in group procedure can be justified through systematic and objective demonstration of their benefits, acceptance of new methods will depend on them being felt to offer something to people for whom there are few other options. Some traditional indications for group psychotherapy can be expressed in terms of needs for particular kinds of integration. For instance, Dennis Brown (1992) confirms that they are especially helpful for people whose internal failure to integrate emotional life is evident in excessive intellectualization, and for people who need to integrate social and psychological development. Jane Knowles (1995) writes of groups' special complementarity with the needs of chronically defended patients for kinds of mirroring that only peers can provide. Beyond these, an assertively integrative group, emphasizing linking and immediate experience, might be particularly useful for people who are isolated within a perception of themselves as particularly difficult or different, or for people who have the unfortunate tendency to use theoretic gleanings from previous experiences of therapy defensively.

What do groups offer integrative practice?

The integrative power of groups has been explored here entirely through therapeutic situations. There are many additional ways in which groups can be used to support therapeutic work as well as providing a medium for it. These range from groups for supervision, support, case discussion, or service liaison to groups in which policy is developed. While the process of each of these can benefit from participation of seasoned group therapists, there is a more fundamental contribution they can make to psychotherapy integration. It concerns the personal challenges of attempting to work in a more integrative way.

While the current explosion of interest in integrative approaches to psychotherapy can be genuinely inspiring, it poses major personal challenges to therapists who were sitting fairly securely behind a definite professional identity. Therapists entering the strange terrain of integrative psychotherapy are often confronted with an identity struggle, reminiscent of that faced by some patients. This is not without its clinical and personal dangers, particularly in the temptation prematurely to adhere to emerging therapeutic recipes before these are properly tried. These may then be quickly surrounded by professional structures as rigid as those of traditional institutes, with the further risk of denying the spirit of exchange and responsible experiment that seeded their development in the first place.

Group psychotherapists are probably more acquainted with living with personal uncertainty and professional identity diffusion than most. As well as enduring the rivalrous suspicion that will attach to any psychotherapist willing and seemingly able to treat many patients simultaneously, they have had to assimilate a wider range of psychotherapeutic theory than many training programmes for individual psychotherapy offer. While this borrowing does reflect a relative lack of original group theory to underpin clinical practice, it can be taken as evidence of dilettantism rather than earning respect for the breadth and flexibility of mind necessary to rework it and apply it. The psychological tension such attitudes engender can be creative but also oppressive.

Exchange between group psychotherapists has to cope with anxieties of these kinds. Indeed, group therapists sometimes seek further training in well-established models of individual psychotherapy for negative as well as positive reasons. However, once trained they are likely to remain adept at using groups for themselves and for one another. This allows personal learning to be pooled and theoretical ideas, however seductive, to be tested against shared experience. One of the understated reasons why psychotherapy groups are inherently integrative is that their members, who are rarely complete neophytes, bring their personal therapeutic models into a common frame with those of their therapists, out of which a local working model will inevitably evolve. Having relied on their common experiences to maintain clinical responsiveness and theoretical openness amid personal uncertainty, group psychotherapists might in their turn assist integrative colleagues to accept insecurity as a necessary cost of innovation.

Part 2
Models and practice

Chapter 6

Integrative developments in cognitive analytic therapy

Chess Denman

What is integration?

The phrase psychotherapy integration is capable of many different interpretations (cf. Chapter 1). Some therapies are integrative in the sense that they borrow and then synthesize practical elements from a number of other therapeutic approaches under a novel theoretical overview. Other therapies are integrative in their manner of synthesizing and reformulating seemingly divergent theoretical perspectives. Yet a further integrative approach sits above different therapies and, arguing that there is a place for each, sets out at least a sketch of that place. The different views of integration in therapy commit their adherents to different conclusions about the value of rival therapeutic approaches. Therapies which bring a range of techniques under a single theoretical overview need to be committed to their own theoretical stance and to regard it as in some sense superior to that of the other therapies they may borrow from. This may seem somewhat imperialistic but it is worth noting that all attempts at integration imply a claim that they are better syntheses than others for if they were not then the integration would have been done differently.

Cognitive analytic therapy (CAT) was developed by Anthony Ryle (1990, 1995a, 1997). It is both a theoretical perspective on human psychological health and illness and a practical therapeutic method involving generally a brief focal input of 16 or 24 sessions. The therapist is active, open, and seeks collaboratively to involve the patient in a process which comprises elements of self-discovery, behavioural, cognitive, and emotional experimentation, and education. CAT is a self-avowedly integrative therapy. It is mostly one of the type of integrations which take a range of concepts and ideas under a single theoretical wing but it also contains elements of the other kinds of integration described. For this reason CAT is to some extent committed to the view that the theoretical integration embodied in CAT has at least some advantages over other integrations. However it is also certain that no CAT therapist would be arrogant enough to suppose that CAT represents the best possible theoretical or practical integration. We still have a lot to discover. This chapter sets out the central theoretical perspective of CAT and delineates the areas in which it claims its theoretical stance offers advantages over other ways of looking at clinical material. CAT also has its theoretical deficiencies. Until recently one of these was the failure to incorporate attachment theory (cf. Chapter 11). This had obvious relevance but had had relatively little detailed impact on CAT. This has been to some extent rectified by recent developments, including an important paper by Jelma (1999) dealing with the topic.

Discussing integration, Ryle recounts how he designed one of the central concepts of CAT, called the procedural sequence model, as an explicit attempt to provide an explanation for the finding announced in the celebrated 'Dodo bird paper' (Luborsky *et al.* 1975) that all therapies were equal in efficacy. The procedural sequence model proposed that all agentful human activity was conducted according to constructed or recalled sequences which involve first, the generation of an aim, second, an appraisal of the environment and the construction and enactment of a plan, and third, an evaluative check of the outcome of action. According to the model, procedures could be malformed in various ways and these malformed procedures result in problems that present to psychotherapists. Ryle argued that each brand of therapy concentrates largely on a single part of the procedural sequence – for example cognitive therapy on appraisal, behavioural treatment on enactment, and psychodynamic therapies on aim. As a result all therapies will be effective to the extent that they repair or improve the underlying procedural malformation. This bit of CAT theory represents a good example of the meta-theoretical integration which is able to point out the individual advantages of different theoretical perspectives.

From this base, CAT developed the integration of CAT with other therapies to different extents. Cognitive–behaviour therapy (CBT) exerted an early important influence on CAT, giving rise to active techniques in therapy such as homework-like diary-keeping. Sadly, though, more recent developments in CBT have been neglected, receiving at most an admixture of approving or disapproving nods, although recent work has tried to rectify this situation (Allison and Denman, 2001). By contrast there were extensive and influential engagements with psychoanalysis both American and English, particularly Kleinian, while Leiman (1992, 1994, 1997) reintroduced Ryle to Winnicott by way of Vygotsky and Backtin. These areas of engagement eventually coalesced into a revision of the procedural sequence model with the introduction of the key concept of reciprocal roles. The debt to analytic thinking remains in the name given to this revised model: the procedural sequence object relations model. The clinical issue which has spurred on most of this development has, in the last 10 years, been the challenge of treating borderline personality disorder.

For this reason the focus in this chapter will be on the treatment of borderline personality disorder. First, with the aid of a disguised case example the key features of a CAT approach to borderline personality disorder are outlined. Then some aspects of cognitive–behavioural approaches to borderline personality disorder are sketched, pointing up areas of similarity and difference. Psychoanalytic psychotherapy approaches are given a similar treatment. The concluding section of the chapter turns to broader integrative issues and uses the considerations outlined by Bateman in his paper on borderline personality disorder and psychotherapy integration (Bateman 1997). It tries to show how CAT's view of the building blocks of human behaviour allows for exactly the kind of integration Bateman is seeking.

The CAT model of borderline personality disorder

An outline

The central idea that CAT uses to analyse borderline personality disorder is that of the reciprocal role template and the procedures that secure it. It is claimed that this model of reciprocal role templates and their relations, known as the procedural sequence object relations model, is capable of providing a complete account of the symptoms of borderline personality disorder. A *state* consists of two complementary roles bound by a relationship paradigm. States can also be thought of as being composed of attitudes to the self, and the world, which involve constellations of characteristic cognitions drives and emotions. The paired roles: caregiver–care receiver, victimizer–victim, and author–reader are all examples of states. They are learned through experience as blocks of reciprocal role pairs. Thus a child who is chastised by her mother for throwing food on the floor can often be observed to re-enact this experience later with a toy and with roles reversed. By far the most important source of learning about roles is the social experience of the child and the roles that they, in consequence of this and of their temperament, enact. In saying this CAT theory is explicitly drawing on the work of Vygotsky, who taught that learning is a social, tool-mediated process (Vygotsky 1986).

CAT has used Vygotsky's description of socially mediated intellectual advance to describe a process of socially mediated emotional development. The developing child first learns social roles by observing them and enacting them with others, and then as development progresses the roles are internalized and become enacted in relation to the self in the form of procedures for self-management and self-control. Thus emotional and social development parallel intellectual development in following Vygotsky's aphorism that 'what was first done with others can now be done alone'.

Another central CAT principle is that, in social situations, the adoption of one pole of a reciprocal role exerts a pressure on others to reciprocate and adopt a congruent pole. So in any situation, the role people adopt will be conditioned partly by the expectancies created by the situation, partly by their own state but also, to a greater or lesser extent, by the roles adopted by other actors in the social setting. CAT claims that it is this feature of roles that is responsible for the phenomena which psychoanalysis subsumes under the terms transference, counter-transference, and projective identification. CAT therapists tend also to make the stronger claim that the concept of reciprocal role relationships and role induction allow for an analysis of the reasons for these phenomena which is more understandable and more workable than the sometimes obscure theoretical underpinning of the equivalent psychoanalytic concepts.

In normal individuals reciprocal roles are numerous and for the most part moderate. Using special procedures which evaluate the social environment they are able to move gracefully and appropriately between varying states – for example, in the course of a day, from teacher to student, then to mother, and finally to partner. In cases where changes of role are abrupt or discontinuous evident social and environmental factors make the sudden change between states intelligible to all. An example might be a sociable and chatty guest at a party who, all of a sudden, becomes taciturn (an abrupt change of role) and makes the earliest excuse to break off the encounter. Later she tells her friend that she had suddenly seen her husband talking to an old flame in a way that looked suggestive (social explanation). Normal individuals are often able to give an historical account of their states and experiences that includes motivational, affective, and cognitive explanations for behaviour and which stitches together past, present, and future in a plausible narrative structure. This is to say that normal individuals have three levels of control, all of which are in good working order. Level one is the nature and number of the reciprocal roles and their attendant states, Level 2 the command and control procedures which govern state transitions, and Level 3 the capacity for conscious self-reflection and conscious accounting for at least some of the other two structures.

In borderline personality disorder often all three levels are grossly abnormal. At Level 1 the reciprocal roles are few in number and stark in nature. So that 'abusing to abused', 'contemptuous to contemptible', 'ideally caring to ideally cared for', and 'abandoning to abandoned' are all too frequently the only states in a borderline patients reciprocal role repertoire.

Joan[1] was a 43-year-old woman referred to the service after sexual boundary violations in another service. Her behaviour was grossly disturbed and over the past year she had spent little time out of hospital. She would suddenly run off the ward and, if successful in leaving, be found wandering near the local railway line. She made repeated parasuicidal attempts by abusing her diabetic regime. She was grotesquely overweight and appeared unkempt and smelly. Staff were sharply divided between those who thought her a manipulative troublemaker and a few who tended to excuse every behaviour.

---

1. It goes without saying that the case example produced here is heavily disguised to protect the patients involved. However, it should also be added that there has also been some fictionalization of the case example in so far as details from two case histories have been combined. This manoeuvre was undertaken to further protect the identity of the patients.

At assessment a number of reciprocal roles were apparent. The assessor found herself literally disgusted by Joan, who she experienced as contemptible and during the interview Joan referred in contemptuous terms both to herself and to the member of staff with whom she had had a sexual encounter. Thus 'disgusting and contemptible' in relation to 'contemptuous and disgusted' was hypothesized to be a powerful reciprocal role template for Joan. Her self-abuse was partly a frustrated response to her self-perceived state of disgusting obesity but also had origins in an early and amply physically and sexually abusive childhood. She exerted strong pulls on staff to abuse her and there was evidence that many staff took a certain guilty pleasure in doing her down in little ways. The assessor, for example, found herself deliberately keeping Joan waiting at the beginning of appointments. From these facts 'abusing abused' was hypothesized as another state.

Partly the paucity and starkness of the Level 1 repertoire accounts for the jerky changes in state that are responsible for the unstable instability of borderline personality disorder. However, patients with borderline personality disorder are also often subject to dysfunctions in Level 2 regulation. States may often be switched between on a hair-trigger basis. This accounts for the very common experience of therapists that patients may suddenly be thrown by an innocuous comment that the therapist has made. Probably this hair-trigger effect is one cause of the methodological debate between therapists who advocate highly boundaried therapy practice with little self-disclosure and clear rules, and those who relax boundaries, allow extra session calls and may be self-disclosing. Both, it seems, are attempting to deal with the hair-trigger effect of Level 2 disruption. One by offering a low stimulus environment with few opportunities for misinterpretations and the other by providing a lot of contextual information in the hope of improving the signal-to-noise ratio.

Joan seemed to leave one session in a very good state. However, she returned the following week having had no thoughts about the previous therapy session at all. It turned out that on her way home from the session she had driven past a graveyard. This had put her in mind of suicide and she had spent the rest of the week planning it. During the next session with the therapist she continued in this 'suicidal', state eliciting an increasingly frantic attempt by the therapist to engage and rescue her. Ultimately she left seemingly no better off. The following week Joan announced that she was coping well and thought the sessions could end soon. This time she denied any real recollection of her previous suicidal state. However, during the session she became convinced her therapist had arranged for someone to listen at the door and launched an attack on the therapist for being scared of her and needing to have someone listen at the door. After some questioning she revealed that while talking to her therapist she had seen the title of a book on the bookshelf, *Aggression in the Personality Disorders*, and had then become convinced she heard someone listening.

The graveyard incident is a clear example of the hair-trigger effect, as is the book on the therapist's shelf and illustrates difficulties in Level 2 switching. The excerpt also demonstrates Joan's difficulties at Level 3. Level 3 disruptions are restrictions of conscious reflection. Ryle anatomizes a number of causes. They may reflect actual injunctions to secrecy by early caregivers, or be the consequence of the jerky progress between states which, combined with state-dependent recall (amply evident in Joan's case), disrupts any hope of sustained reflection, or be consequent on trauma-induced disassociation.

The CAT model of treating borderline personality disorder

Cognitive analytic therapy aims to treat patients with borderline personality disorder chiefly by promoting integration and Level 3 self-reflection. If dissociation is the key pathology and if the different roles and states have no or little effective knowledge of each other, then a first step in therapy must be to try to repair this state of affairs. To do so involves constructing with the patient joint tools for self-reflection. Frequently tools for self-reflection have never been accessible to the patient and, once they are fashioned, patients often seize on them with alacrity. Gaining the patient's collaboration in this task is vital. This collaboration is developed through the use of description and cooperation as the vehicle of understanding, and by stressing the *joint* fashioning of 'tools for self reflection'. One key tool a CAT therapist will make with her patient is a narrative account of current difficulties and a pictorial map of the succession of reciprocal roles and self-states which the patient occupies. Ideally these will be the result of a joint process of investigation and dialogue that frequently involves considerable extra session work by both parties.

Despite her chaotic state of being Joan did manage to write an account of her early life for the therapist. This was fractured in its chronology, leaving out huge tracts of time, and was also a flat and unemotional document that detailed a catalogue of abuse in an emotionally detached way. It was read in the session by the therapist who commented that Joan's early life must have been a long nightmare. Joan waved her hand negligently and the therapist commented that she experienced Joan as dismissing the horrors of her own past. Joan responded that it was pointless to discuss her past as nobody ever listened to her or did anything about it. The therapist responded that she was listening. Joan became furious and pointed out that it was quite all right for the therapist to talk as she didn't have to put up with the memory of her past on a daily basis. Chastened, the therapist invited Joan to consider a simple diagram, based

partly on her own emotional responses, which she sketched. It involved two reciprocal roles 'abusing' to 'abused' and 'pathetically inadequate helper' to either 'politely
acquiescent but secretly furious' or 'shut off sullen and inaccessible'. Joan responded
by giving a number of further accounts of childhood events that mirrored this pattern and were more emotionally involving.

As the sessions progressed further the therapist was able progressively to expand and
elaborate the diagram. Joan was able to keep a diary of her days and was encouraged to
make her accounts as rich and inflected as she was able. She was also encouraged to use
writing as an escape behaviour when she felt overwhelmed by feelings and wanted to
harm herself. Once the diagram was complete a copy was given to Joan and the different
states on it were colour-coded (the colours having been selected collaboratively). Joan
was invited to highlight sections of her diary in different colours, depending on the state
she judged she had been in during the events she was recounting.

Integration and non-collusion

All the techniques described above promote integration of the different parts of the personality. Another emerging feature of modern CAT practice in the treatment of borderline personality disorder is a stress on non-collusion with dysfunctional reciprocal roles.
Because the roles that borderline patients can adopt are stark and emotionally
under-modulated, and because roles in general exert social pulls to reciprocate, the
therapist and all other people in the orbit of borderline personality disordered patients
are likely to be the recipients of strong 'invitations to join the dance'. The counter-
transference enactments which result are various. Some are discordant with the professional and personal role repertoire of the therapist, in which case they are generally perceived rapidly. Joan's therapist, for example, quickly noticed when she started
deliberately making Joan wait extra time for her session to start. Other counter-
transference enactments are concordant with the professional and personal repertoire
of the therapist, in which case it may be very hard for the therapist to notice an intensification of what they would in any case expect to be doing or feeling. An example in Joan's
case was when the therapist was pulled deeper and deeper into trying to rescue Joan
from her suicidal state. From a CAT perspective it is important to avoid becoming
drawn into reciprocal role enactments with the patient because this tends to work
against integration by reducing the therapist's capacity for reflection and by reinforcing
a single part of the patient's psychic structure at the expense of the rest. Recently work in
CAT has focused on the analysis of small transcribed segments of therapies for subtle
collusions on the part of the therapist. There is some evidence that therapists who are
good at spotting pulls into reciprocal role enactments and describing rather than enacting them tend to be associated with good outcome therapies (Bennett and Parry 1996).

During the therapy with Joan the therapist was in general able to avoid collusion with Joan's reciprocal roles although there was a strong tendency for the therapist to agree with Joan too readily when she described ways in which she had been maltreated by a range of healthcare workers in her current life. This was partly because of an invitation by Joan to emphasize a fantasy of 'ideal care to ideally cared for' versus 'abusing bastard to abused victim'. It was also partly due to a tendency on the part of Joan's therapist to hold some mental health services in low regard. Supervision concentrated on showing the therapist how Joan repeatedly deprived herself of what, albeit inadequate, help was offered because of this fantasy, and in disentangling personal, professional, and induced responses in the therapist herself.

Once the patient begins to develop the capacity for an overview of their differing states it is possible to turn to symptomatic areas and use that overview as a strategic location from which to plan a range of interventions which help to manage difficult state transitions or symptomatic procedures. Intervening in symptomatic procedures too early is conceived in CAT as potentially counterproductive because it may provoke state changes which disrupt work on the identified system and hinder new learning.

The evidence base in CAT

The evidence base for CAT is considered in a recent review by Margison (2000). He rightly points to the existence of a large number of single case reports or small uncontrolled series and to the existence of a large theoretical literature. Some controlled trials do exist, however. Of these the earliest was by Brockman *et al.* (1987), who reported a controlled trial of 16-session CAT and Mann's time-limited therapy. CAT was superior to Mann's therapy on some grid-derived measures of change, although both therapies were equally effective on more conventional psychometric measures. This rather inconclusive study probably lacked the power to detect differences. Fosbury (1994) showed that CAT was superior to nurse education in producing sustained HbA1 levels in diabetics, and similarly, controlled studies have shown the value of CAT in increasing compliance in asthmatics (Bosley *et al.* 1992).

Currently Ryle and Golynkina (2000) are gathering a growing series of patients formally diagnosed as suffering from borderline personality disorder who have received CAT delivered according to strictly supervised criteria. They report on a series of 27 patients who entered therapy and attended a 6-month follow-up, and on the 18 who also attended a follow-up at 18 months. At 6-month follow-up 14 patients no longer met formal criteria for borderline personality disorder and in those who attended at 18 months there was a continuing decline in psychometric scores.

Other preliminary work supportive of CAT's effectiveness includes an ongoing Cambridge-based study. All patients treated with CAT were given a measure of relating called the PROQ2 (Birtchnell *et al.* 1999). Preliminary results show significant drops in

PROQ2 scores at the 16th session compared with the score at the first. Even more encouragingly, at 3-month follow-up preliminary data show that 38% continued to improve and a further 46% had slipped back somewhat but were still improved. It should be stressed that the sample is, as yet, small ($n = 21$ at session 16, and $n = 15$ at 3-month follow-up) and, in the absence of a control group a specific effect for CAT cannot be conclusively claimed. However, the important feature of this study is that it used a measure of relating which has good links to attachment theory (Birtchnell 1997) and, for this reason, good face validity as a measure suited to more psychodynamic therapies.

A CAT perspective on CBT for borderline personality disorder

Cognitive–behavioural therapists have taken an increasing interest in borderline personality disorder. There have now been quite a few contributions in the field so that there cannot be said to be a single CBT treatment for borderline personality disorder. However, Young's (1990) schema-focused approach is gaining acceptance and is highly congruent with CAT.

Young distinguishes schema-focused therapy for borderline patients from cognitive therapy for depression in that the former places greater emphasis on the therapeutic relationship, affect, and on the childhood origins of disorder. In this, schema-focused therapy resembles CAT, which also emphasizes the need for a change of perspective when treating borderline patients. The central idea is of the baleful influence of early maladaptive schemas, which are defined as broad pervasive themes regarding oneself and one's relationships with others, developed during childhood and elaborated throughout the lifetime and which are dysfunctional to a significant degree. This concept has obvious commonalities with that of a reciprocal role template. Indeed reciprocal role templates can be seen as a hypothesis about the morphology of a particular kind of interpersonal schema and an early paper by Young concerning the clustering of schemas together shows an uncanny resemblance to CAT (Young 1990). In CBT as in CAT schemas are seen as deeply entrenched and often self-perpetuating. However, CAT criticizes the schema concept for lacking any superstructure and for being insufficiently relational. Young's schemas are loosely related to Bartlett's notion of a schema, which he introduced as a way of theorizing phenomena associated with defective recall.

Here the schema represents a kind of 'default template' against which interesting deviations can be recorded. Thus, to take a non-clinical example, the default template for a restaurant would include low-level lighting, and in relation to this template one might tend to think a brightly lit one was queer. When we recall events, lacunae in our recall are filled in by the schema, making for a characteristic pattern of errors. Young's schemas are in effect default generalizations about the working of the world and our place within them. He lists 18 schemas relevant to borderline personality disorder but does not order them into relationship structures as he did in an earlier paper, nor does he introduce any idea equivalent to that of the sequential diagrammatic representation in CAT.

A sequential diagrammatic representation is a diagram which sets out the main reciprocal roles (often represented as paired boxes) on a single page. It also seeks to show the way in which patients move predictably between roles as a result of their own actions and the actions of others. The sequential diagrammatic representation also allows for rapid predictions of the role induction pressures exerted on others by the patient and the likely result if induction does occur. Schema-focused CBT, lacking this ordering of schemas, finds it hard to theorize rapid switches between schemas. The reciprocal role concept also provides CAT with a ready tool for understanding the effects that the patient has on the therapist and on other actors in their interpersonal field. Because it is an interactional concept, the reciprocal role theory introduces the notion that the environment is to some extent shaped by the individual who experiences it. Schema-focused CBT, by contrast, is predominantly intrapsychic rather than interpersonal in its focus (cf. Chapter 2). Some schemas are held to be maintained by cognitive distortions like selective generalization. Other schemas are avoided, as in phobic phenomena, and yet others are compensated for in elaborate ways. These schema processes are similar in some ways to procedural sequences but crucially, from a CAT perspective, they lack the interactional and social elements built into the procedural sequence object relations model.

Practically, therapy is divided into an assessment phase, during which schemas are identified and linked to presenting problems and life history, followed by a focus on change using typical tools of empathic confrontation, reality testing, cognitive restructuring, and behavioural pattern breaking. CAT, by contrast, does not move rapidly into a change phase. After the assessment phase known as *reformulation* the next stage is *recognition*, which has the aim of helping the patient see in 'real time' how they are moving between states. CAT argues that if the patient is started on symptom-focused change too early, vital parts of the personality may be left out of the picture, indeed therapist and patient may collude to silence them. For example, if the patient has a strong, coping, 'pull-your-socks-up' state, this may cut in and silence other areas that are less cooperative. Only once recognition is established can revision begin. It may well involve many of the techniques used in CBT, although there is far less prescription and far more reliance on the patient's serendipity in the design and use of change techniques.

Young lists some of his overall treatment objectives for therapy: empathizing with and protecting the abandoned child, helping the abandoned child to give and receive love, and fighting against and expunging the punitive. While CAT would acknowledge that many of these aims are important, it would argue that Young does not appreciate the complexity and ambivalence of motivation in borderline personality disorder patients. Listening to and validating parts of the patient which are experienced as abandoned and

neglected is vital, but CAT therapists would worry that simply siding with the abandoned child and expunging the punitive parent does not do justice to the ambivalence
and complexity of the reciprocal role templates which emerge from a highly emotionally, physically, or sexually abusive childhood. From a CAT perspective, therefore, the
CBT approach demonstrates a certain naivety about the likely internal reciprocal role
patterns, combined with a failure of the schema-focused approach to theorize higher
functioning (levels 2 and 3) or to structure schemas into an ordered pattern. Since from
a CAT perspective there is as much damage at the level of the sequencing of reciprocal
roles (the hair-trigger problem) and the capacity for self-reflection as there is at a single
role level, this is a major limitation of the theory. This in turn limits treatment by focusing attention at Level 1 rather than building an integrated overview at Level 3. CAT
would therefore predict that a CBT treatment might run the risk of leaving the patient
dependent on the therapist to provide their Level 3 functioning (i.e. self-monitoring and
self-reflexive capacity) rather than having a 'portable' one of their own.

A CAT perspective on psychodynamic therapy for borderline personality disorder

Psychoanalytic psychotherapists invented the term borderline and, for a long time, their
approach to its treatment claimed uncontested therapeutic supremacy. However, this
long-standing interest and the wealth of theory that accompanies it generated no great
commonality of approach. More recently controlled trials have been appearing. and
important amongst these are the work of Stevenson and Meares (Meares *et al.* 1999;
Stevenson 1999; Stevenson and Meares 1992) using twice-weekly psychodynamic psychotherapy along Kohutian lines, and Bateman and Fonagy (1999, 2001) who report a
randomized controlled trial of psychoanalytically oriented hospital treatment. From
these trials and from clinical report it does seem that some kinds of psychodynamic psychotherapy can help in the management of borderline personality disorder. However, it
should be noted that Bateman and Fonagy's trial included a wide range of therapeutic
elements, not all of which were centrally related to psychoanalytic theory.

No one approach can be singled out as entirely representative of the field, but certain
approaches do stand out as having been systematized and also as manifestly dealing with
the kinds of patient and levels of severity typical of hospital-based practice. My review of
psychoanalytic approaches draws heavily on Higgit and Fonagy's review (1992).

Kernberg

Kernberg (1975) delineates a kind of psychic functioning he calls the 'borderline personality organization'. It is characterized by ego weakness, irrational thinking, less
mature defences such as splitting and projective identification, and identity diffusion, all
consequent on the ill effects of fragmented and strongly charged object representations.

Influenced by Melanie Klein, he propounds what might be called an 'explosion model' as the cause of this state of affairs. In this model early innate destructive impulses cannot be contained by the weak ego of the developing infant and the individual arrests in paranoid schizoid position. That is in a state of desperately trying to keep good and bad fragmented internal objects apart in order to avoid damage to the good ones.

For Kernberg the grandiosity, contempt, and profound dependency displayed by borderline patients result from a manic defence aimed at maintaining a sense of an invulnerable self. This may involve attacks on caregivers precisely because their care reminds patients that they are vulnerable. Self-mutilation is ascribed to a whole range of motives including regaining a sense of control, manipulating caregivers, enacting rage on an object, or the infiltration of the self with destructiveness similar to that found in sexual perversions.

Ryle (1997) is sharply critical of Kernberg at a theoretical level on a number of counts. He finds Kernberg's description of borderline functioning unduly complex and focused on reified internal objects and conflicts for which there is little evidence. Ryle is especially worried by what he sees as a tendency in Kernberg's work to blame and criticize borderline patients, and an excessive focus on destructiveness and hostility.

For Kernberg the treatment of choice is transference-focused psychotherapy at a frequency of about three times a week. Interpretation is the central therapeutic tool. Kernberg aims by interpretation to diagnose and then 'interpretively transform' primitive internalized object relations from split off or 'part' object relations into integrated or 'total' object relations'. Central to interpretation is analysis of the transference. However, interpretation is, according to CAT, bound to fail. It places the therapist in the position of privileged knower in relation to ignorant known and can frequently cause the therapy to deadlock in whichever of the patient's states most resembles this relation. In place of interpretation CAT substitutes joint *description* as the therapeutic manoeuvre. This is not purely a semantic matter. Therapist and patient cooperate together in the construction of tools for self-reflection. They sit up. They try things out. They do what it takes. Nothing is left of the need to keep some kind of pure bloodless field of the analytic situation. Neutrality, a vital part of Kernberg's work, is replaced by active engagement and struggle, which arguably results in an integration of patient and therapist perspectives. Here we see the dialectic of integration and differentiation at its most stark. CAT draws on ideas from object relations theory, but is also highly critical of them, and tries, through its collaborative commitment, to create an integrative framework with the patient.

In one respect Kernberg's description does mirror current CAT practice. His attention to detail and his use of the idea of self and object representations is reminiscent of the detailed microanalysis of role enactments currently practised by Ryle's group. A second feature of Kernberg's approach, with which CAT shares some aspects, is the introduction of a highly structured system for setting and maintaining a contract with the patient. It seeks to deal with threats to therapy ranging from suicidal risk to non-payment of fees. Kernberg's contract-setting is worked out in the greatest detail and has at its heart the aim of getting the patient back to the therapy to talk things out. Kernberg abandons interpretation as soon as a contractual violation has occurred and resumes it only once the patient is in line again. CAT similarly incorporates some elements of contract-setting in the early sessions. Understandings of reciprocal role patterns are used rapidly – even before reformulation – to predict and discuss the kinds of threats to therapy and the patient that might arise, and to discuss ways in which these might be avoided. However, in contrast to Kernberg who abandons interpretation, CAT makes explicit use of joint understandings as tools to understand and deal with problematic behaviours.

Kleinian approaches

Although Klein and her followers would find much to agree with in Kernberg, they probably would agree with CAT's reservations about contracts believing that borderline patients are not able to agree to a contract in an uncomplicated and single-minded way. This is because for these analysts motivations in borderline patients are complex and conflicted and not necessarily operating in the patient's best interests. However, this potential criticism of Kernberg in relation to contracts has certainly been extended by Kleinian commentators to many aspects of CAT. When Ryle, in a series of papers (1992, 1993, 1995a) engaging with Kleinian thought, critiqued a number of senior Kleinian authors, responses from Kleinians or those sympathetic to a Kleinian position voiced just such a criticism: 'cognitive analytic therapy presupposes the existence of a stable therapeutic alliance: Joseph's approach by contrast, illustrates the way in which a patient can set his heart ruthlessly, if subtly, against change as well as seek it' (Scott 1995).

Put another way, for a contemporary Kleinian, CAT would stand in great danger of 'training' the patient to comply by producing surface level compliance at the price of reinforcing deeper levels of pathology.

These criticisms hit home only to the extent that the underlying assumptions they contain about unconscious self-destructive motivations are accepted. Ryle denies that unconscious self-destructive motivations play any great part in human motivation, though not all CAT therapists follow him in this. For example, contemporary Kleinians have been influenced by the work of Steiner, who outlined the concept of a *pathological organization*. This compromise structure is described as lying between the paranoid schizoid position and the depressive one, and serves to allow the patient to advance from the paranoid schizoid position without having to bear the pains of the depressive one. Because of its defensive role the pathological organization is said to produce intractable resistances in analysis. Ryle has argued that these apparent resistances are in fact products of the analytic situation *itself*, in which a combination of 'opacity, omniscience and interpretive attributions of negative motives' induce the patient into the least exposing reciprocal role available. Ryle is thus claiming that it is analysis rather than CAT that 'trains' the patient. Cognitive analytic therapy certainly depends on a positive alliance with the patient but it does not assume it. Many elements of CAT practice are designed to foster a working alliance – an open, transparent, genuine, educative, and collaborative approach. By contrast the analytic approach, particularly in its Kleinian variant, is, Ryle argues, highly likely to foster suspicion, anxiety, distress, and hostility.

A repudiation of Klein (and thus a highly selective 'integration' of psychoanalysis) has been a central developmental force in shaping CAT's relationship to psychoanalysis – indeed in relation to Kleinian thought CAT's position is largely one of theoretical or even moral opposition. CAT, while opposing Klein, has at the same time embraced and modified a more Winicottian version of object relations theory. In this respect the version of psychoanalysis CAT has sought to integrate is independent group in flavour.

Fonagy

More recently, and with the support of a certain amount of experimental evidence, Fonagy and his co-workers have proposed a model in which a child who experiences early abuse may be unable to bear seeing their caregiving figure as hostile and abusive (Fonagy and Target 1997). To protect him or herself against this the child defensively inhibits the capacity to think about self and others, thereby reducing reflective self-functioning. This reduced reflective self-functioning then secondarily results in much of the psychopathology of the borderline patient. Fonagy argues that the crucial element in treatment involves increasing reflective self-functioning. Fonagy's reflective self-functioning has clear similarities to Level 3 capacities in Ryle's model. But implicit in Fonagy's model is a conflict between the self-awareness and avoidance of the pain which such awareness might produce. Ryle, on the other hand, adheres to a deficit model in which the failure to develop Level 3 is far more the consequence of lost opportunity than of opportunity refused.

There are further differences in approach. Fonagy recommends psychoanalysis or psychoanalytic psychotherapy centred on interpretation as an important treatment modality. Additionally he advocates deliberately avoiding any exploration of the details of the patient's early abusive experiences, commenting that 'Explorations of the patient's past and interpretations using childhood experience as an explanation of current behaviour are unlikely to do more than divert attention from the pathological nature of the patients current behaviour.' Ryle's response is sharp: 'It is at this point that, for me, reasoned argument can easily give way to anger. The failure to acknowledge the reality of a person's experience is itself an assault' (Ryle 1997, p45).

Criticism can be levelled here at both Ryle and Fonagy. The concept of reflective self-functioning and Ryle's 'Level 3' potentially share an abandonment of one of the key insights of CAT, which is that the acquisition of higher mental functions is a social and cultural achievement. Both the term Level 3 and reflective self-functioning tend to make the capacity to give an account of oneself to oneself a mental capacity rather on a par with memory or depth perception; that is, one developed solipsistically or autonomously and relatively uninfluenced by cultural and social forces. Self-reflection and self-management are, however, not universally similar across cultures but depend crucially on the social environment in which the self was developed and currently exists.

The growth of Level 3 capacities for self-reflection seem evident in the early self-talk of children as they babble to themselves, often in a sing-song voice, while they play. This self-talk is itself an extension of the dialogues with caregivers, essentially about self, self-control, and motivation that have been going on since birth. Mothers can be observed talking to babies from their earliest moments in monologues which contains narrative elements that involve the hypothesized intentions, memories, desires, and motivations of the infant. Later the infant responds by gesture and then in words, and it is this dialogue which becomes a central part of the child's capacity to talk to and relate to itself. In this way the child, having learned socially to talk with others, begins to talk with itself and this internal talk can be equated with Level 3 self-reflection. It is an inner dialogue between two poles of a reciprocal relationship narrated–narrator. Thus what CAT calls Level 3 psychological function is in its origin and essence a social construction formed out of reciprocal roles.

Conclusion: integration and meta-theory

This critique of cognitive and psychodynamic approaches to borderline personality disorder has tried at the same time to illustrate the ways in which CAT views the same phenomena. One aim has been to demonstrate that CAT is not capable of being classified as an offshoot of either cognitive or of psychodynamic psychotherapy. Instead I argue that CAT may represent a sketch of the kind of meta-theory that is needed to unify cognitive and psychodynamic approaches.

Bateman (1997) undertakes a similar project in his paper 'Borderline personality disorder and psychotherapeutic psychiatry: an integrative approach'. He sketches out three areas of difference between cognitive and psychodynamic therapy – irrationality and the self, a focus on intra or extrapsychic causes of behaviour, and a focus either on affect and motivation or on cognition. It is instructive to see how CAT is situated in relation to the debates which surround these nodal areas, each of which will need to be negotiated for any successful integration to occur.

Irrationality and the self

One problem of psychological approaches to symptomatic behaviour lies in the apparent irrationality of the symptom. When apparent behaviour and avowed motivations are at odds, practical reasoning on the basis of conscious beliefs and desires fails to account for behaviour. Either the actor must be thought no longer an agent (the action was, say, an accident or biologically caused) or psychological theorists are forced to seek some deeper reason for the apparent irrationality. In such a case one of two concepts must yield. Either the conscious self is not united but divided, or else the parts of the self responsible for the apparently irrational behaviour are hidden from the apparent self so that it cannot attest accurately to its motivations. Psychoanalytic theorists since Freud have opted to maintain the unity of the self at the price of proposing an unconscious realm of motivations which supplies the missing but now congruent motivations that in turn restore the breach in practical reason. Exposing and explicating the unconscious thread of missing motivations represents the key task of insight-oriented therapy

Therefore it is not surprising that Bateman, writing from an analytic tradition, highlights the irrationality of borderline patients by pointing up discrepancies between the conscious representations that borderline patients make of themselves and the unconscious self-representations which are evidenced by their behaviour. Cognitive therapists take a different route. They aim to seal the breach in practical reason by proposing powerful underlying misconceptions about the world – patterns which, once understood, make the patients' motivations rational once more by altering the presumptive belief structure which informs decision-making. In the context of practical reason, using the belief–desire pairing, analysts appeal to hidden desire and cognitive therapists appeal to hidden belief. However, Bateman argues that powerful underlying misconceptions turn out to be inadequate to fill the breach in practical reason and in consequence cognitive therapists are forced to ignore, dismiss, or explain in over-complex ways, behaviour which threatens it.

Ryle, too, criticizes CBT for adopting a piecemeal approach to higher-order phenomena and would agree with Bateman that it is not capable of explaining the full range of phenomena seen in borderline personality disorder. However, Ryle is also critical of psychodynamic approaches, which he argues assume that behaviour can be explained by a set of hypothesized motivations whose presence is inferred in the patient as much for reasons of theory as on the basis of evidence. At worst psychodynamic therapists fill the explanatory breach with fanciful theoretical constructions built out of observations of what are essentially artefacts of an unusual social situation created by analytic technique itself. As we have seen, Ryle is particularly critical of the way in which such inferred motivations can lead to accusations both of 'failure and destructive intent'. It is also clearly a natural danger that a theory which supposes as of necessity the existence of unseen (unconscious) forces may easily stray far beyond what is warranted on the basis of observation.

CAT's explanation of irrationality takes the other route – that of questioning the unity of the self. At first sight questioning the unity of the self might appear a self-defeating move since it is central to the notion of a self that it should be united. In order to understand how this can be a valid route it is important to understand how CAT sees the development of the self.

According to CAT, no primordial self exists in the infant. Instead, there are primitive capacities and motivations, attachment drives, propensities to recognize faces, possibly capacities to read emotions, and so forth. However, the child is taken by others to have/be a self from long before birth; it is treated as a self. The child is regarded as an intending, motivated communicator and agent. Selfhood is acquired out of the repeated interactions with others who take the selfhood of the child as given (even though it is not); thus, like many cultural capacities the self is a donation. It is something we have because we are born into a culture. CAT's story about borderline personality disorder is a story about how that process goes wrong in a variety of ways.

So, for Ryle the self is socially constructed through dialogues with caregivers that build up the reciprocal role repertoire and self-management procedures, and is socially maintained by virtue of its current interpersonal interactions; consequently his model is intensely interactionist. Radical discontinuities in the self signalled by incongruities of avowed aim and intent result from the intelligible responses of a self with intensely impoverished resources to what are often highly deprived social circumstances consequent on previous cycles of difficulty. Both the internal and the external world are dialogic and social processes build up and maintain personal unity – or are unable to do so. CAT hypothesizes that breaches in the unity of the self are the result of 'deficiency and dissociation rather than [of] conflict and defence'(Ryle 1997). The pathologies of borderline personality disorder result from a range of disruptions to the unity of the self. As a result the true aim of treatment should be integration.

Consequently CAT criticizes cognitive and psychodynamic therapies whenever they seem to advocate doing things which promote a disunited view of the self. Ryle discusses Young's work on schema-focused approaches to CBT in the following terms. 'In the example quoted the card reads ". . . I feel angry drained and ignored because schemas prevent me from expressing my needs." This form of words places schemas alongside internal objects as quasi-autonomous agents and is likely to detract from the development of a sense of responsibility and control.' (Ryle 1997) From a CAT perspective, splitting off and reifying a part of the psyche is a profoundly anti-therapeutic move when working with borderline patients. This is a criticism Ryle has also levelled at British object relations theorists in the Kleinian tradition when they use the idea of bad internal objects or of defensive pathological organizations. He argues that these terms, particularly ones like Rosenfeld's internal mafia or gang, require the propounding of semi-autonomous sub-personalities over which the subject has no control.

Extrapsychic versus intrapsychic origins of behaviour

Another area of debate which forms an axis for integration is the issue of extrapsychic versus intrapsychic causes for psychopathology.

Commenting on the appeal to environmental causes central to the approach of dialectical behaviour therapy (DBT) (cf. Chapter 9) to disturbed behaviour, Bateman remarks wryly that 'for DBT the culprit is the environment, for psychodynamic psychotherapy it is the mother'. Bateman worries that a concentration on current environmental causes of behaviour may 'reinforce distortions and maintain maladaptive patterns'. He asks 'If the rage and anger are valid, what becomes of the oft-reported accusations, denigration, and contempt of the therapist? They too must be valid.' This response to DBT is a little extreme since acknowledging the reality of experience can be important in therapy and it is often the case that patients with a personality-disorder label have much to complain of in the healthcare system.

However, not all environmental influences are in the present and Ryle takes DBT to task for being insufficiently environmental in ignoring the past. He argues that it allows insufficient room for the environment in relation to the causal role of abusive early experiences. CAT strongly emphasizes early environmental influences in the aetiology of borderline personality disorder. It tends to accept patient's accounts of their early life as more likely to be true than otherwise. But it also leaves room both for biological or temperamental factors, and for psychological events, including later misconstructions of experience, defensive dissociation from experience, and also for profoundly ambivalent reactions to experience.

Debates about the intrapsychic or extrapsychic origins of behaviour do not in any event resolve neatly across analytic versus cognitivist lines. For example, different analytic schools stress influences on pathology which range from innate levels of aggression through to traumatic early experiences. Cognitive therapists vary in the kinds of environmental influence which they think important. They have tended until recently to ignore past influences in favour of an analysis of current perpetuating features. More recently, though, in schema-focused work entrenched schemas formed in earlier life are theorized to override current environmental influence to cause symptoms.

On a CAT analysis, if the external world is primary this does not remain entirely true for long. The developing self becomes a self in interaction and forms its internal parts out of interaction. Selfhood is then maintained and conditioned permanently by two environments: the internal social environment of stored reciprocal roles and the external social environment of relatedness. So, once adulthood is reached neither internal nor external explanations will stand alone when seeking to plot out borderline psychopathology. Instead, only an interactional approach will serve. CAT criticizes both psychoanalytic and cognitive approaches for their exclusive concentration on the individual and their internal processes, or for seeing only one-way environmental influences. Both lose sight of the social nature of the self and in so doing create many of the paradoxes about the causes of behaviour which they then seek to explain.

Affect, motivation, and cognition

Interactional approaches have intuitive appeal but are often highly complex in practice. CAT offers two devices to serve as building blocks for the complex analyses that must follow. These are the concepts of reciprocal roles as templates for social and intrapsychic relationships, and procedural sequences as building blocks for aim directed actions. These two blocks also provide a different approach to the debate over the primacy of affect, motivation, or cognition in driving human behaviour. Bateman criticizes cognitive–behavioural approaches to treatment for 'doing gymnastics to explain clearly motivational phenomena on cognitive grounds' and for contorting themselves over issues of motivation and emotion. Equally, he suggests that psychodynamic approaches lack attention to cognitive detail. CAT therapists might add to this comment the difficulties created by psychodynamic psychotherapy's approach to therapeutic change. Analysts possess only one main tool as agent of change – the transference interpretation. However, we can agree with Bateman that any complete description of human experience and behaviour must theorize and synthesize cognitive, affective, and motivational processes.

CAT welds emotion and feeling together in the procedural sequence object relations model. Procedural sequences begin with aims and then proceed along affective and cognitive lines to actions in the service of the aim and retrospective evaluations of the consequences of action. Motivational processes appear both within the aim of the procedural sequence and within the structure of the reciprocal role templates which are often oriented towards a specific aim – say caregiving to care-receiving. However, there are still difficulties with this model. Conflict of motivation remains largely untheorized within CAT. This is partly because, clinically, motivational conflict does not turn out to be difficult for individuals once the nature and structure of their reciprocal roles has been elucidated and softened. Partly, though, it is due to the uneasy way in which motivational structures are distributed within CAT between elements of our social knowledge base (reciprocal roles) and as close cousins of affective and drive structures.

CAT can, in my view, be expanded to encompass a much better theory of motivation. One way to do this is to return to Freud's original views in which drives and their objects were at first not necessarily related. Motivations can then be theorized as resulting from the attachment by classical conditioning of basic drives onto self-states, environmental circumstances, and social situations in which experiences of satisfaction occur. Motivations grow to take more complex forms as repeated successful procedural enactments groove the object (in this case the procedural sequence and its associate reciprocal roles) onto drive.

CAT: a springboard

In this chapter I have argued that CAT offers a strong base from which to develop the necessary meta-theory for psychotherapy integration. It is neither a cognitive nor a psychodynamic theory but one which, while drawing on both bodies of thought, gives primacy to the most important part of our lives and the one most seriously neglected by psychodynamic and cognitive therapists – the social. There is clearly scope here for further integrationist work with those in the group-analytic tradition (see Chapter 5) in that they, too, emphasize the social nature of the self. CAT sketches out a new view of selfhood which, because it is not monolithic, does not require profound contortions to understand irrationality. It takes a clear stand on the primacy of the environment in development but, because this is a social environment and the resulting self an 'internally social' one, it can develop an interactional account of behaviour which welds self and environment together. Last, in relation to different aspects of mental functioning, it is capable of at least a partially unifying account and I hope I have added a sketch as a further step in that process.

Chapter 7

Psychodynamic interpersonal therapy

Frank Margison

Introduction

Psychodynamic interpersonal therapy (PIT) integrates psychodynamic, interpersonal, and humanistic approaches to therapy (see Barkham *et al.*, in press; Guthrie 1999). Integration here means that the elements are part of one combined approach to theory and practice, as opposed to eclecticism which draws *ad hoc* from several approaches in the approach to a particular case (cf. Chapter 1). To this extent the model exists as a 'stand-alone', manualized therapy which has been evaluated in several randomized controlled trials.

However, the tradition to which PIT owes its origin is called the conversational model of Robert Hobson (Brown 1999; Hobson 1985; Martin and Margison 2000). Hobson's vision was based on fundamental principles of how therapy might be practised. These principles can be used to enhance the practice of therapists across a wide range of other models. In this chapter the origins of PIT are described in the context of a generic model of therapeutic change. As will be discussed later, it is neither helpful nor accurate to attempt to claim ownership of these principles for any particular model of therapy, but they are stated in this chapter from the perspective of PIT. The underlying theoretical principles are presented in terms of a theory of developmental psychopathology linked to a theory of practice.

The chapter briefly reviews the research basis for the model, applications in practice, models of teaching, and supervision, with a concluding section on future developments.

General principles of therapeutic change applied to PIT

If a therapy is integrated within a scientific tradition, it is sometimes believed that this will inevitably influence the position of the therapy on the continuum between *responsiveness* to the client, and *detachment*. In our view, the balance between these two seemingly opposed features is central to psychotherapy. The PIT approach is committed to an evidence-based approach to practice but also to the principle that a practice-based approach to evidence is needed (Margison *et al.* 2000).

In the earliest writing on this model of therapy, Hobson stressed this *experiential* and *responsive* quality to the therapy combined with a *scientific attitude*. On the one hand the therapist is immediately engaged with the here-and-now nuances of the conversation, aware of 'minute particulars', but also able to see how this particular meeting shares common patterns with other meetings. Although expressed in the language of poetics, this is close to basic scientific method as applied in a clinical setting. This preoccupation with observation and simultaneous engagement is also reflected in the teaching methods described later.

Principles and values

There are fundamental human values involved in psychotherapy, as well as technical skills (Holmes and Lindley 1991). The ethical issues involved in any therapeutic work apply in PIT and so the therapist needs to be aware of professional issues such as confidentiality, the duty of care to patients and (at times) to other family members, and the need to be aware of the intrinsically asymmetric power relationship between patient and therapist.

Hobson (1985) stresses the aspects of therapy which are about 'persons' involved in a mutual conversation:

> [S]ix qualities of a personal relationship . . . are at the heart of conversational therapy: it happens between experiencing subjects, it can only be known from 'within', it is mutual, it involves aloneness–togetherness, its language is a disclosure of private 'information', and it is shared 'here and now'.

This definition is central to Hobson's approach to therapy. In those six points he sums up some of the key principles of ethical practice, dealing with the need to respect the autonomy of the other person, whilst engaged in a fundamentally human rather than technical activity.

A generic model of change in therapy

PIT can be seen as attending in particular ways to a therapeutic conversation so as to maximize the possibility of change. This approach is inherently integrative in focusing on the basic requisites for change to take place. The fundamental aspects of change used in this model of therapy can be summarized as:

- Capacity for intimacy
- Personal problem solving
- Use of the relationship with the therapist
- Extending self-reflective capacity
- Hope and the capacity for change
- The use of the working alliance in therapy

Capacity for intimacy

Hobson introduced the concept of 'aloneness–togetherness'. This describes a state of intimacy which avoids extreme states of detachment and loneliness on the one hand and pseudo-intimacy and clinging arising from the dread of abandonment on the other, or states where these two poles alternate abruptly. These concepts are closely allied to Bowlby's notion of a secure base for exploration (aloneness–togetherness) and the diffi-culties with attachment characterized by compulsive self-reliance, clinging attachment, and the mixed or ambivalent states with features of both.

Therapy is not normative in the sense that it is 'correct' to move towards a particular type of relationship, but stresses the need to be free from pervasive anxiety about rela-tionships that characterize many clinical states.

Personal problem solving

The model of change was summarized by Hobson as 'personal problem solving'. By this he meant solving problems *in* interpersonal relations and also *through* the relationship with the therapist. This stresses two generic features of psychotherapy. First, clinical states are seen as arising in the context of disrupted relationships. These may be in the external world and the immediate focus of distress for the client. Or, they may be mani-fest internally as abnormal thoughts, beliefs, internally condemning 'voices', or simply as maladaptive relationship 'templates' which the person follows blindly.

Second, the *goals* of therapy are defined and worked upon within the therapeutic relationship.

Use of the relationship with the therapist

Through the therapeutic relationship and attempts to link to other relationships in the person's life there is an increase in understanding of general relationship patterns. Some models of therapy, such as PIT, see the use of the relationship with the therapist as cen-tral, but even in models where the emphasis may be elsewhere it is crucial to maintain a 'good enough' relationship.

Extending self-reflective capacity

Insight is a change factor commonly cited within the psychodynamic tradition. It is better to view insight as a *capacity* than as the discovery of a previously hidden truth. Therapy can be seen as a reconstructive process through which memories, desires, and beliefs are integrated, along with the developing capacity to stand outside difficult situa-tions and see connections with past experiences. In some traditions the term *meta-cognition* is used to refer to this capacity for self-reflection. Success in therapy can be measured in terms of an increase in this meta-cognitive capacity even under pressure.

Hope and the capacity to change

One of the generic factors described by Jerome Frank (1988) is the instillation of hope. Simply attending for an initial assessment and filling in self-report forms has a substantial positive effect. Also, patient 'expectancy' (hope expressed in other terms) has a substantial impact on outcome.

Some models of therapy (such as motivational interviewing for example) pay particular attention to *motivation*, but 'hope' is a subtly different concept. It refers to an existential state, and models such as PIT focus on the experience of 'loss of hope of change' as central to the person's engagement with therapy. Articulating this existential position in a shared-feeling language can allow therapy to progress, sometimes for many years, whilst co-existing with suicidal thoughts.

The use of the working alliance in therapy

The therapeutic alliance has been shown to be among the most stable and powerful predictors of therapeutic outcome (Luborsky *et al.* 1988). Those capable of forming an alliance relatively easily can use therapeutic help to greatest effect and so therapists need to pay particular attention to ensure that the alliance shifts to the optimal level. The alliance needs to be *monitored* constantly within sessions as one of the 'vital signs' within a therapy. This can be seen as a generic property of therapies, but its implementation is a particular feature of some therapies such as PIT.

Thus the 'feel' of the session may suddenly change. Kohut (1977) described this as a sudden threat to the cohesion of the self, manifest by a sudden change of affective tone. Hobson emphasized the shift in voice quality at these times, or the change in posture, expression, or gaze. These 'minute particulars' are part of the second-by-second monitoring of the alliance. A marker of a skilled therapist is to be able to maintain this monitoring at a high level whilst also allowing conversation to flow.

All therapists need strategies for *repairing the alliance* when attention to these early markers has been insufficient. A common generic strategy is to 'step outside the frame' by suggesting that something has gone wrong and to invite exploration of this experience.

Early development of PIT by Robert Hobson

PIT involves the integration of a number of traditions. As is often the case, the impetus came from dissatisfaction with then current approaches. Hobson was uncomfortable with some features of traditional practice that he saw as persecutory. His own unique blend of influences led to the development of the conversational model. The influences are difficult to prioritize, and do not form a chronological sequence, but Table 7.1 summarizes some of the key influences that are mentioned elsewhere in this chapter.

Table 7.1   Influences on PIT

Influence	Key figures	Examples of key concepts
Literary	William Wordsworth, Samuel Taylor Coleridge, and the Romantic poets	Metaphor Imagination and construction of meaning Attention to 'minute particulars'
Philosophical	Ludwig Wittgenstein	Language games
Christian writers	Martin Buber	'I-Thou' relationship
Existential writers	Rollo May	Phenomenology and experience of self
Person-centred counselling	Carl Rogers	Focus on immediate experience Non-hierarchical relationship in therapy Analysis of therapeutic skills
Analytical psychology	Carl G. Jung	Symbolical attitude Focus on 'here and now' The dialectical nature of meeting and conversation
Interpersonal psychology	Harry Stack Sullivan	The 'self' only existing interpersonally
Psychoanalysis	Sigmund Freud and the British 'Independent School'	Disclaimed actions and the unconscious 'Good enough' parenting
Self psychology	Heinz Kohut	Affect shifts and disturbances of the self
Attachment theory and developmental psychopathology	John Bowlby Daniel Stern	The 'secure base' concept for therapy Stage development of the self

Although Hobson had developed his description of the conversational model from the late 1960s, his book *Forms of Feeling: The Heart of Psychotherapy* (1985) is the fullest exposition of the underlying principles and practice. Although for current descriptive purposes (as in this volume) the term psychodynamic interpersonal therapy is used, the fundamental principles are drawn from the conversational model and for most purposes the terms can be used interchangeably.

Literary, religious, and philosophical influences

Literary influences, in particular Wordsworth and the Romantic poets, have been important in Hobson's development of the concept of a conversational model. Central to the model is a particular kind of feeling-based, associative language. Wittgenstein's description of situation-specific 'language games' also influenced how Hobson saw the detailed analysis of the context of language in psychotherapy (Hobson 1985, pp. 46–9).

Hobson has also extended the domain of psychotherapy into the spiritual. The Christian influence is seen in the idea of 'aloneness–togetherness' as opposed to 'loneliness', where the image of being forsaken has deep resonance in Christian culture, and Buber's notion of the 'I–Thou' relationship was pivotal to his notion of an equal yet asymmetric relationship (Hobson 1985, pp. 18–20). Hobson was also aware that aloneness can be seen existentially, and he drew widely from the Continental European tradition of existential psychology to expound the idea of 'loneliness'.

Hobson developed the ideas of imagination and fantasy as central aspects of his method, drawing widely on literary sources. He cites (Hobson 1974) Samuel Taylor Coleridge's definition of fantasy as 'a union of deep feeling with profound thought'. Fantasy is a part of Hobson's wide definition of 'imagination' (Hobson 1985, pp. 95–114). A further development is to Jung's idea of active imagination where a conscious effort is made to dwell on fantasy images and other materials (Hobson 1985, p. 102).

The influence of other models of practice

Table 7.1 shows that the conversational model integrated a diverse set of influences. Hobson was personally influenced by Carl Jung and the three principles of symbolic amplification, immediate experience in the 'here and now', and the dialectical nature of the conversation became founding principles.

Hobson was also influenced by a wide range of psychodynamic theorists and practitioners, although he was highly critical of the 'blank screen' approach to therapy. Sullivan's model of interpersonal psychology provided a radically interpersonal view of psychopathology, and existential theorists like Rollo May provided a theoretical base for Hobson's conception of 'loneliness'.

Despite some clear similarities with client-centred counselling, Hobson's approach to the interview situation came from different roots, although he exchanged videotape material with Rogers and co-workers, and the teaching methods were strongly influenced by the skills-based model originating with Rogers and co-workers.

Developmental theorists

From early in the development of the conversational model, Hobson recognized the importance of developmental theory and was influenced by Bowlby's attachment theory (Holmes 1993) as an explanatory model for some patterns of relating. Stern's concept of the emergent self then formed a theoretical bridge to a developmental theory formulated by Meares (1993).

All of these individuals and approaches have influenced the model that Hobson developed. However, one paper on the 'persecutory therapist' (Meares and Hobson 1977) could be considered as highlighting the dissatisfaction with the approaches then current, prompting the synthesis that became known as the conversational model, and latterly psychodynamic interpersonal therapy.

The persecutory therapist

Hobson and Meares began to develop a model of therapy by describing what elements of a conversation were anti-therapeutic or even persecutory (Meares and Hobson 1977). They had a clear idea of how certain aspects of a bad therapeutic relationship resonated with failures of parenting, so persecutory therapists were intrusive, derogatory, invalidating, opaque, made impossible demands, gave conflicting messages, and made conflicting demands within an unclear structure. By spelling out these negative therapeutic behaviours (which are now part of the therapist rating manual) the link between failures of parenting and failures of therapy are made clear.

Following the description of the persecutory therapist Hobson and co-workers in Manchester began defining this model, and its related theory of the origin of interpersonal difficulties.

Theory of the origin of interpersonal difficulties

The development of the 'self' in relation to others

A crucial aim in psychotherapy is to re-create self-esteem, including, Hobson points out, the specific aspect of feeling at ease with '*myself*'. His model assumes that persons who seek psychotherapy have typically experienced a disruption to their sense of personal existence. In developing his ideas on how we form a sense of *self*, he drew on Kohut's self psychology, Piaget's observations of infant development, Winnicott's concept of 'good enough' parenting, Bowlby's attachment theory, and Stern's notion of attunement.

Attunement to the baby's early attempts to engage the parent in a conversation, and later developments such as the capacity to hold a secret (Meares 1993), underpin the conversational model.

Early in life, the baby has remarkably well-developed capacities for interacting with the caregiver. The infant is highly sensitive to nuances of interaction and can communicate in sophisticated ways. However, as the infant's capacity for cognition is limited, the baby's concept of self is assumed to be limited to a prototypic 'I'. By the age of about 15 to 18 months, the infant is able to point to its own image in the mirror, and seems to recognize it as an objective self – a '*me*'. The crucial point about this process of development of a sense of self is that it occurs *interpersonally*. If all goes well, it is the mother (or caregiver) who, in her responses to the baby's '*proto-conversation*', has modelled a stable image of 'me' during those early months, so that 'I' can internalize a sense of myself as cared for and worthwhile.

However, the baby's communication is reflected back, subtly altered to incorporate messages about the mother's emotional state. The 'me' is the germ of the child's view of himself in others' eyes. If the mother or caregiver distorts the early communication, saturating it with her own unmanageable feelings, the child may develop with a sense of being unworthy in the eyes of others.

Hobson, though, extended this *duplex self* (James 1962) into a notion of a *tripartite self*, with the added element he called '*myself*' (Hobson 1985, pp. 147–60). This is a complex concept, which extends to the idea of multi-layered internal voices and conversations. For the purpose of this chapter, however, it is enough to note that this influences the nature of the therapeutic conversation, through explicit recognition of a parallel internal conversation with 'myself'.

Meares (1993) has speculated further on the ways in which the developmental processes outlined above may be disrupted. If the carer does not provide the possibility of resonance with another, the growing individual feels unconnected. The result may be that he learns to focus solely on the outside world, and attends exclusively to stimuli originating from it, particularly those that impinge upon the body. He may become preoccupied with *somatic* or bodily symptoms, and attempts at conversation feel boring or dead, emotional life residing solely in distressing physical symptoms inaccessible to thought or reflection. Hobson describes a meeting with 'Freda', who is 'talking *about* her symptoms – as if they are "out there." She is treating herself as if she were only a thing, and talking at me as if I were a thing, not talking with me as a person.' (Hobson 1985, pp. 21–8.)

Alternatively, the growth toward a stable and valued sense of 'myself' may be disrupted by multiple trauma, many not being remembered. Traumas which have the potential to disrupt the emerging sense of 'myself' include threats of or actual abandonment, shame, and ridicule, all of which deny the separate existence of the child. In adult life, many patients who have experienced such traumas will live with an enduring and profound inner emptiness (Hobson 1985, p. 274).

Internalized conversations, voices, and signs

Given this emphasis on the emergent self in relation to other internalized conversations and selves, PIT must be fundamentally dialogical in approach. As well as the overt emphasis on the actual conversation between the client and therapist, the model focuses on how role relationship patterns are embedded in language. Internalized conversations with caregivers are accessed at times of stress and can act positively to soothe and contain, or can recapitulate hostile, derisive, and humiliating comments from the past. These conversations can become dissociated and be experience as semi-autonomous voices. In extreme states they can be experienced with marked dissociation as hallucinatory voices or as partially autonomous separate 'selves'.

Some of the earliest case descriptions of this model were with patients with schizophrenia. 'In some people labelled "schizophrenic", separate selves act as partial personalities, as for example when in hallucinations alien voices comment or mock . . . The understanding of such psychotic phenomena ... also demonstrates a loss of the capacity to symbolise and use figurative language' (Hobson 1985, p. 158).

These internalized voices may be derived from early disruption of the development of self in settings where parenting is flawed. However, this model of therapy is non-dogmatic about the origin of such voices, recognizing that they can also arise through acquired brain injury, intoxication, or other disease processes. The *results* of these processes are, however, then manifest in the present in disrupted relationships and a disordered relationship to 'self'. These problems in relating can either be avoided by becoming 'cut off' from others, or the relationship problems can be endlessly re-enacted.

Complexes

Hobson used Jung's term 'complex' to describe these multilayered patterns of relating. The concept is closely allied to that of 'schema' and is defined as a simultaneous activation of thoughts, feelings, perceptions, and bodily sensations linking current and past experience. Usually the source of activation is only partly conscious in the early stages and one of the key aims of therapy is to allow the triggering events to be brought into awareness.

In PIT the recurrent patterns are assumed to be played out in all significant relationships, and so are potentially open to examination and change in minute-to-minute here-and-now experience in the therapy.

A theory of practice

PIT integrates many theoretical strands as described briefly above. It can also be seen as having a theory of practice.

The types of intervention characterizing a model can be described fairly easily, but a common misunderstanding is to assume that a therapy is defined by its characteristic interventions. Therapies can be described in terms of characteristic, unique, and 'forbidden' interventions (see Waltz *et al.* 1993), but in practice it may be better to develop more refined descriptions of *strategies* for intervention, rather than simply differentiating the interventions used. In support of this principle, PIT has developed a theory of practice, based on the underlying principles of the model.

Optimal anxiety for exploration

Hobson stated that therapy maintains a 'level of anxiety or fear which is necessary for recognizing and solving problems in relationships'. He sees the therapist's task as monitoring the second-by-second changes in the level of anxiety and helping the patient to maintain anxiety at the optimal level for exploration. He was acutely aware that excessive anxiety can narrow the possible zone of exploration. In some cases anxiety can be so high that the patient consolidates maladaptive patterns of avoidance. If anxiety is too low, however, change does not occur and well-established patterns are simply replayed without any revision being necessary.

Scaling

Drawing on principles from education, the level of conceptualization possible will vary with the level of anxiety, but also with the subject's ability to stand 'outside' the narrative. One aim is for this capacity to increase as therapy progresses. In PIT the therapist tries to develop an overall formulation, but the 'level of magnification or scale' may vary from client to client and session to session within a therapy. So, in some sessions there may be detailed work on what seems to be a 'tiny piece of the jigsaw', whereas others may link patterns of experience to very broad existential themes.

In clinical supervision Hobson would sometimes stay with a few seconds of audio tape and explore the material in exacting detail, attending to every nuance and inflection. The underlying belief behind this process was that psychological meaning was embedded more like a hologram than an architectural site. In every phrase of a therapy there would be subtle features reflecting the whole in every part. This is essentially a view derived from Romanticism, that the organizing principles of the universe can be perceived in every leaf or grain of sand.

The psychodynamic interpersonal therapist should move from the big picture to detail very fluidly, at times staying for a whole session with associations to a smell which has brought back a flood of childhood memories, at other times making explicit thematic links (often expressed in the form of metaphor). PIT emphasizes this quality of *multiple scaling* as an essential feature not only of therapeutic practice but also as a model of how mental life is organized.

The secure base

Many models incorporate a model of the therapy (or the therapist) as a 'secure base' from which exploration is possible. The metaphor of secure base is derived from attachment theory (Holmes 1996b, 2001). In PIT there are the usual conventions of consistency of time, place, and approach. However, despite overt consistency in the therapist's behaviour, there are differences of approach based on sensitivity to the developmental complexity of the current therapeutic task. At times the therapist needs to provide a secure base in the sense that even the most minor change in routine is intensely anxiety-provoking. At other times the therapist is more like an encouraging mentor or teacher, at yet others someone to be 'left behind' as 'out of touch' or 'out of date' as the client consolidates their identity an individual person. All of these positions can be seen as linked by a consistency of underlying language, but the nature of the secure base will vary with the developmental task at any particular moment.

Using therapist errors

In PIT the therapist will openly acknowledge and use error. Hobson (1985, p. 197) states:

> A personal conversation is a movement; it progresses not by comfortable agreement but by correction of mistakes. In intimate relationships we constantly miss the mark and it is out of the gap that new possibilities emerge. But the miss must not be too great. Some adjustment must be possible if 'misses' are to be recognized. Then it is possible to explore jointly the nature of the misunderstanding.

So, the therapist in PIT focuses more on getting things optimally wrong rather than as 'correct' as possible, in that the 'emerging shared feeling language' is seen as a central aspect of therapeutic change.

Developing the conversation

The 'imaginative elaboration of feeling' is part of the process of 'personal problem solving'. The patient's interpersonal problems are located as they manifest themselves within the therapeutic conversation and are gradually formulated in interpersonal language. This will reveal ways in which the patient has habitually avoided pain, and so may mean rediscovering actions that were formerly denied or *disclaimed*.

The therapist aims to build a relationship with the patient which is *mutual* yet *asymmetrical*. The therapist is not '*opaque*', like a 'blank screen', but present in the conversation. This does not imply significant self-revelation about the therapist's own life.

Elements of the model

The sections above have focused on the underlying principles, but there has been considerable work in PIT in defining interventions unambiguously. Table 7.2 summarizes the main elements of the approach, as described in the manual used in PIT research, to check adherence to the model. Some of the elements are explicitly generic: facilitative conditions are present to a greater or lesser extent in any therapy. But, even those skills described as specific are shared to varying degrees with other therapies (sometimes with different terminology). Manualizing a therapy draws attention to how much integration has already occurred between ostensibly different approaches. However, techniques form part of a coherent 'blend' of style, approach, and strategy often seen most clearly in the style of problem formulation used.

Formulation of difficulties

The method of formulating problems is systematic and yet tries to express interpersonal themes in the language that the patient used in the sessions. In short-term therapy the formulation may need to be made explicit and clear goals set. This is less marked in long-term therapy, but may still help at times. For example, some therapists will build in a 'review of progress' when a different style of conversation is seen. The style then is

Table 7.2 Skills for PIT

Specific skills
Rationale for exploratory therapy
Providing a rationale
Relating interpersonal change to therapy
Shared understanding
Negotiating style
Language of mutuality (I and we)
Metaphor
Use of disclosure
Understanding hypotheses
Focus on 'here and now'
Cue basis
Focusing
Confrontation
Focus on feelings
Exploration of feelings
Acknowledgement of affect
Acceptance of affect
Limitations
Gaining insight
Patterns in relationships
Linking hypotheses
Explanatory hypotheses
Structure
Sequencing interventions
Structuring the session
Facilitative conditions
Supportive encouragement
Convey expertise
Therapist's communication style
Involvement
Warmth
Rapport
Empathy
Lack of formality

more focused with the aim of producing a clearer, and agreed, map of the territory to be explored.

The formulation is derived from the principle of linking together themes which arise within the therapy sessions. An example is given of both the format and style of formulation and how these can be linked to session notes. In brief therapy the essence of a whole therapy should be encapsulated, if possible, within one or two sentences.

The following case example is over-simplified to show the general principles, and the key themes of the formulation are shown in Table 7.3.

Table 7.3 Formulation

Information	Problems / issues	Metaphors / key phrases
Client self-description	Depressed and cut off from people Lonely and hopeless about the future	'I just can't feel it's like I'm a robot'
Current relationships	Gets extremely close, demands a lot and then is rejected	'I just feel I am going to burst, like I have to stuff myself before I am on my own again'
Past relationships	Father: away a lot organizing cancer care for children in Africa Mother: ill a lot, needed caring for when she had migraine	'He was such a loving man, I feel ashamed that I took up so much of his time' 'My mum loved me so much, I did everything I could to make her comfortable'
Relationship with Therapist	Worried about breaks at holidays, feels she is a burden on me, concerned about my health	'You don't look after yourself enough, you'll end up getting flu'
Hidden feelings	Possible hidden feelings of anger and resentment at having to care for others with no-one to care for her	Only evident in a 'griping' pain in her stomach

Interpersonal dilemmas

If I care for others I feel I am worth something, but they take advantage of me and I am left alone. But if I ask for proof that people love me then I still get left alone.

Links between people, events and feelings

Griping pain tends to be worse when facing a loss, however small.

Over-concerned about therapist's health and 'holds back' her needs.

Expects to only get 'the crumbs' when other people's needs have been met (link to father's work and mother's overwhelming needs)

Metaphor of 'stuffing myself' emotionally to protect against future starvation

Formulation expressed as hypotheses

I have to put others first, then someone (like my father) will love me.

Feelings are dangerous: they drive people away, or make you /me ill.

Planning

(1) Goals

Reduce depression

Reduce stomach pains

Reduce her 'cut-offness' from her children and others

(2) Methods

Link fears regarding abandonment with pain, and later develop 'griping' metaphor

Link her placation and care of me to relationship with mother, and her need for my approval with father

Use any opportunities arising from fear of loss to examine 'here and now' somatic symptoms

Link her father's care of others who are sick and her mother needing care because she was sick and also her fear (?wish) that I was sick and so she could care for me

Mrs White was a 35-year-old woman who had been depressed for about 2 years since her mother's death. Her husband had left her and she blamed herself for that because she was not there for him. She found it difficult to relate to the children in case she became a burden to them.

She had had a recurrence of 'griping' pains which had taken her to the doctor, who thought they might be related to her depression.

She came across at the initial interview as contained and able to manage, but there were clear suggestions that she had not grieved for her father's death 12 years ago and had not cried since her mother's death. She had a pattern in relationships of asking for very little, but then would suddenly shift to demanding a lot in a 'greedy way', which tended to confirm her fear that she would drive others away if she expressed any needs.

Her relationship with her father as a wonderful carer was idealized and she actually had had very little support or love from him at a time of great difficulty in her teens when she had become pregnant. Her mother was a demanding woman who was 'sickly' and retired to bed where she had to be cared for.

Even in the first session she was worried about my health and asked about future breaks. Over the sessions she began to explore the links between her pain and 'gnawing hunger' of her needs, but it was much more difficult for her to see that her word 'griping' also suggested that she might feel angry. This only came out after she had expressed her feelings of upset when I had had to cancel her session one day.

By the end of the 20-week therapy she was less depressed and more responsive to her children. She had made some connections between her 'caring' but unavailable father on whom she modelled herself. She also saw how she had learned from her mother to use physical symptoms as a 'disowned' method of communicating. Her pain was a little better but not fully resolved.

Most strikingly, she had become intensely needy towards me at about the mid-point of the therapy, but by the end felt she could cope with the back up of a review session in two months.

Research base

The research falls into three main types:

+ clinical conditions
+ the therapeutic change process and
+ teaching the model

Clinical conditions

Depression

Two randomized comparative studies carried out in Sheffield (Shapiro 1987, 1994) showed broad equivalence between this model and a model derived from cognitive–behaviour therapy.

In a further randomized study of '2 + 1' sessions of therapy of less severely depressed in a typical service setting, PIT was again of comparable efficacy to cognitive–behaviour therapy (Barkham and Hobson 1990). This study showed that PIT can be given in a coherent way even with a very small number of sessions, although in the previous studies there were suggestions that 16 sessions might be preferable to 8 sessions in more severe depression.

A randomized controlled study against treatment as usual looked at the effectiveness of eight sessions of PIT in patients who had been unresponsive to routine psychiatric treatment for a minimum of 6 months. The study showed a significant reduction in symptoms *and* a reduction in health-care costs (Guthrie *et al.* 1999). Many of the patients had several diagnoses, the most common being depression.

Somatization

Guthrie and colleagues (1991) showed in a randomized controlled study that PIT is an effective treatment for irritable bowel syndrome (IBS) in terms of both associated mood symptoms and physical manifestations of the syndrome. Current work is in progress on upper gastro-intestinal disorders and to replicate the IBS study with a larger sample.

Borderline personality disorder

Stevenson and Meares (1992), in a well-designed open study using a variant of PIT influenced by Heinz Kohut (1977), showed a reduction in symptoms and disturbance at 1- and 5-year follow-up and suggested economic benefits from therapeutic intervention.

Psychosis

Two case studies have been published showing that PIT can be an effective adjunctive therapy in severe psychosis treated in long-term in-patient settings (Davenport *et al.* 2000).

Deliberate self-harm

A randomized controlled study has demonstrated the usefulness of PIT in deliberate self-harm (Guthrie *et al.* 2001).

The therapeutic change process

Part of the research strategy in the evaluation of PIT has been to use a 'process–outcome model'. In each of the studies described above, therapeutic change has been studied by looking in detail at process as well as simply looking at the outcome of therapy. A wide variety of methods has been used including measures of the therapeutic alliance, helpful aspects of therapy, depth and smoothness of therapy, and tape-assisted recall of sessions (Elliott *et al.* 1994) and the assimilation model (Stiles *et al.* 1990).

An example of the change processes studied was the development of insight (Elliott *et al.* 1994). In comparison with cognitive–behaviour therapy where insight was often at a procedural level, in PIT there was often a use of extended metaphor to pull together disparate themes into a problem formulation.

Teaching the model

The early studies on PIT focused on accurate description, replicability, development of adherence measures, and teaching methods. The studies can be summarized in the following stages:

Defining the key elements of the model	(Goldberg *et al.* 1984)
Developing a rating system	(Elliott *et al.* 1987)
Developing a training system	(Maguire *et al.* 1984)
Evaluating teaching tapes	(Margison and Moss 1994)
Clinical seminar group teaching	(Margison 1991, 1999)

The preliminary stage consisted in the development of robust and reliable descriptions incorporated in a rating method (Goldberg *et al.* 1984). The rating method was then further tested as part of an international comparison of six rating systems, showing that the method had good reliability (Elliott *et al.* 1987).

The model was refined by checking how therapists who were trained in the model differed from equally experienced therapists not exposed to the model, and the results of that preliminary study were used as the basis for developing a teaching method (Maguire *et al.* 1984).

The main body of the research on teaching used a combination of videotape and clinical teaching. A set of three teaching tapes was supplemented with eight sessions of clinical discussion. The trainees showed very considerable differences in interview style as a result of the teaching, moving from an interrogative to an exploratory style.

Further studies demonstrated that the teaching effects persisted with little decay over time and could be replicated in other centres. Further analysis of the results using a combined cluster- and factor-analysis approach supported the initial description, with factors representing a 'here and now' focus and an 'exploratory style' (Margison and Moss 1994).

Trainees also reported high satisfaction with the training and found it helpful in their general psychiatric work 2 years later.

Role play has been developed as an adjunct to supervised experience. The disadvantage of role play is that it is an artificial situation which can sometimes lack veracity. These problems are outweighed by the flexibility of examples to which trainees can practice at no risk to clients. Role play has particular advantages which warrant its wider use as a teaching method in developing high-level therapeutic skills as well as practice of basic therapeutic elements (Margison 1999; Margison and Moss 1994).

The videotape and role play methods can be supplemented with a self-teaching approach taken at the trainee's own pace.

The first phase of this training encourages the trainee to listen accurately to a session by transcribing the whole session as accurately as possible. The trainee is asked to transcribe the session annotating the length of pauses, sections where both participants talk together, hesitations, non-verbal vocalizations, dysfluencies, and changes in intonation. This is a very time-intensive process, but it has the advantage of helping the trainee to realize the extent to which they are processing communications in multiple 'channels' simultaneously in the session.

Supervision of PIT

There are several overlapping roles for supervision. At its most basic level it is a form of quality control to ensure that the practitioner is, and remains, competent in the basic skills of the model being taught. The discussion earlier in this chapter points out that this model lends itself to this approach in that there are a number of specified behaviours that are consistent with the model and some which are only used exceptionally. So, the supervisor can attend to an audio- or videotape or even a transcribed and summarized account to draw attention to times when the therapist veers away from a conversational style.

It is helpful for a supervisor to have a *developmental framework* in mind for the trainee so that attention can be given to the areas that are most relevant to the trainee's developmental stage.

Models of competence

This approach to supervision allows a supervisor to consider trainee therapists and fully fledged practitioners as having different levels of *competence*. Competence goes beyond the concept of simple *adherence* to a method, but subsumes it. As well as adherence the therapist shows increasing flexibility in using a model with growing competence (see Margison *et al.* 2000).

For PIT the model of competence includes the ability to avoid the qualities described in the 'persecutory therapist' (Meares and Hobson 1977), and also increasing levels of mastery in demanding situations.

By developing PIT from descriptions of practice it has become clear that therapists can mimic, or accommodate, a model of therapy whilst still not assimilating it fully. The assessment of competence used in PIT involves demonstration of ability to stay in mode under intense pressure: structural engineers have known for a long time that models perform differently 'under load'. The training approach used in PIT works on the assumption that this 'proving' should take place at minimum risk to the patient, and so should involve careful analysis of role play of stressful situations prior to undertaking actual therapeutic sessions wherever practically possible.

Current developments

Just as it may be used for working with a wide variety of clients and clinical problems, so the model lends itself flexibly to a range of settings. It has been used principally in the context of the British National Health Service until now, but is also used in independent practice. It was first developed in hospital settings, with both outpatients and inpatients. The model has been intensively evaluated in terms of descriptions of practice, adherence and competence measures, efficacy and effectiveness studies, and models of change.

Current developments are focused on using PIT in particularly challenging secure settings, and with clients who have not responded to other types of therapy. The emphasis is in building on what is already known about the client or the setting. The therapy is integrative in synthesizing the best aspects of practice and suggesting alternatives where existing methods are blocked.

PIT can be seen as a 'stand alone' therapy in research studies, but, in the spirit of its founder, Robert Hobson, it is perhaps best seen as a broad approach which can enhance the skills of therapists from various traditions, whether novices and experts. It focuses on best practice, but also describes explicitly what *not* to do as a therapist. So, PIT training has been used in developing the therapeutic skills of a wide range of mental health-workers – doctors, psychologists, nurses, social workers, and others – who do not necessarily see themselves primarily as psychotherapists.

The title given to this model by its founder has been superseded in research by the term psychodynamic interpersonal therapy, but there is something about the term 'conversational model' that summarizes the importance of attention to detailed conversation between persons that characterized the work of Robert Hobson, which continues in this tradition of integrative therapy. Attention to the nuances of a conversation is relevant in developing the effectiveness of mental health staff across a variety of settings as well as being a specific model in its own right.

Chapter 8

Interpersonal therapy

Laurie Gillies

Introduction

Interpersonal therapy (IPT) was developed by Gerald Klerman and Myrna Weissman in the 1970s and early 1980s as a brief treatment for depression (Weissman *et al.* 2000). The main thrust of this chapter is an exposition of IPT as an integrationist therapy bringing together an number of different techniques: guided grief; cognitive–behavioural methods to help deal with changes of role; marital therapy; and methods that originated in humanistic therapies such as role play. It starts, however, with a brief review of some of the research evidence showing its efficacy compared or combined with antidepressants – an example of organizational integration (see Chapter 1).

IPT was included as a treatment in the National Institute of Mental Health Treatment of Depression Collaborative Research Programme (NIMH TDCRP) (Elkin *et al.* 1989). It was compared to cognitive–behaviour therapy (CBT), imipramine with clinical management, and placebo with clinical management for the treatment of major depression. In this carefully controlled randomized clinical trial, IPT was superior to placebo for the more severely depressed and functionally impaired patients. Sotsky (Sotsky *et al.* 1991) examined patient predictors in NIMH TDCRP and found that in the IPT group patients with better initial social adjustment had superior outcomes compared to patients with lower social dysfunction. Klein and Ross (1993) re-analysed the NIMH TDCRP data and found that IPT was superior to placebo on the Hamilton Depression Rating Scale (HDRS) (Hamilton 1960) and the Global Assessment Scale (Endicott *et al.* 1976). They also found that IPT was superior to CBT on the Beck Depression Inventory (Beck *et al.* 1961) for both the end point and completer samples. IPT did particularly well in comparison to CBT with moderate to severely depressed patients; this is an important finding because it is among the first to indicate that psychotherapy alone can be effective with severely depressed patients.

IPT was first used in a clinical study conducted by Weissman *et al.* (1979). They combined IPT with amitriptyline and found that IPT was more effective for the treatment of depression when compared to either treatment alone or a control condition. It is important to note in terms of study design that the amount of amitriptyline used was relatively low by today's standards. The patients treated with IPT (both alone and with amitriptyline) showed significant improvement in social functioning at 1-year post-treatment (Weissman *et al.* 1981). IPT has been used more recently for a number of different treatment populations (see Weissman *et al.* 2000). IPT has been used with both different diagnostic groups (for example, dysthymic patients and patients suffering from anxiety) and in different modalities (for example, group, telephone treatment, conjoint therapy). Most recently, IPT has been used in two neuroimaging studies. Martin and Martin (1999) followed 28 patients in a comparison of venlafaxine and IPT; they used single photon emission computed tomography (SPECT) imaging pre- and post-treatment. They found both IPT and venlafaxine patients showed changes in the dorsolateral prefrontal cortical area. However, the venlafaxine patients showed additional changes in the angular gyrus while IPT patients showed changes in the limbic central cingulate area. Brody *et al.* (in press) compared paroxetine with IPT and used pre- and post-treatment positron emission tomography (PET) scans to examine brain changes. They found that the paroxetine-treated patients showed a better outcome (as measured by the HDRS scores) compared to the IPT patients. Both the paroxetine patients and the IPT patients showed decrease in normalized prefrontal cortex and left anterior cingulate gyrus metabolism. Both these studies are important in that they demonstrate change in regional brain metabolism following psychotherapy (IPT) alone. While the studies must be viewed with caution given the small sample sizes, the differences in treatment outcomes are intriguing and indicate a need for further future research.

Interpersonal therapy: theoretical origins

The work of Klerman and Weissman has been influenced by Meyer, Sullivan, Bowlby, and Brown and Harris. Klerman and Weissman integrated aspects of the work of each of these theorists and researchers, the common thread being the impact of loss on mood. Adolf Meyer was one of the driving forces in the development of the American philosophical school of Pragmatism founded by William James (Klerman 1979). Meyer coined the term psychobiology, which has come to stand for an integrationist approach to the psychological, social, and biological mechanisms that interact to affect mood and behaviour. Meyer was among the first to emphasize the psychological and social aspects of mental illness. He adapted the work of Darwin to include a fluidity of direction between biology and environment. He and his followers were particularly interested in the factors in the social environment that affected the development of mental illness.

Harry Stack Sullivan was also interested in the impact of social factors on mental illness. He led a group of psychoanalysts in the Washington–Baltimore area in the 1930s and 1940s, at times including Frieda Fromm-Reichman, Erich Fromm, and Karen Horney. Sullivan came to view the domain of psychiatry as equivalent to the study of interpersonal relationships. He and his colleagues were among the first to include family members in the treatment of the mentally ill. For Sullivan, the treatment of the patient was based on understanding the patient's interpersonal world at different points in time. Sullivan's work is particularly important to the development of IPT in that it emphasized the ameliorative effects of companionship. Sullivan was among the first to point out the importance of confiding peer relationships. This work was later picked up and amplified by Brown and Harris (1978) in their seminal work on the social origins of depression in women. Brown and Harris note that women at high risk for the development of depression in adulthood due to the loss of a mother in childhood did not develop depression at rates higher than that of the general population if, and only if, they had a confiding relationship with an adult friend. To put it another way, Brown and Harris found that an intimate, confiding relationship was protective against depression following the loss of a key relationship. The lack of an intimate confiding relationship can be seen in this work as a vulnerability or risk factor for depression.

Bowlby's (1969) early work on attachment and loss articulated many of the theoretical constructs that were later realized in the research of Brown and Harris. He noted that frequent, prolonged separations from primary caregivers resulted in infants and children with attachment problems, who in turn were vulnerable to depression and mental illness as adults. The work of Brown and Harris and Bowlby influenced the development of IPT in that it delineated both the risk of depression in vulnerable individuals when their social attachments were impaired and the strength of such attachments in minimizing the risk of depression.

Integration of other perspectives in IPT

Interpersonal therapy appears to be an amalgam of both psychodynamic and behavioural approaches. In addition, it shares some common factors with cognitive therapy. Both CBT and IPT aim to provide symptomatic relief from depression, albeit through differing mechanisms. CBT attempts to alter target thoughts, whereas IPT attempts to improve interpersonal communication skills, thereby improving current interpersonal problems. Psychodynamic psychotherapy is aimed at promoting personality change; this is decidedly not the aim of IPT, although Weissman *et al.* (1979) have shown that individuals with personality disorders and depression are as successfully treated with IPT as those depressed individuals without personality disorders; however, patients with dual diagnoses relapse more quickly. Psychodynamic therapy and psychoanalysis ideally occur within the context of a stable environment for the patient. IPT is similar in that a strong social support network is associated with better outcomes in IPT compared to patients with impoverished or unstable networks.

Psychodynamic and interpersonal approaches share an emphasis on experiencing affect in the sessions. Identifying and tolerating difficult feelings is key to both approaches, and the therapist clearly plays a role in this. In psychodynamic work the therapist tends to interpret and reflect while in IPT the emphasis is more on prescription and exploration. The IPT therapist actively works with the patient to reduce interpersonal difficulties associated with family and friends or work; this is done by improving interpersonal communication. Apart from conjoint IPT for marital couples, family and friends are not generally included in IPT treatment, except for the occasional early session where the therapist educates the key social supports of the patient with regard to depression. IPT is more similar to psychodynamic therapy than cognitive therapy in this approach, as in cognitive therapy the spouse frequently has a role as an objective reporter. In psychodynamic work full individual confidentiality is generally the norm.

IPT shares with CBT an emphasis on adhering to a specific treatment regimen. The IPT therapist needs to be comfortable and able to adhere to very specific treatment strategies. There are tasks in IPT sessions that need to be clearly accomplished. Research carried out by Frank *et al.* (1991) showed that patients whose therapists adhered most closely to the model had the best outcomes in treatment. Clearly, it is easier to maintain a focus and use strategies with some patients compared to others. Frank and her colleagues found this to be the case in their research; the IPT therapists who were best able to adhere to the treatment also had difficulty maintaining adherence with some patients. Therapists who have a strong preference for an eclectic approach may find IPT a difficult treatment to provide. Thus IPT is a good illustration of a therapy that is integrative in theory, but highly 'pure' and specific in practice.

The role of the therapist in IPT is that of an advocate. The IPT therapist plays an active role in coaching the patient, while respecting the patient's ability to determine the best choice of actions. IPT resembles CBT in both the relatively high-activity level of the therapist and the coaching stance. The IPT therapist needs to be comfortable in the role of 'expert' about depression. Part of the therapist's job is to educate the patient about depression and help enable the patient to educate key members of their social network about depression. The IPT therapist is not neutral in the psychodynamic sense, rather, she or he is actively optimistic and models optimism for the patient. The IPT therapist shares with the psychodynamic clinician an interest in understanding emotional receptivity and feeling states. The IPT therapist differs from the psychodynamic therapist in that material from the patient's past is rarely discussed. IPT is a very 'here and now' treatment and the interpretation of dreams or discussion of events from the distant past are not within the model. While an IPT therapist coming from a psychodynamic background may use the dynamics of the patient's early experience in order to formulate the case, these dynamics are rarely discussed in the treatment itself.

There is sometimes a tendency for therapists with a CBT background coming to IPT to shift to rational propositions and sometimes move the patient too quickly away from feeling states. The cognitive therapist training in IPT needs to include feeling states and give them greater emphasis in comparison to cognitions.

Part of the role of the IPT therapist is to educate the patient about depression as a medical illness. This may be quite different from either a cognitive or a psychodynamic approach, where intrapsychic factors may be given more precedence. In practice, it can be difficult for therapists to feel comfortable suggesting that the patient withdraw from some activities, as would be the case with any other serious illness. Therapists may also have personal and philosophical difficulties in conceptualizing depression as an illness, particularly when it requires a re-examination of their own values regarding work and illness.

Finally, in terms of role, the IPT therapist needs to be satisfied with discreet gains. The goals of IPT are to reduce depressive functioning and increase social support. These goals tend to be identified more with brief treatment and therapists working in long-term psychodynamic psychotherapy or long-term CBT may find it difficult to reduce their expectations with regard to treatment outcome. This tends to be an issue for anyone shifting from a long-term to a short-term treatment.

The IPT treatment model

Tasks of the early sessions

There are a number of tasks to be completed in the first four sessions of IPT. These include a complete review of depressive symptoms, taking an inventory of interpersonal relationships, the provision of the sick role, and assessing the need for medication. Educating the patient about depression is a critical responsibility in the early sessions; this includes examining the patient's present level of understanding about depression and its treatments and correcting any misinformation he or she may have gathered in the past.

The review of depressive symptoms

The review of depressive symptoms serves a number of purposes. It enables the patient to become familiar with all of his or her symptoms of depression and to understand and distinguish normal sadness from a full depressive episode. It also has explanatory value for the patient in understanding symptoms that the patient may have perceived as due to other illnesses or medication side effects. It is also important for both patient and therapist to have clear markers of depression because in IPT the weekly review of depressive symptoms helps both parties to assess the efficacy of the treatment on an on-going basis. Not infrequently, a depressed patient may not identify changes in depressive symptomatology until they are recounted in the treatment session because memory difficulties and negative thoughts can make it difficult for the patient to monitor change.

The interpersonal inventory

This is one of the aspects of IPT that sets it apart from other treatments. Trainees recount experiences of working with patients they thought they knew well and being astonished at how little of their social support network they were able to recount. The goal of gathering the inventory is to assess potential strengths and weaknesses in the network, and the therapist generally spends a session or two doing this. The therapist looks for departures from the network, difficult or challenging relationships, as well as strong supports. Distant supports are important to assess; often ties from the past can be re-strengthened and are important in helping the patient to become well. The IPT therapist also needs to be aware of omissions in the network of key members that one would expect to be there, for example a parent or a child. It may be that such relationships are avoided because they are difficult and it is especially important for the IPT therapist to carefully assess these relationships. It is also helpful to understand how the patient has handled the loss of relationships in the past, whether these have been through relocation, dispute, or death of a loved one.

Examining the quality of the patient's relationships is crucial in developing an understanding of the patient and choosing a focal area for the treatment. It is important to know who in the network will provide emotional support to the patient as well as instrumental aid, whether or not the network is densely connected or more distant, and whether or not the network as a whole is characterized positively or negatively by the patient. Very occasionally the patient's network is seen primarily as negative (for example, with drug addictions); in such cases the work of the treatment may require building a new support network if the patient makes changes in drug use behaviours.

The sick role

In Western culture, there are very few times when one is allowed to 'opt out' of responsibilities. The death of a close family member or a serious illness are among the few acceptable reasons for the temporary reduction of responsibilities. Giving the patient the sick role accomplishes the task of allowing the patient to temporarily withdraw from some onerous activities and to re-engage in previously pleasurable activities. Both these areas of functioning can be tremendously stressful for the patient and changing behaviours within each realm is often challenging. Many depressed patients fear being a burden to others and are very reluctant to ask others for help. In addition, because of depressive cognitions, they may have difficulty recalling activities that they previously found pleasurable and have great difficulty initiating such behaviours. The role of the therapist is to encourage the patient to try to make changes and to troubleshoot each week with the patient about difficulties that arise from these attempts.

Choosing a focus

In IPT, there are four choices of foci. The task of the therapist is to work with the patient to choose an appropriate focus within the first four sessions of treatment. The foci include grief, interpersonal disputes, role transitions, and interpersonal deficits. While a secondary focus may be chosen, it is most often the case that one area is worked on throughout the treatment. There are a number of cues provided by the patient as to the most appropriate focal area. A careful time line helps to establish the beginning of a depressive episode. Often the onset of the depression can be linked to a specific focus. It is important to confirm whether or not there have been any deaths, transitions, or serious disputes occurring at the same time the symptoms began. It is also helpful to ask about the interpersonal events that occur during the week between treatment sessions. Evidence of an unresolved grief reaction or a dispute will often present itself between sessions. In the case of interpersonal deficits, the isolation will become apparent when the therapist questions with whom the patient has spent time in the past week. Evidence of transitions may also present themselves, for example, the patient may discuss aspects of a new job or a recent move when questioned about the events of the past week.

The IPT therapist may choose to discuss all four foci with the patient and decide on a focus together or she or he may simply chose a primary focus. Most often the therapist will narrow the choice of focus down to two or perhaps three areas and discuss these with the patient in order to choose the most appropriate area. If there is a dispute between patient and therapist regarding the area of focus, the patient's choice takes precedence. Given the limited time for treatment, it is counterproductive to spend time arguing about a focal area. It is quite rare for the wrong area of focus to be chosen. Difficulties with choosing a focus often have more to do with difficulties in the therapeutic alliance than the choice of focus per se.

The middle phase of treatment

The middle phase of treatment generally comprises sessions 4 to 9 or 10. In these sessions, specific strategies and techniques related to the four focal areas are used by the IPT therapist to help the patient work through difficulties within the chosen focal area. In terms of technique, IPT shares with CBT the clarification of cognitive and affective markers; IPT, however, places its main emphasis on the markers that precede highly charged interpersonal events. IPT also uses the active problem-solving techniques found in CBT, although these techniques are again used specifically in relation to interpersonal events in IPT. In the middle sessions the therapist continues to actively provide support and assurance to the patient. In addition, role-play techniques may be used from time to time.

The four foci of IPT

Grief Grief is an area of focus in IPT only when there has been an actual death. Events such as job loss or divorce are considered as transitions in the IPT model and appropriate mourning can be carried out in those areas. The goal of IPT work with grief is to reactivate a stalled mourning process and help the patient to reconnect to relationships in the present. The process of the reactivation of grief is a difficult one for the patient. He or she must recount the details of the death, as well as the funeral, and the periods before and after the death. The sole exception to this is when there has been a very traumatic death that has been observed by the patient, for example, a decapitation or observing a number of deaths during war. In such cases, research indicates that reliving the actual death may actually retraumatize the patient and serves no useful purpose. It is still important, however, for the patient to reconstruct the relationship with the deceased in the treatment. When a patient is able to recall both the positive and negative aspects of the relationship, grieving tends to proceed normally.

Often when the grieving process has been disrupted it is due to an unsuccessfully resolved conflict that has resulted in an idealization of the deceased. For example, an elderly man treated in clinic described his wife as 'a saint'. As the treatment progressed it came to light that he had been contemplating a divorce after a long and difficult marriage when his wife contracted a terminal illness. He felt guilty about his wish to leave the marriage and following her death he gradually idealized their relationship. For him, an important part of the treatment was to reconnect with other family members and to discuss in a more balanced way the positive and negative characteristics of his wife. This is in keeping with the second goal of IPT grief work, that is, re-establishing, initiating, and strengthening relationships with others. Frequently in IPT the treatment involves renewing relationships with family and friends that have deteriorated as the depression has progressed. The patient initially felt too uncomfortable seeing other people because he did not want to speak badly of his wife. However, after discussing the marital relationship in therapy he was able to have a more balanced view of it.

Transitions Transitions are generally related to life events. These events can be positive, for example, a job promotion or the birth of a longed-for child, or negative, for example, a catastrophic illness or a job loss. The goals in working with transitions are to mourn the old role and to gain access to interpersonal relationships that help the patient to develop expertise and a sense of mastery in the new role. Transitions are difficult for most people. For the depressed patient they may tip the balance into a depressive episode. When confronted with new role demands, most people experience a loss of self-esteem because they lack the skills and resources needed for the new role. With the passage of time skills develop, but for the depressed patient isolation and depression may set in before a new behavioural repertoire is in place.

In transition work it is generally most helpful to examine the positive aspects of the old role first and to help the patient to immerse him- or herself in mourning for the lost role. Once this has been accomplished, the patient is often freely able to offer examples of negative aspects of the old role. For example, a senior financial officer lost his job and subsequently presented with a major depression. He missed his glamorous high-powered life but after appropriate mourning took place he was able to discuss the intense emotional costs of this high-pressure job. He regretted not having spent enough time with his children when they were growing up and vowed to do better as a grandparent.

The second aspect of role transition is to master the new role. This generally requires learning from others who have successfully done so. In a healthy transition, the individual is able to access help from a number of people who function well in the new role. For the depressed patient, the symptoms of the depression coupled with low self-esteem make it very difficult for the patient to approach others who have the necessary expertise.

There are two areas of role transitions that are particularly difficult to work with: those due to catastrophic illness, and, paradoxically, seemingly positive transitions. In the former, finding positive aspects of life is the key to improvement. A dying AIDS patient spoke of the beauty of sitting on his balcony on a sunny summer day. In fact, he was only able to tolerate sitting there for a few minutes but felt those few minutes to be both precious and positive. Many patients with serious illnesses are initially angry in treatment and take the view that anyone would be depressed with catastrophic illness. It is important to help the patient to understand that depression is a separate illness and that treating it effectively will improve quality of life. It is also worth pointing out to the patient that many patients with medical illness do not become depressed.

With positive transitions, such as a job promotion, the patient may feel guilty and ashamed about not enjoying the new role. They may also feel quite isolated because they are not comfortable discussing their apprehension in the new role with either their former colleagues, whom they may now supervise, or their new colleagues, with whom they may be in active competition. Often as the depression recedes, the patient is able to connect with new colleagues and is helped to gain a sense of mastery in the new role as a result. As such relationships develop there is often an opportunity to discuss concerns about functioning in the new role.

Disputes Role disputes may be experiences in a number of relations or one key relationship. Disputes arise when there are differences in values, goals, and role expectation. Often, there are non-reciprocal role expectations in disputed relationships. For example, in a workplace one team member may expect certain compensations; these expectations may not be shared by the manager. Lack of communication may fuel disagreement, as do differences in values and goals.

One of the tasks in working with role disputes in IPT is to assess the state of the dispute. In the renegotiation phase the dispute is very active and patients frequently present for treatment because the relationship is on the edge of dissolution. In the impasse phase there is no active dispute readily apparent, but there is a lack of intimacy and connection in the relationship. Often the partners in such a dispute have seemingly 'agreed to disagree', but on closer examination there has been no resolution to the dispute. It may be that several critical areas in the relationship cannot be discussed because attempts at discussion in the past have resulted in unresolved conflict. When the relationship is at the impasse phase, the task of the IPT therapist is to encourage renegotiation. The patient may experience the relationship as worsening before it improves because renegotiation is frequently difficult and affect-laden. When the differences cannot be negotiated, the third phase, dissolution, is reached. The dissolution phase is characterized by mourning for the lost relationship and beginning the search for new relationships that will substitute for what has been lost.

An exception to dissolution in IPT work is very long-term relationships. In relationships that have lasted several decades, it may be more realistic for elderly patients to learn to accommodate to the relationship rather than dissolve it. In such cases, the IPT therapist works with the patient to establish ways of minimizing conflict in the key relationship and strengthening ties with others who can support the patient.

In the renegotiation phase, one of the tasks of the treatment is to examine communication style. In disputes there is often fractured or unsuccessful communication. The IPT therapist asks the patient to recount in detail the most recent argument in the disputed relationship. This may take on a 'script-like' quality where actual dialogue from the argument is recounted in the session. The patient frequently has difficulty recollecting arguments initially, but this usually improves over the course of treatment. When discussions are recalled in such detail the IPT therapist can listen for examples of miscommunication. Communication difficulties can be gross, for example, a person walking out of an argument, or subtle, where silence is used to squelch communication. Other examples of miscommunication include 'mind reading', where one partner expects the other partner to intuit what is being thought or felt, and assuming communication has occurred simply because it has been attempted. Difficulties in communication frequently worsen disputes and helping the patient to communicate more effectively frequently improves the relationship.

Deficits Interpersonal deficits are characterized by long-term loneliness and isolation. They are not the result of normal transition, such as moving to a new city where some initial isolation and loneliness is to be expected. Deficits are the most difficult area to work with in IPT and research indicates that treatment is least likely to be successful with such patients (Weissman *et al.* 2000). In working with deficits, the IPT therapist may need to make use of both past relationships and the therapeutic relationship because of a paucity in present-day relationships. While IPT is generally focused on present-day relationships, with the deficit patient there may be too few such relationships to work with effectively. The therapist may need to role play in order to help the patient develop effectiveness in communication.

The patient with deficits frequently lacks both breadth and depth in interpersonal relationships. The goals of IPT treatment with deficit patients are very straightforward: they are to increase the quality and quantity of interpersonal relationships. It is important to have modest goals in working with deficit patients, and it may be some time before changes in the interpersonal network are observed. She or he may also need to help the patient examine what contributed to the dissolution of past relationships.

Final sessions

The final sessions of IPT (typically sessions 12 through 16) are taken up with reviewing coping strategies and strengthening the patient's interpersonal ties. The patient and therapist continue to work on interpersonal interactions that occur from week to week, as well as reviewing depressive symptoms weekly. The IPT patient should be so familiar with his or her own depressive symptoms that they can be easily recognized should they begin to reappear. Considering that depression is a chronic illness for the majority of those suffering from it, it is essential that the patient be able to identify early symptoms of depression and seek appropriate help. The patient and therapist should work together to evolve a plan for dealing with future episodes of depression. A key part of this plan is increasing social interaction at the first sign of mood changes.

For the patient who has suffered multiple episodes of depression, maintenance sessions should be considered. Frank *et al.* (1991) found that monthly maintenance sessions of IPT could significantly lengthen the period of time between episodes. Maintenance treatments most frequently takes the form of monthly sessions with work continuing in the focal area. Even when the therapist and patient have agreed to maintenance treatment, it is important to mark the end of the intensive weekly phase of treatment and to focus on termination issues.

Treatment failure

When IPT has failed to bring about improvement, it is important for the IPT therapist to offer treatment alternatives. Since both therapist and patient will be aware of a lack of improvement because of the weekly review of symptoms, treatment referral should be openly discussed from the mid-phase of treatment through to termination. The patient will need to express his or her disappointment and frustration about the lack of improvement and it is important for the IPT therapist to clarify that the treatment failed the patient rather than vice versa. It may well be the case that the patient has exhausted all other effective treatments before seeking IPT. When this is the case, the IPT therapist needs to help the patient face his or her despair but to also point out that depression is a chronic intermittent illness and that naturally occurring periods of wellness can be expected with the passage of time for most people (a strategy integrated from solution-focused therapy, see Chapter 4). It is helpful for the IPT therapist to be well informed about current research trials into novel treatments for depression and to offer to refer the patient where appropriate. Given the difficulties in most health-care systems, with waiting time until treatment begins, the IPT therapist should be setting referrals in motion during the mid-phase of treatment. In the event that the patient improves late in treatment, such referrals can be cancelled.

We end this chapter with a case illustration which exemplifies the technical eclecticism that typifies the IPT approach to integration.

Case example

In the brief outline of the treatment of a depressed patient, aspects that are typical of IPT are highlighted in bold. However, IPT does not consist simply of applying prescribed techniques. The skill, as in any therapy, is in weaving all the different aspects together in a way that is understandable and meaningful to the patient.

Patient

Miranda is an 86-year-old emeritus professor of classics, a proud and somewhat austere woman. She has been widowed for 30 years and has no children. She lives alone in a small university town in southern England and continues to work 3 days a week in her office at the university. She has been depressed for 6 months with symptoms that include early morning wakening, weight loss, joint aches and pains, headaches, poor memory and concentration, and anhedonia. She reluctantly agreed to treatment following the prodding of an old family friend, and after her family doctor assured her that her memory difficulties were not due to dementia and might be improved by psychotherapy.

The treatment

Miranda and her IPT therapist agreed to work together for 16 consecutive weekly 1-hour sessions. Miranda was referred through her family doctor, who had advocated antidepressant medication as well, which Miranda had declined. The therapist **discussed medication early in the treatment** to ensure that Miranda did not have any inaccurate ideas about it and to inform her that the question of medication would be revisited in the event that the IPT failed to improve her symptoms.

The early sessions

Miranda was initially very sceptical about the treatment and treated the therapist somewhat condescendingly, taking a rather paternalistic attitude.

The therapist handled this initial presentation sensitively and **educated Miranda about her depressive symptoms.** Although the therapist felt somewhat attacked and belittled, she did not address these feelings directly but **framed them as part of the depression:**

Therapist: Well I expect you do feel like dismissing the treatment, that's part of depression. One feels half dead, helpless, hopeless – those are all symptoms. I wouldn't expect that you would think this treatment would be effective. That would require you having hope and that simply isn't on when one is depressed.

The therapist acknowledged that the IPT treatment might not be fully effective for Miranda, but if this was the case they would look together at what else to try. She spent the remainder of the first session educating Miranda about the treatment and encouraging her to take on **the sick role.**

Giving the sick role

Miranda, a keen gardener, had been very proud of her garden but had been overwhelmed by the prospect of weeding for several weeks. She was reluctant to let to ask for any help but, in discussion with the therapist, finally agreed that she would try to ask a family friend (who knew of her depression) to help her weed the garden. Sara was the only person she would allow to see the garden in its present state. The therapist encouraged Miranda to rest from work for a few weeks, as is standard practice in IPT. Miranda simply could not do this at first with regard to the garden but was able to relinquish some of her tasks (such as volunteer tutorials) during the second and third week of treatment. As is often the case with the sick role, this change encouraged her to **connect with other people** since they need to be approached to help with essential daily tasks.

She asked a young colleague, John, to take over her tutorials and to her surprise was able to acknowledge that she had begun treatment for depression. John was relieved to hear this since he had been worried that she was seriously physically ill but had been reluctant to pry. John and his wife invited Miranda around for tea and she was able to go and enjoy their company. John also confirmed her feeling that she had a particularly difficult tutorial group this year. This was very reassuring for Miranda. She had thought they were a difficult lot but had more often felt the fault was her own, that she was 'losing her touch' as a teacher. She discussed this with her therapist who pointed out the **self-blame was a common symptom of depression.**

The interpersonal inventory

Miranda had an extensive network of colleagues and former students but had lost touch with many of them as she became depressed. Two of her closest friends and colleagues had died of old age in the past year and another had moved away. She was close to her neighbours but had felt too drained and demoralized to see much of them in the past few months. She worried about being a burden to others and feared imposing her low mood on them. She stopped attending university functions and avoided her colleagues as the depression worsened.

Miranda had an especially rich network of distant ties. Many of her former students had become colleagues and had moved across Great Britain and the United States as their careers had developed. Prior to her depression Miranda had made a couple of trips a year to visit former students and had often attended a conference or two that kept her in contact with old friends.

In terms of family, Miranda had a number of nieces and nephews located in small towns around the university; she had been a frequent visitor in the past to these families. She also had a large network of cousins spread throughout England and had enjoyed reciprocal visits with these families as well as her husband's family. As a childless widow, Miranda had made an excellent series of connections and enjoyed a rich social world prior to her depression.

The goal of treatment was **to re-establish and re-strengthen these ties**, as well as reducing her depressive symptoms.

Choosing the focus

While the therapist initially considered choosing **grief** as a focus, given the timing of Miranda's most recent losses, on further questioning she decided not to because Miranda appeared to have coped well and appropriately with these losses. As she herself put it:

Miranda: I felt very sad, especially losing Paul, but one goes on. I still think of him, but the pain isn't as long or as deep now. I'll find myself reading a magazine and seeing a photo of a place we'd been to, and I have a moment where the sadness washes over me, then it passes.

The therapist confirmed that Miranda didn't idealize any of the people she had lost, as is often the case with pathological grief. She could speak of both their strengths and their foibles and didn't have a sense that no one in the present network could adequately compensate for the loss of these relationships.

Miranda and her therapist decided to work on the area of **transitions**. Miranda's physical health was becoming frailer and she had had a myocardial infarct 6 months prior to becoming depressed. She found the post-myocardial infarct period very difficult; she had always seen herself as a strong, independent person and while her energy had slowed somewhat with age she prided herself on her strength and stamina. After the MI, she would frequently push herself too hard and then have a debilitating bout of angina. She found this very difficult and became angry and frustrated with her condition. She had begun making the rounds of specialists, hoping to hear that there was something that could be done to give her back her old energy. She was furious each time moderating her activity level was suggested.

The middle sessions

Kaitlin, the wife of Miranda's colleague John, was a warm, young Australian woman at home with a young baby, who began making a point of coming around a couple of mornings a week on her daily walk with the baby to visit Miranda. Kaitlin had taken a year off from reading law and welcomed the chance to discuss intellectual material with Miranda. Miranda initially found it difficult to manage these visits but after a couple of weeks began to look forward to long walks with Kaitlin and the baby, Freddie. Freddie was an especially jolly baby and Miranda enjoyed spending time with him, and eventually offered to baby-sit once a week. Kaitlin agreed, but only on the condition that Miranda come for Sunday lunch each week. Kaitlin also insisted on giving Miranda a 'care package' of leftovers each week and this was especially helpful because Miranda's appetite had not returned and she found it difficult to muster energy for cooking. The Sunday lunches reconnected Miranda to some old colleagues as well as introducing her to a group of young academics and their families. All this had been discussed in therapy with the therapist **emphasizing the importance of social interaction as a way of improving and regulating mood.**

In the therapy sessions, Miranda had difficulty talking about the limitations her heart condition precipitated. The therapist helped her by asking her first to **talk about the old role**, what it had been like to be a very healthy 86-year-old, with no real physical impediments. Miranda was able to grieve the loss of this old role as she tearfully recollected it over several sessions:

Miranda: I could spend days in the garden before my heart failed. I would be up killing slugs before dawn and deadheading last thing at night. I'd rest, but it would be to have a cup of tea in the garden. Now, I'm useless (crying). I can't bend without being winded, I'll weed a half a plot then need to lie down, I hate it.

Therapist: You must miss those times very much.

Miranda: I do. I really do. (Miranda cries for several minutes.) And it's the same with my work, I can't stay at it as long, I have trouble concentrating, even being motivated. I've never in my life had trouble preparing a lecture, now I face it with dread.

The therapist helped Miranda to relive her days as a productive, busy scholar. She had enjoyed the work as well as the day-to-day connections with her colleagues, something she had taken for granted before her myocardial infarct. Miranda had normal fears and frustrations about ageing but had made a good accommodation to the process until she became depressed. After several weeks of talking about the period of wellness prior to her depression, Miranda was able to see some **positive aspects of the new role**. She especially enjoyed her times with Kaitlin, John, and Freddie and thought that she might not have had time for them in her old role. She hired a part-time gardener and gardened with a friend, and found it a pleasant change. As her depression improved she exercised more and found most of her aches and pains disappearing. She visited family and friends more, and partly as a result decided to reduce her university hours from 3 days to 2 days a week. She seemed relieved to be lightening her university load and compensated well for the potential lost companionship by arranging a weekly lunch with colleagues.

The final sessions

Miranda had done well in IPT treatment and by the ninth session most of her symptoms were gone. She continued to have early morning wakening and eventually saw her family doctor, who prescribed a sleeping tablet for a few weeks. This was very helpful in giving Miranda a feeling of being well rested. She tapered off the medication over a few weeks and her sleep remained good.

She was functioning well and had comes to terms with the physical limitations imposed by her heart condition. The therapist felt pleased that Miranda was neither a 'cardiac invalid' nor was she risking her health by ignoring chest pain or fatigue and said so towards the end of treatment. Miranda felt that she had also found a more realistic balance in her work and social life. She allowed herself to do less academically and to use some of that energy to **strengthen her social ties which had been strongly emphasized throughout treatment**. The friendship with John and Kaitlin was a warm reciprocal one and also served to introduce her to a group of younger people, an essential set of relationships for successful ageing.

In the final session the therapist discussed with Miranda the progress she had made and **reviewed the symptoms** that had led to the initial presentation. They agreed that Miranda would call the clinic if any of the symptoms were to reappear for more than a few days. The therapist spoke of the pleasure she had had in treating Miranda and told her that she hoped to have a similar life (minus the depression) when she was in her eighties. Miranda was very touched by this and presented the therapist with a bouquet of flowers from her garden.

Chapter 9

Dialectical behaviour therapy

Heidi L. Heard

Introduction

In psychotherapy integration, different theories and techniques are combined and synthesized in an attempt to develop a maximally efficacious therapy. In this way, the goal and process of such psychotherapy integration resembles the goal and process of psychotherapy itself. In one way or another, most psychotherapies foster synthesis, whether by targeting the incorporation of new skills into the client's behavioural repertoire or by attempting to help the client integrate disparate aspects of the self, with the ultimate goal of enhancing the client's enjoyment of and effectiveness in life. In dialectical behaviour therapy (DBT) (Linehan 1993a, b), the emphasis on observing and creating syntheses within the theory, process, and content of the therapy is an integral part of helping clients achieve their ultimate goals. DBT is integrative in the 'dialectical/developmental' sense of the word (Stricker and Gold 1993) referenced in Mahoney (1993), meaning that it emphasizes the 'open-ended dialogical process in which differences are examined and novel integrations are welcomed' (p. 7). Thus, while at any given moment DBT constitutes a single, unified psychotherapy, it is also in a continuous process of change in which new developments are accepted rather than avoided, rather like a client participating in therapy.

   This chapter elaborates the various integrative aspects of DBT. First, it will provide a context for discussion by briefly describing the therapy. Next, the chapter will define and discuss 'dialectics', and demonstrate some of the ways in which the dialectical philosophy performs various synthesizing roles throughout the therapy. Then follows a discussion of the relevance of integration to the structure and strategies of DBT. It will trace the origins in behaviour therapy and Zen practice of the many procedures employed in DBT, though it will not attempt to construct a genealogy of every piece of literature or procedure that the therapy has integrated, nor to catalogue every similarity between the therapy and other treatments. Finally, the chapter will summarize the results of several outcome trials designed to examine the efficacy of DBT.

Overview of DBT

Theory

Linehan (1993a, b) originally developed DBT as an outpatient cognitive–behavioural intervention for individuals meeting criteria for borderline personality disorder (BPD) and engaging in parasuicidal behaviour. To explain the aetiology and maintenance of problematic behaviours associated with BPD, she combined capability deficit and motivational models of behavioural dysfunction to suggest that: (1) individuals who meet criteria for BPD lack important skills, including emotional regulation, interpersonal effectiveness, impulse control, and problem-solving skills, and (2) personal and environmental factors both inhibit skilful behaviour and reinforce problematic behaviour. Linehan further proposed a transactional theory of the aetiology and maintenance of BPD that combines biological, developmental, and social research.

To change the problematic behaviours, Linehan applied the principles of traditional cognitive–behaviour therapy that had lead to the development of efficacious treatments for so many other disorders. Clinical experience, however, suggested that these principles alone would prove insufficient when treating BPD clients, and that the greatest problem was cognitive–behaviour therapy's continuous focus on change. To balance the emphasis on change, Linehan began to integrate the principles of Zen practice, which describes *acceptance* at its most radical level. The tensions between the principles of cognitive–behaviour therapy and those of Zen practice required a framework that could house opposing views. The dialectical philosophy, which highlights the process of synthesizing oppositions, provides such a framework. Through the continual resolution of tensions between (1) theory and research versus clinical experience, and (2) western psychology versus eastern practice, DBT thus evolved in a manner similar to the theoretical integration model described by psychotherapy integration researchers (Arkowitz 1989, 1992; Norcross 1992).

Structure

The modalities of delivering DBT were based on the capability deficit/motivational model. In standard DBT clients receive concurrent weekly group skills training, which primarily targets capability deficits, and individual psychotherapy, which primarily targets motivational issues. Individual therapists also offer clients coaching sessions, usually via the telephone, on an as-needed basis between sessions. Finally, the therapists meet together regularly for consultation.

Each modality of treatment has a behavioural target hierarchy that guides the agenda of a session. Behaviours in the target hierarchy typically include suicidal behaviour, therapy interfering behaviour (here the therapist is as likely a suspect as the client), behaviours relevant to other diagnoses (e.g., abusing alcohol, purging or dissociating), or behaviours that are unsafe or destabilizing (e.g., shoplifting, behaviours leading to unemployment or to homelessness). Within individual therapy sessions, the therapy often weaves between targeting behaviour that occurred outside of therapy since the last session (e.g., self-harm, purging, shoplifting) and behaviour occurring within the current session (e.g., client refusing to collaborate, client dissociating, therapist lecturing).

Strategies

DBT has four basic sets of therapy strategies. The core strategies (problem solving and validation) create most of the content of the therapy sessions, while the stylistic strategies (irreverence and reciprocity) refer to the manner in which the content is presented. The case management strategies (consultation-to-the-patient and environmental intervention) describe how the therapist interacts with other professionals in relation to the client. Finally, the dialectical strategies refer to how the therapist interweaves the use of the other strategies and employs specific techniques that inherently reflect characteristics of a dialectical philosophy. While DBT primarily employs methods adapted from standard cognitive–behavioural therapies and Zen practice, it also incorporates techniques from other treatment orientations, such as crisis intervention, and areas of research, such as social psychology. DBT modifies this psychotherapy integration approach of technical eclecticism (Arkowitz 1989; Norcross 1992), however, by requiring that all fit within a dialectical framework that joins behaviourism and Zen. Relying on such an interwoven framework for support and guidance may prove particularly important when treating complex disorders such as BPD.

Dialectical assumptions in DBT

As the underlying philosophy of DBT, dialectics describes the process by which the development of the therapy and progress within the therapy occurs and by which conflicts that impede development or progress are resolved. The *American heritage dictionary* defines dialectics, in part, as 'The Hegelian process of change whereby an ideational entity (thesis) is transformed into its opposite (antithesis) and preserved and fulfilled by it, the combination of the two being resolved in a higher form of truth (synthesis).' To apply the dialectical philosophy to DBT, Linehan used Basseches' (1984) work on the development of dialectical thinking in adults and the work of evolutionary biologists (Levins and Lewontin 1985). DBT emphasizes three dialectical assumptions regarding the nature of reality, that it is (1) oppositional or heterogeneous; (2) interrelated or systemic; and (3) continuously changing.

Opposition

Dialectics emphasizes the way that reality is comprised of opposing forces in tension: the thesis and the antithesis. Development occurs as these oppositions proceed toward synthesis and as a new set of opposing forces emerges from the synthesis. The philosophy suggests a heterogeneous world in which reality is neither black nor white nor grey.

In therapy, tensions can arise within the client, within the therapist, between the client and therapist, or between the therapist and the larger treatment system. Examples of tensions that occur between the therapist and the client might include:

- the client's belief that taking drugs is the solution and the therapist's belief that taking drugs is the problem;
- the client's belief that only hospitalization will prevent suicide now and the therapist's belief that hospitalization may increase the probability of a future suicide;
- the client's wish for more contact with the therapist and the therapist's wish to observe his or her own limits.

To resolve conflicts the therapy searches for syntheses. The most effective syntheses are generally those that validate some aspect of both sides of the debate and move toward more effective behaviour. For example, in the first scenario above, if the client considers drugs as a solution because they decrease overwhelming anxiety, the therapy may achieve a synthesis by identifying anxiety reduction as a valid therapy goal. With this as the accepted goal, drug abuse would no longer be a valid solution, as it will tend, directly and indirectly, to increase, not decrease, anxiety in the long term. The therapy would instead focus on the client developing more skilful means to prevent and/or manage anxiety.

According to Linehan (1993a), the central opposition in psychotherapy occurs between change and acceptance. The fundamental relationship between change and acceptance forms the basic paradox and context of treatment. Therapeutic change can occur only in the context of acceptance of what is, and the act of acceptance itself is change. Moving rapidly, the DBT therapist balances acceptance strategies, which acknowledge the client as he or she is in the moment, and change strategies, which attempt to alter the client's behaviour. The therapy strives to help the client understand that responses may both prove valid and present a problem to solve. For example, the client's fear that he or she will not have sufficient skills to cope when the therapist leaves town for a holiday is a valid response from a client who has few coping skills and functions better when the therapist remains in town. On the other hand, the client must learn new skills to cope with the separation because the therapist will leave town. One solution may be to schedule an extra session prior to the holiday to focus exclusively on acquiring skills to cope with the therapist's absence.

The ability of the DBT therapist to balance change and acceptance is enhanced through combining aspects of Zen practice with cognitive–behaviour therapy. While cognitive–behavioural therapies provide the technology of change, Zen practice provides the technology of acceptance. Through experiential, rather than experimental, evidence, Zen students learn that each moment is complete by itself and that the world is perfect as it is. Zen also encourages students to use skilful means and to find a middle way. Of course, the categorization of behaviour therapy and Zen practice into change and acceptance is only relative as each practice contains elements of both acceptance and change. Behaviour therapy, like all other therapies, includes at least some elements of acceptance in that it acknowledges the client's behaviour in a non-judgemental way. Equally, as mentioned, change or impermanence is a crucial concept in Zen.

Interrelatedness

Dialectics also attends to the interrelatedness and unity of reality. The dialectical philosophy emphasizes relationships within and between systems and the complexity of causal connections. Levins and Lewontin (1985) describe this aspect of dialectics: 'Parts and wholes evolve in consequence of their relationship, and the relationship itself evolves. These are the properties of things that we call dialectical: that one thing cannot exist without the other, that one acquires its properties from its relations to the other' (p. 3). To analyse the factors that maintain problematic behaviour, the therapist considers two basic levels at which the client may experience dysfunction within the systems that influence their behaviour. The first level includes overlapping and mutually influential systems within the individual, such as biochemical systems, affective regulation systems, and information-processing systems. For example, if a client's serotonin uptake is dysregulated, this may lead to affective instability. Affective dysregulation often interferes with cognition. If the cognitive dysregulation includes a disruption of problem-solving abilities, this disruption could lead to a crisis that, in turn, further increases affective dysregulation. While multiple dysregulations may require multiple treatment interventions, a systemic approach also foresees how any single treatment interventions may influence multiple systems. For example, effective pharmacotherapy may regulate serotonin intake such that the chain described above never begins. Alternatively, enhancing emotion-regulation skills may help the client to cope effectively with biological changes such that information processing and problem solving are not impaired. (This is an example of 'Type A' integration, combining two effective treatments – drug therapy and psychotherapy; see Chapter 1).

The second level of systemic dysregulation involves the many interpersonal systems, such as family and culture, and other environmental systems that influence behaviour. To obtain an accurate understanding of the client's behaviour, the DBT therapist performs 'dialectical assessments' that attend to these influences. Many clients live in or interact with systems that reinforce problematic behaviour or punish skilful activity. For example, the hospitalization of a client in response to self-harming actions may actually reinforce those actions if the hospitalization provides desirable consequences such as more warmth and caring from staff than the client receives elsewhere, or fewer onerous responsibilities (e.g., coping with children, finding housing) that the client cannot otherwise avoid. Alternatively, a client's attempts to search for employment may be punished by a family in which everyone else lives on unemployment benefits.

Within the process of therapy, the DBT therapist attends to the system of the therapeutic relationship and to the tensions or therapy-interfering behaviours that can arise. Dialectics specifically directs the therapist's attention toward transactions that occur between the therapist and client and accepts that the therapist is part of and, therefore, influenced by the therapeutic context. The DBT therapist views therapy as a system in which the therapist and client reciprocally influence each other. For example, one can easily imagine that if a client became verbally aggressive every time the therapist tried to address a presenting problem, the therapist may become less likely to target that problem. In this scenario the client would have punished the therapist's therapeutic behaviour, and the therapist may have reinforced the client's aggressive behaviour. Altering transactional developments such as this can prove rather difficult when one is part of the system. DBT therapists, however, participate in a second system, the consultation team, designed to counteract such developments in the therapy by providing the motivation for the therapist to stay on track.

Both cognitive–behaviour therapy and Zen recognize the importance of interrelatedness. While all cognitive–behavioural therapists are trained to include the external environment in their search for controlling stimuli and to evaluate the effect of behavioural consequences as well as antecedents, the contextualist position described by Hayes (1982) most clearly resembles the dialectical emphasis on attention to interrelatedness and the whole. Zen (Aitken 1982) and other Eastern practices (Wilber 1979) discuss the experience of connectedness to the universe and letting go of personal boundaries.

Change

Dialectics highlights change as a fundamental aspect of reality. To some degree, all therapies foster change (few clients or health-care purchasers pay for things to remain exactly the same), but they differ in what type of change they promote and to what degree. In addition to promoting change in the client's behaviour, DBT allows the therapist extensive freedom to change as well. For example, as the therapeutic relationship develops, the therapist may become willing to expand various limits (e.g., willingness to accept phone calls, using examples of self as a coping model) as one would expand limits in any other relationship over time. This natural change is allowed to occur so that the therapeutic context matches, as closely as possible, the 'real world' (cf. Asen's systemic account of context in Chapter 4). Alternatively, such limits may also contract as a result of changes in the therapeutic relationship (e.g., client begins to phone the therapist too often or shares the therapist's self-disclosure with other clients) or the therapist's life (e.g., therapist has a baby, is studying for exams). The therapist does not try to protect the client from natural change but instead tries to help the client learn to cope with such change.

Both cognitive–behaviour therapy and Zen discuss change but in slightly different ways. Behaviour therapy promotes change by using interventions such as contingency management, exposure, problem solving, or skills training that require the client and/or the therapist actively try to alter emotions, thoughts, overt behaviour, or the environment. In contrast, in Zen practice neither the student nor the master intentionally try to change but instead mindfully observe experiences as they occur. According to Zen everything is impermanent and comes and goes like waves in the ocean. Behaviour therapy and Zen practice thus offer two approaches to change in therapy. For example, while behavioural procedures can reduce suicidality by teaching the client how to actively reduce suicidal urges, Zen practice can impact on suicidal behaviour by teaching the client how to allow and observe the urges without acting on them. These behavioural and Zen approaches to parasuicide reciprocally enhance each other. On the one hand, an important step in reducing self-harming urges is to increase awareness of those variables that control the urges. On the other hand, if one observes the urges without reinforcing them through action, the urges will naturally decrease over time.

Structure

Tasks and modalities

Linehan has identified five primary treatment tasks based on her capability deficit/motivational model of the development of the disorder. These tasks consist of

♦ enhancing client capabilities;
♦ improving client motivation;
♦ generalizing client capabilities;
♦ structuring the environment;
♦ treating therapists.

The therapy's dialectical model would suggest that while tensions may arise amongst the various tasks, the successful completion of any task depends upon how well it is integrated with the others.

To address the assumed capability deficit, the treatment first requires a modality of therapy that enhances the client's capabilities. Various modalities, ranging from self-help books to pharmacotherapy (which enhances the client's physiological capabilities), may address this task. Standard DBT employs psycho-educational skills training (Linehan 1993b) as the primary modality of enhancing capabilities. The DBT skills trainer teaches four modules or sets of skills. These can be divided into those that promote change, consisting of the emotion regulation and the interpersonal effectiveness modules, and those that promote acceptance, consisting of the mindfulness and the distress tolerance modules. Linehan (1993b) derived the change skills primarily from traditional cognitive–behavioural techniques (e.g., Linehan and Egan 1983), and the acceptance skills from Zen practice (e.g., Aitken 1982) and Western philosophy (May 1982). In skills training, the client first learns a wide variety of skills and then works to integrate these skills into a repertoire. The client's job resembles that of a technically eclectic psychotherapist who may select from a variety of techniques to solve a therapeutic problem. For both, the key question is: 'What is effective in this situation?'

From an integrative perspective, the mindfulness skills, which focus on enhancing awareness of reality, are of particular interest because they are an inherent part of the other skill modules. Before one can change what is, one must first be aware of what is. As one of their early assignments in the emotion regulation module, for example, clients must practise observing and describing the prompting event, interpretations, facial expressions, actions, etc. associated with a particular emotional episode. Only after becoming aware of the many factors contributing to a single emotional episode can clients learn skills to change those factors and thus better manage the corresponding emotion.

In addition to having a repertoire of skilful behaviour, one must also have sufficient motivation to engage in skilful behaviour. The therapy therefore requires a second modality that focuses on improving motivation. A variety of modalities, ranging from inpatient milieus (e.g., settings that provide incentive systems, peer support/pressure) to pharmacotherapy (e.g., anxiolytics may decrease fear that inhibits interpersonal skills), may address this function. Standard DBT primarily addresses this task in individual psychotherapy, where the therapist conducts an extensive analysis of the factors that motivate the client and employs various strategies to improve motivation. The individual therapist also integrates the skills training described above into the individual therapy (e.g., suggesting skills as solutions to problems, rehearsing the implementation of those skills, and reinforcing the use of skilful behaviour). Also, if the client has a problem with the skills-training group (or any other mode), the individual therapist consults with the client as to how the client can best solve the problem. Similarly, the client could seek consultation from the group therapist regarding a problem with the individual therapist.

Just as the therapist cannot assume that the client will have sufficient motivation to apply new skills, the therapist cannot assume that skills practice will automatically generalize from therapeutic settings to 'real' life settings. The context of applying skills may differ substantially from the context of learning skills, particularly in terms of the client's degree of emotional dysregulation and the environment's likelihood of providing a reinforcing response. As a behavioural treatment, DBT emphasizes the need for *in vivo* treatment so that learning will generalize beyond the therapeutic context. Possible treatment modalities include inpatient milieus, occupational therapy, or *in vivo* practice/exposure with a social worker or therapist (all these providing examples of 'organizational integration' described in Chapter 1). Standard DBT provides clients with the opportunity to phone or otherwise contact a designated member of the DBT team for brief coaching interventions between individual therapy sessions. These coaching interventions generally function to help the client apply skilful solutions to an immediate problem. Similarly, the treatment's fourth function focuses on helping the client to structure their environment in a way that promotes progress in other contexts (this can be compared with the emphasis in interpersonal therapy on building social networks as a bulwark against depression; see Chapter 8).

Finally, the therapy's dialectical model would suggest that the treatment must also address the capabilities and motivation of the therapist. With difficult clients, in particular, the transaction between client and therapist may be such that the client punishes therapeutic behaviour and rewards iatrogenic behaviour. Treating the therapist as well as the client thus reinforces the dialectical frame of the therapy by attending to the two primary subsystems within the therapeutic context. Supervision or consultation meetings among therapists usually address these issues.

In the community, one of the frequent consequences of such a complex network of treatment modalities and care-providers is that tensions arise amongst the providers. Therapists on DBT consultation teams adhere to a set of agreements that seem to reduce the likelihood of such tensions. For example, the consultation-to-the-client agreement states that therapists do not instruct each other about how to interact with a client; instead they coach the client on how to interact effectively with members of the team. This removes one of the greatest causes of tension: care-providers telling each other how to do their jobs. The consistency agreement states, in part, that all team members need not have a consistent response to a client. For example, a therapist covering for an individual therapist on leave may provide more hours of phone availability but may hospitalize more quickly if the client threatens suicide. Such inconsistencies offer the client an opportunity to learn, with the therapist's coaching, how to cope with the inconsistencies and changes occurring outside of therapy.

Targets

Although the practice of defining and hierarchically arranging treatment targets is traditional to behaviour therapies, the way in which this is done in DBT is influenced by the integration of Zen practice. The definition of treatment targets highlights a tension between behaviour therapy and Zen and a paradox within Zen itself. While the behaviour therapist helps the client to define where he or she wants to go, the Zen master helps the student to realize that he or she is already there. Within Zen a paradox exists because while one may enter the practice to achieve enlightenment, the more one focuses on enlightenment as a goal during practice, the less likely one is to experience it. The DBT therapist balances requiring the client to work on treatment targets with appreciating the strengths inherent within the client. Of course, the therapist must also attend to the many ways in which attention to treatment targets can interfere with their achievement. For example, how the client's fears of not being able to stop drinking may actually cause an increase in drinking to avoid the anxiety.

The inclusion of therapy-interfering behaviour (i.e. in psychodynamic terms 'acting out', see Chapter 2), which includes any action by either the client or the therapist that impedes the progress of therapy as a potential target, is particularly influenced by both cognitive–behaviour therapy and Zen practice. Cognitive–behavioural therapists have developed strategies to directly target problems with treatment compliance (Meichenbaum and Turk 1987; Shelton and Levy 1981). DBT integrates these strategies with Zen in which the primary essence of the practice is overcoming any 'delusions' (e.g., in cognitive–behaviour therapy terms, interpretations, desires, automatic assump- tions) that interfere with the practice, or the attainment of enlightenment (Aitken 1982). Thus in DBT, therapy-interfering behaviours are not obstacles to be avoided or simply solved so that therapy can proceed, but instead are assessed in terms of their rela- tionship to problematic behaviours that occur in the client's life outside of therapy and viewed as opportunities to treat relevant behaviours *in vivo*. If a client fails to complete the weekly diary card, the therapist would target the non-compliance, not only because it would interfere directly with the therapy itself but also if the non-compliance is related to the client's other target behaviours. For example, shame may be the crucial link in the chain leading to a client's non-compliance, just as it is a link leading to the cli- ent's suicide attempts. By addressing the shame leading to the non-compliance, the therapist directly targets a therapy-interfering behaviour and indirectly targets suicidal behaviour. There are clear integrative parallels here with transferential work in psychodynamic therapy, in which the therapist uses problematic aspects of the *in vivo* therapeutic relationship to illustrate and work on more general themes in the client's life.

Strategies

It is among the DBT treatment strategies that the influence of integration and synthesis occurs most substantially. First, Linehan (1993a) developed technically integrative sets of strategies by including many different procedures and techniques adapted from a variety of areas in psychology in each set. Second, she organized the primary sets of strategies into pairs, with one member of the pair most strongly emphasizing change and the other most strongly emphasizing acceptance, which provide a point and coun- terpoint to each other. Linehan also developed the dialectical set of strategies to facilitate the synthesizing of the other strategies. The relationship between the strategies resem- bles a figure skating pair in a single rink (Linehan uses many metaphors of this sort which can be seen as inherently integrative in that they coalesce a number of complex strands of thought into a single memorable image). The members of the pair have different steps, but the steps must flow together and balance each other, with one member's moves enhancing, not competing with, the moves of the other. Attaining balance is difficult, of course, particularly since the balance point continuously changes across clients and across time for a single client. That the session is no longer flowing (i.e. the therapist has encountered 'resistance') is the primary indicator that one or more of the pairs of strategies have become imbalanced. Unfortunately, the therapy does not include any guidelines to help the therapist decide which way to move when an imbalance occurs!

Dialectical strategies

The dialectical strategies permeate the application of all other DBT strategies. Dialectical strategies refer both to a specific set of techniques which inherently include elements of acceptance and change and to strategies which facilitate dialectical processes within the session, that is, the development of syntheses in place of tensions. With respect to developing syntheses, the therapist and client must attend to the entire context of a problem, frequently asking what has been forgotten or ignored. As discussed above under dialectical assumptions, when tensions arise, the therapist and client must search for the validity of various viewpoints and the syntheses between them. The therapist also responds to dialectical tensions by interweaving change strategies with acceptance strategies. Furthermore, the therapist must balance adherence to the treatment manual with responsiveness to the client, just as a ballroom dancer must follow both the steps of the dance and the movements of his partner. Indeed, therapy should feel a bit like dancing with a partner, albeit sometimes dancing by the side of a cliff (more metaphorical discourse!).

While balancing, integrating, or synthesizing may prove the most effective ways forward, *how* to balance, integrate, or synthesize in any particular situation is not always obvious or easy. Success requires comprehensive and detailed assessments, rapid movement amongst the strategies and rigorous application of the therapy as a whole. Such demands can be intellectually and emotionally exhausting for the therapist and client alike. The therapy can stop or even reverse if the therapist then becomes emotionally dysregulated or cognitively distracted by worries of what may happen next, by beliefs that they should be able to find a synthesis more easily, by judgements that the client shouldn't have placed them in this situation in the first place, or any similar thoughts. One of the keys to not becoming overwhelmed by the demands of therapy is to remain mindful throughout the session. Being mindful requires the therapist non-judgementally to focus on the moment and what is effective, to be aware of any distractions from this focus, and to return to this focus when distracted.

Specific dialectical techniques all share an inherent synthesis of acceptance and change. For example, the therapist may guide change by the art of persuasion in the manner of ancient Greek philosophers who employed dialectics as a method of debate that involved refuting an opponent's argument by hypothetically accepting it and then leading the opponent to admit that it implies contradictory conclusions. While some of the techniques, such as metaphor and playing devil's advocate, are traditional psychotherapy interventions, other techniques are adapted from Eastern practices. 'Entering the paradox' and extending, two of the techniques influenced by Eastern practices, are discussed below.

'Entering the paradox' requires the therapist to highlight the contradictions within the client's behaviours, the therapy process, or reality in general, to tolerate the ambiguity and to help the client to solve the paradox by finding a synthesis of the various positions. For example, a client may frequently respond to the needs of others at the cost of caring for herself. The paradox for this client is that caring for oneself is a way of caring for others. The presentation of paradoxes in DBT somewhat resembles the koans, or practices, presented to students in Zen. In both, the solution must be experiential, not intellectual. The ultimate paradox in Zen, for Westerners at least, may be the coupling of the proposition that 'the essential world of perfection is this very world ...' (Aitken 1982, p.63) with the proposition that '. . . life is suffering' (p. 49). Thus quietly summarizing and confronting the client with the paradox, without any attempt to resolve it, may be helpful and stimulate the client to begin to find her own solution.

'Extending' is a translation of a technique used in Aikido, a Japanese martial art. Extending is a strategy whereby the therapist produces change by 'extending' or taking more seriously than the client a position taken by the client in an effort to pull the client slightly off balance so that movement or a shift in direction is forced. It is akin to the technique of 'unbalancing' used by systemic therapists (see Chapter 4), in which, by taking a particular behaviour to its limit, a sudden 'flip' back to a more balanced position often occurs. The therapist joins with the client, allows the behaviour to progress naturally to the point intended by the client, and then extends the behaviour beyond the point intended by the client. The challenge for the therapist is in deciding what to extend. For example, a client may say 'You're a horrible therapist, I'm going to write a complaint about you', with little intent of writing a complaint but with the expectation that the therapist will resist the client's threat and will focus on repairing any damage to the therapy relationship to prevent the client from writing. A therapist using extending, however, would accept the client's desire to write such a letter and, extending the client's threat, may offer to spend the session time helping the client to write the letter because it's the therapist's job to help the client to be as effective as possible.

Core strategies: problem solving and validation

Problem solving

Most DBT problem-solving strategies are direct applications of traditional cognitive–behaviour therapies, though Linehan also integrated research from social psychology. Problem solving begins by defining the problematic behaviour and conducting a behavioural chain analysis to identify environmental events, cognitions, affect, etc. that are causally related to the problem. The behavioural analysis itself represents a synthesis of acceptance and change. On the one hand, completing a behavioural analysis requires the client to acknowledge, without judgement, the occurrence of a target behaviour and the relationship of that behaviour to other links in the chain. In this way, behavioural analyses resemble the Zen practice of observing without 'delusion' (Aitken 1982). On the other hand, conducting a behavioural analysis may in itself produce change. For example, behavioural analyses may decrease parasuicidal behaviour by modelling problem-solving skills that the client can apply to situations that elicit parasuicidal urges.

The therapist continually interweaves solution analyses into the behavioural analysis. Links in the behavioural chain present opportunities to apply solutions. As solution strategies, DBT therapists employ cognitive–behavioural change procedures, such as exposure, contingency management, skills training and cognitive modification procedures (e.g., Spiegler and Guevremont 1993). Therapists adhere to the traditional principles underlying these procedures, but Linehan (1993a) has adapted the application of the procedures to the problems associated with BPD clients. For example, exposure was primarily developed as a treatment for anxiety, but DBT therapists employ exposure to treat a variety of emotional responses. If a client becomes aggressive to escape from feelings of shame elicited by criticism, the therapist may expose the client to the cue of criticism and block attempts to become aggressive to escape from feelings of shame. In the case of contingency management, Linehan adapted these procedures by emphasizing the use of the therapeutic relationship as a contingency. For example, if a client finds the therapist's warmth and approval reinforcing, the therapist might withdraw warmth and approval and become matter-of-fact and confrontational in response to therapy-interfering behaviour by a client. When the client ceases the therapy-interfering behaviour and engages collaboratively with the therapist, the therapist would then respond with warmth and approval. Such an oscillation in warmth and approval by one individual based on the behaviour of the other individual more closely resembles the contingencies in relationships outside of therapy.

While DBT therapists sometimes formally apply a single type of cognitive–behavioural procedure as a solution, in usual practice therapists weave the procedures together informally. For example, if a client avoids asking the therapist for help because the client fears that the therapist will respond with rejection, exposure would probably be the primary intervention. Prior to the exposure, however, some interpersonal skills training might increase the likelihood that the client asks for help in a way that the therapist can reinforce, while a cognitive intervention might increase the client's collaboration with the exposure procedure. Finally, the therapist would reinforce the client's request for help.

Validation

Balancing the focus of problem-solving strategies on change, validation strategies focus on acceptance. Linehan (1993a) describes validation as occurring when 'the therapist communicates to the patient that her responses make sense and are understandable within her current life context or situation' (pp. 222–3). Linehan (1997a) identifies six levels of validation:

- listening and observing;
- accurately reflecting;
- articulating the unverbalized;
- validating in terms of sufficient causes;
- validating as reasonable in the moment;
- treating the person as valid or being radically genuine.

(There are clear overlaps here with Hobson's existential approach in psychodynamic interpersonal therapy; see Chapter 7.)

Levels 5 and 6 are most definitional of validation in DBT. Level 5 validation requires the therapist to communicate how a client's response makes sense or is normal in terms of the current context, rather than in terms of the client's psychiatric disorder or learning history. For example, in a response to a new client who indicates some distrust of the therapist, the therapist might say, 'It makes sense that you have difficulty trusting me considering that we have just met and you don't know me well.' Level 6 requires the therapist to interact with the client simply as a fellow human being, rather than as a fragile or volatile individual who is incapable of learning. For example, a therapist may notice that a female client, who complains that the male clients in her skills training group stare at her, wears very revealing clothing to group. If the therapist hypothesizes that the clothing contribute to the stares, a radically genuine response would require the therapist to share this hypothesis with the client. The therapist may then validate both the client's 'right' to dress as she wants and the normalcy of the male clients' responses to her dress. These last two levels of validation most clearly reflect the emphasis in Zen on the current moment, on searching for truth or enlightenment, and on this truth and the capability of discovering it being inherent within oneself. In his discussion of Zen, Aitken (1982, p. 6) observes, 'All beings are the truth, just as they are.'

While validation is an end in itself, it is also a means to facilitate change. Linehan's theoretical development of validation has been strongly influenced by recent research indicating that the verification of an individual's beliefs about the self tends to enhance the processing of new information (Linehan 1997b; Swann *et al.* 1992). This research would suggest that interweaving problem solving with validation might increase the likelihood that the client will process the information provided by the problem solving. For example, a therapist may validate the function of a target behaviour ('Yes, it makes sense that you want to stop feeling so distressed, and overdosing is very effective at immediately numbing your feelings'.), challenge the use of the target behaviour ('But overdosing keeps creating more distress in your life.'), and then suggest alternative skills to achieve the same function ('We must find more effective ways to help you tolerate your distress.') In addition to balancing problem-solving strategies, validation may function directly as a change strategy by providing information about what is valid, modelling how clients can self-validate, and reinforcing skilful behaviour.

Stylistic strategies: reciprocal and irreverent communication

The stylistic strategies refer to the manner in which the therapist interacts with the client. These strategies attend to the how, as opposed to the what, of the therapist's communications to the client. The therapist balances the tension between two opposing sets of strategies: reciprocal communication and irreverent communication.

Linehan (1993a, p. 371) defines the reciprocal communication style by 'responsiveness, self-disclosure, warmth and genuineness'. Part of reciprocal communication requires attending to the client in a mindful manner by noticing even subtle responses by the client and by not allowing preconceptions or judgements to interfere with the attention. Zen applies a similar responsive approach to achieving a state of the mind at rest: 'Nothing carries over conceptually or emotionally. [. . .] we do not react out of a self-centred position. We are free to apply our humanity appropriately in the context of the moment according to the needs of people' (Aitken 1982, p. 42). As another aspect of reciprocal communication, the therapist self-discloses personal information to the client to encourage self-disclosure by the client, to model coping with problems, or to validate the client's perception of the therapist. The emphasis on self-disclosure in DBT is based on findings in social psychology literature (see Derlega and Berg 1987 for a review) which suggest that self-disclosure by one individual facilitates self-disclosure by another. This would be an example of radical disjunction between psychodynamic therapies and DBT – the dialectic of integration and differentiation. The emphasis on warmth and genuineness was influenced, of course, by Rogers' (1986) humanistic approach.

In contrast to reciprocal communication, Linehan (1993a) defines the irreverent communication style as 'unhallowed, impertinent and incongruous' (p. 371). These strategies temporarily 'unbalance' the client by shifting attention or by introducing a new viewpoint. Procedures include reacting matter-of-factly to a client's extreme communication and directly confronting dysfunctional behaviour. Therapists enquire about topics that clients may prefer to avoid. For example, if a client harms herself by inserting shards of glass into her vagina and the therapist hypothesizes that this behaviour has a sexual function, the therapist would share this hypothesis with the client. Therapists also reframe behaviours and situations in unorthodox ways. For example, if a client commits to decreasing frequent judgemental thinking, the therapist might respond to in-session judgemental statements by light-heartedly saying 'Did you notice that you were judging? We know that you already have that skill, so you don't need to practise it any more. Let's practise a skill that you don't have yet. Try describing rather than judging what happened.' Linehan emphasizes that these strategies must be applied upon a foundation of compassion and caring. The irreverent strategies integrate techniques from Whitaker's (1975) irreverent style in family therapy and were influenced by Ellis' (1962, 1987) style in his rational emotive therapy. The irreverent strategies also reflect the style of unorthodox responses employed by Zen masters with their students (Braverman 1989). Such responses function to interrupt habitual thinking patterns that interfere with a student achieving enlightenment.

It is important to note that within the context of DBT, irreverence refers to behaving in an offbeat manner, not behaving disrespectfully or sarcastically toward the client. The therapist must interweave warmth, vulnerability, and closeness with matter-of-factness and confrontation. As in Zen practice, the therapist strives toward both compassion and detachment. A primary function of balancing of these strategies is the preservation of the therapeutic alliance as a context for client change. If the therapist maintains reciprocal vulnerability (to the extent of the client's vulnerability), he or she is likely to feel overwhelmed or suffocated and to want to leave the relationship, whereas if the therapist maintains extreme imperviousness, the client is likely to feel ignored or abandoned and to want to leave the relationship for a new therapist.

Outcome

The initial randomized, controlled trial (RCT) of standard DBT compared 1 year of the therapy to treatment-as-usual in the community (Linehan *et al.* 1991, 1994). The subjects in this trial were women who met criteria for BPD and had a recent history of parasuicidal behaviour. The results of this trial suggested that after 1 year, subjects receiving DBT had significantly fewer parasuicides, less medically severe parasuicides, lower treatment dropout rates, fewer psychiatric inpatient days, lower anger, and higher social and global functioning. The two groups did not differ, however, with respect to depression or suicidal ideation. Results were weaker but generally maintained during a 1-year follow-up (Linehan *et al.* 1993). Linehan and colleagues are currently attempting to replicate the initial trial, though with a more rigorously designed controlled condition this time.

Two other randomized, controlled trials examining the efficacy of DBT for BPD have been completed. First, Koons and colleagues (Koons *et al.* 1998) compared standard DBT to a treatment-as-usual condition that was primarily cognitive–behavioural. The subjects were female veterans who met criteria for BPD but who did not necessarily have a history of parasuicidal behaviour. The results of this trial suggested that, after 6 months of treatment, subjects receiving DBT had a significantly greater reduction in suicidal ideation, depression, hopelessness, and anger. The two groups did not differ with respect to treatment retention.

Second, Linehan and colleagues have completed a randomized, controlled trial that examines the efficacy of modifications to standard DBT for the treatment of substance abuse (Linehan *et al.* 1999) to treatment-as-usual. The subjects in this trial were women who met criteria for BPD and either substance abuse or substance dependence. The results of this trial suggested that after 1 year subjects receiving DBT had significantly greater reductions in substance abuse and a trend toward greater treatment retention when compared to subjects receiving treatment-as-usual. The two groups did not differ with respect to psychiatric inpatient treatment, anger, social functioning, or global functioning. During a 4-month follow-up, however, DBT subjects had significantly greater gains in global and social adjustment and reductions in anger, as well as significantly greater reductions in substance abuse. Linehan and colleagues are currently attempting a replication of this trial as well.

Several studies that have not employed randomized, controlled designs have also produced results favouring DBT. These studies have examined the impact of DBT on an inpatient unit consisting primarily of parasuicidal BPD patients (Barley *et al.* 1993) with suicidal, BPD outpatients (Stanley *et al.* 1998). Though the results of these studies generally favour DBT, the findings must be replicated in more tightly controlled trials before clear interpretations can be made of the findings.

Conclusion

DBT is a comprehensively integrative psychotherapy. At a theoretical level, DBT employs the primary assumptions of a dialectical philosophy to synthesize the principles of behaviourism with the principles of Zen. Structurally, the therapy integrates several therapeutic tasks and modes in a manner that allows each task or mode to facilitate the completion or application of the others. The strategies of DBT balance acceptance and change, while its techniques draw from social psychology, crisis intervention, and various psychotherapies, in addition to behaviour therapy and Zen practice. Research results foretell a positive future for this approach to treating clients who meet criteria for BPD. Due to its dialectical foundation, DBT is a therapy that strives to constantly evolve by synthesizing clinical and research data from new and multiple sources.

Chapter 10

The therapeutic community

*Theoretical, practical, and
therapeutic integration*

Kingsley Norton and Rex Haigh

Introduction

To integrate means (1) to combine into a whole or (2) to facilitate equal membership of society. Both definitions have relevance to therapeutic communities (TCs) in relation to the theme of integration within psychotherapy. The aim of the therapeutic community, within the field of mental health, is often to achieve greater integration of the personality. This is achieved through the patient inhabiting an environment which is deliberately structured to integrate the aims of its formal psychotherapy sessions with those of the unstructured time. As a result, psychotherapy and sociotherapy can complement, rather than conflict with, one another (Edelson 1970).

In practice it is often hard to harmonize the goals of psycho- and sociotherapy. However, in the course of a successful therapeutic experience, an enhanced sense of self is accompanied by a corresponding capacity to differentiate self from other people. This helps the individual to diminish any sense of marginalization and alienation, which most of those who encounter therapeutic communities as clients will have felt previously – whether by virtue of the stigmatizing of those with mental illness or by membership of other marginal groups within society. Intrapsychic, interpersonal, and social benefits deriving from TC membership accrue concomitantly.

Combining into a whole

Theoretical base of TC

There is no single or sufficient theoretical model of the TC. Valuing plurality is part of the approach. Although individual units might call themselves 'therapeutic communities' by adhering to a particular type of programme or holding specific theoretical principles, what all different TC have in common is simply a belief that the experience of living together in a structured therapeutic environment can be beneficial. The ways in which those environments are structured, and the theoretical bases of them, differ widely. The definition used for selecting studies in the recent international systematic review (Lees *et al.* 1999) was:

> A consciously designed social environment and programme within a residential or day unit in which the social and group process is harnessed with therapeutic intent. In the therapeutic community the community is the primary therapeutic instrument.

Models used within TCs in mental health care derive from two sources. The first involves an integration of individual and group psychoanalytic traditions, represented by the pioneering work which took place in the two so-called Northfield experiments. Wilfred Bion set up the training wing of Northfield Military Hospital as a therapeutic community in 1942 (Bion 1961). There were numerous groups and a daily '12.15 parade' – the prototypical community meeting – in which the battle-shocked soldiers could 'step outside their framework and look upon its working with the detachment of spectators' (p. 16), aiming to integrate the differing perspectives. The second experiment was conducted with greater sensitivity to the military structures within which it operated and worked successfully until after the end of the war. Amongst its staff were Tom Main, Michael Foulkes, John Rickman, and Harold Bridger (Harrison 1999). Of these, Main took an institutional perspective and coined the term 'therapeutic community' in 1946.

For Main, the TC embraced the ideal of an 'immediate aim of full participation of all its members in its daily life with the eventual aim of resocialization of the neurotic individual for life in ordinary society' (Main 1946). This included the need for the integration of as much of everyday 'social reality' into the daily workings of the institution as was safely possible. For it to retain its therapeutic potential the community of staff and clients needed to establish 'a culture of enquiry . . . into personal, interpersonal, and intersystem problems and study impulses, defences, and relations as these are expressed and used socially' (Main 1983).

The second source incorporated both anthropological and sociological approaches. Maxwell Jones was another wartime doctor, who was treating soldiers with 'disorderly action of the heart' at Mill Hill Hospital, near London. He noted that the soldiers who had been present for some time in treatment became very effective at teaching the newcomers on the programme. A dry theoretical presentation by staff became an emotional sharing of meaning, and more effective for it. This led to development of a democratic approach where patients were constructively used to help one another and gradually took a more equal role with staff in some administrative and social activities. Jones noted that patients' reactions in the hospital 'were similar to their reactions outside, and the study of these real life situations [in the hospital] gave a great deal of information about the patients problems'. The evolving structures included 'more open communication, less rigid hierarchy of doctors, nurses, patients, daily structured discussions of the whole unit, and various sub-groups' (Jones 1968). Ideally, sociotherapy and psycho-therapy complemented one another (Edelson 1970)

Modern TCs have developed on the basis of other ideologies, for example, attachment theory. Haigh proposes a developmental model in which the essential experiences of emotional development were reworked in sequence: attachment, containment, com-munication, inclusion, and agency (Haigh 1999). Tucker and colleagues have empha-sized concepts of dialogue and dwelling: the fundamental human significance of being in contact with others, and the psychological significance of having a place one can call home. In addition to group theory they draw on the writings of Buber, Heidigger, Lacan, Habermas, and Wittgenstein amongst others and a range of contemporary sociological ideas (Tucker 2000).

The therapeutic community has recently been conceived as a 'modality' rather than a specific treatment in itself. Within this approach there is room for any number of theo-retical models which, given sufficient integration and harmonization, could provide for the needs of their client groups (Kennard 1998). This approach might be seen as a liber-ating one, releasing exponents of therapeutic community from a slavish dependence on a particular preferred ideological model and avoiding some of the preoccupation with resolving the problems of integrating individual psychodynamic and group theories.

Practicalities

Psychotherapy for inpatients can be delivered in three main ways (Hinshelwood 1988). First, it can be seen as an essentially distinct ingredient, that is, not integrated with the residential setting, in terms of its goals and necessary preconditions. An example would be of an inpatient who leaves the ward, say weekly, to attend an individual psychother-apy session or, alternatively, when a therapist visits the patient in the ward. Second, the psychotherapy takes place in a setting which is expressly designed to support the ther-apy, while of itself not being acknowledged to have a primary therapeutic function; that is, a group conducted on an inpatient ward that is otherwise run along traditional lines. Third is the situation (otherwise known as the TC) where psychotherapy and the struc-tured residential environment are both designed to complement one another, recogniz-ing the potential for a summative therapeutic (Edelson 1970). This planned environment for living together, and the way in which it is used to scrutinize the human relations of the participants, is more fundamental to therapeutic community work than any single theoretical framework. Numerous practical aspects follow: domestic; admin-istrative; clinical; supervisory and managerial.

Within most TCs there is a flattening of the usual staff–patient and staff–staff hierar-chies. This represents an integration of the total human resource of the institution, all members being combined into a whole. This is to deny neither difference nor hierarchy but to exploit the potential of active participation of all within their particular environment – a more or less equal membership of the TC as a microcosm of society, as mentioned in the definitions of integration above. Further evidence of integration is the blurring of roles which occurs both between staff and between staff and clients. This does not mean an amorphous or imprecise role definition but rather a knowledge and understanding of role and a capacity to deviate flexibly from this, albeit within pre-scribed limits (Burns 2000). (This would be an example of the 'integration in practice' described in relation to mature clinicians in Chapter 1.) For example, staff often share meals with residents of a therapeutic community, although only some staff will be responsible for helping to prepare those meals. Which residents do the cooking will be determined by the whole community, but which staff are available will be determined by external factors, over which the residents of the community will not have authority.

The diversity of approaches demands theoretical integration at several levels. In an individual unit with psychotherapy staff, psychodynamically trained therapists may work alongside those with humanistic trainings, and have joint supervision. Behav-ioural techniques – such as setting and reviewing goals, imposing sanctions, and writing contracts – are commonly used in programmes which also deploy group analytic psy-chotherapy (Rawlinson 1999). Members and residents of such programmes naturally integrate different theoretical approaches in their discussions and relationships. Psychi-atrists, psychologists, nurses, social workers, occupational therapists, researchers, and clinically untrained staff will talk about their experience in the same groups: integration is inevitably present, at least to a degree, in any TC which is working successfully.

To relate to superordinate systems, management must ensure that their TCs are coor-dinated with other services upon which they rely for referrals, resources, and good will. Communities must be integrated with their systemic environment. For example ter-tiary-level TCs within the NHS need to have a more or less clear identity and place alongside community mental health teams and other secondary-tier services. For their continued survival, therapeutic communities need to respond in an integrated way to socio-political demands – such as for openness, accountability, and evidence of effectiveness.

In practice, none of the above aspects are smoothly negotiated or enacted. The ideol-ogy of a flattened hierarchy is attractive to many staff, but not necessarily for similar or socially desirable reasons. For example, an anti-authoritarian or irresponsible motive may underpin such attraction to the ideal. These staff attitudes can readily translate into overt or covert behaviour which is anti-therapeutic. Thus, those lower in the hierarchy may be inappropriately challenging to, or denying of, the legitimate authority of their seniors – 'flattened' being misunderstood as 'flat'. Likewise, seniors may abdicate responsibility, by delegation or lack of clarity for ownership of decision-making, and inappropriately expect junior colleagues to function above their actual capacity or beyond the proper limits of their subordinate role.

Blurring of roles is difficult to achieve in practice since it requires a prior understanding of the professional role in order for it to be therapeutically blurred. Developing and maintaining a clear sense of role, in an environment of 'blurring', can be problematic. As a result it is possible for even basic traditional role responsibilities, for example those surrounding an evaluation of patients' physical needs, to become corroded. As a consequence legitimate physical medical needs are downgraded in importance or psychologized by staff.

Where there is a prominent use of the multidisciplinary team, as a forum in which to make a range of management-related decisions, it can be easy for the group, and for its individual members, to lose sight of personal responsibility. Different members of the team, reflecting different personal and professional attitudes and trainings, may hold opposing views on a range of important work-related topics; for example, moralizing versus sympathetic attitudes to a patient's violent history. These may be more or less overtly expressed. Even when openly expressed, 'splitting' effects can be difficult both to diagnose and to deal with, especially where other staff can readily align themselves according to pre-existing 'fault lines' such as shift-working staff and '9 to 5' staff (Norton and McGauley 1997).

Supervision and sensitivity staff groups are required to facilitate the regular scrutiny of both attitudes to clients and attitudes to fellow staff, to minimize destructive splitting and to maximize their use for the examination of counter-transference. Thus 'integration' – of staff and patient, of different therapeutic philosophies – can be both a source of creativity and strength and have anti-therapeutic potential. Constant monitoring and self-awareness at an individual and community level is needed to foster the former and counteract the latter.

Facilitating equal membership

The TC needs to be aware of its 'system' environment and its degree of integration within that system. Ignorance of this or inattention to it may result in the demise of TCs, as has been seen in the past. This can be seen in a Darwinian way, where the TCs that are not well adapted to their higher-order environment do not survive. Here the TC can be represented as an organism which is either well integrated within its organizational eco-system (making its survival likely) or poorly integrated (making its demise likely). The issue of leadership is important in this respect, leaders being required to be 'Janus-like', facing in two directions at the same time – into the TC and out towards the wider-systems world (Norton 1992). In the period of innovation of any TC there is a potential role for charismatic leaders. Subsequently the dangers of routinization are well-described (Manning 1989).

Facilitating equal membership of the small society which comprises the TC may itself convey therapeutic and other values. Indeed the therapeutic community approach has been applied to a number of marginalized populations otherwise experienced as having pariah status. Through the internalization of the structure provided by the therapeutic community not only is an increased level of intrapsychic integration achieved but also a greater capacity for individuals to integrate with the wider society, which previously rejected them or was at least experienced as being rejecting and alienating.

Some of the client groups for whom TCs have provided personal and interpersonal integration include: those with learning difficulties, troubled children; adults with life-long emotional difficulties (including those with personality disorder), people with drug and alcohol misuse problems, some of those suffering from psychotic illness, and some of those imprisoned for a variety of sexual and/or violent offences.

Our discussion centres on TCs in the UK and is mostly concerned with integration within mental health services, but a brief description of each of these different areas follows. Some of these point to an integration of principles across very different areas of endeavour, in addition to a means of equalizing access to mainstream society – integration in a wider, social sense.

Mentally afflicted pilgrims

A very early type of provision, which might be seen as a TC, was for 'mentally afflicted pilgrims'. They were looked after by foster families in Geel, Flanders from 1250 onwards. Their humane and compassionate treatment was accomplished by integrating them into wider society. The 'pilgrims' came to the holy shrine of St Dymphna and were occupied as workers in agricultural smallholdings. The project was brought under Belgian state control in 1862, with the setting-up of an assessment and new boarders unit, which also looked after the 'temporarily unmanageable' and served as a social centre. Families who took in boarders received an allowance from the state, and it was a matter of great pride to look after their boarders. Success was acclaimed by the boarder's weight gain and it was seen as a disgrace to have a boarder removed (Bloor *et al*. 1988).

Those with learning disability

Rudoph Steiner's 'anthroposophy' was a view of humans as spiritual beings, which integrated sacred and profane aspects of life. His thinking influenced Konig, who set up the Camphill Village Trust in 1938. This was described as a 'therapeutic state of communities' and it remains a successful charity to this day, with many communities around the UK. Their growth has been silent and unremarked and largely without professional input (Bloor *et al*. 1988). They are relatively inexpensive and provide self-evidently good care for many of those with learning difficulties.

Delinquent and troubled children

Homer Lane was a New England woodwork teacher who became superintendent of the Detroit children's playgrounds at the beginning of the twentieth century. He was particularly interested in working with delinquent boys, and he set up 'The Boys' Republic' in 1907. The integration he attempted was between the rules and structures for establishing social order in wider society and the rules and structures needed for effective care of a small community of disturbed boys.

The Boys' Republic was on a 70-acre farm 20 miles out of Detroit. Lane's first action was to make the boys rebuild it, including digging the foundations and making the bricks for its walls. The community had an elaborate set of procedures based on the United States constitution, and all those over 10 years old had a vote. Lane, using example and influence, replaced close supervision and individual task performance with collective and individual responsibility for behaviour. He moved to Britain and set up the 'Little Commonwealth' as a reformatory in 1913. Here, the predominant emphasis was on affectionate relationships, and less on transgressions and the need for order. It closed after a few years in the wake of allegations of sexual impropriety.

A. S. Neill was a keen pupil of Lane, and went on to found Summerhill, a recognized TC school to this day. The 1920s and 1930s were golden years for therapeutic schools: the place of progressive education was secure and valued, and numerous experiments were tried. George Lyward set up Finchden Manor, charismatically run and known for the doctrine of 'tough love'. David Wills set up the Hawkspur Camp, the Q-camps with Marjorie Franklin in 1934, and Hawkspur Green for delinquent 16–19-year-old boys in 1936 (see Pines 1999). They worked with the principles of 'love and shared responsibility'. This meant all were worthy of love, whatever their appearance, habits, or disposition, and domination of one person or group by another was seen as abhorrent. Several such projects and schools continued through the mid-twentieth century. Peper Harow opened in 1970 (Rose 1997). Although it closed some 20 years later after a fire, it spawned the Charterhouse Group, which remains active in coordinating the activities of a number of residential TCs for troubled children, and lobbies for therapeutic childcare in other settings.

Adults with enduring personal, interpersonal, and behavioural difficulties

The work with people with lifelong emotional difficulties arose from experiments in the Second World War at Mill Hill and Northfield, as described above. The therapeutic community approach is especially applicable in mental health settings to those whose needs are complex and enduring, such as those diagnosed as having severe personality disorder. These are people who have considerable difficulty understanding themselves, relating to others, or functioning effectively in the world. Above all, these individuals require the provision of a psychosocial environment which holds, tolerates, and thinks about their disturbance – in order to support their developing abilities to contain and verbalize their emotions. Such an environment needs to blend challenge and support and be sensitive to a range of boundary issues, especially relating to attachment and separation. There is also a need to integrate the referring system into the TC so that entry and exit are rendered as untraumatizing as possible (Norton 1999). Sharing information across the boundaries of the TC may involve using different languages to different referrers and different workers within health care, probation, social services, and carer groups. Individuals with severe personality disorder have difficulty in maintaining a continuous sense of self. This therefore needs to be modelled and supported and there are many structures that help in integrating experiences from the past with today and encouraging a reality-based planning for the future (Norton 1992).

Offender patients

Therapeutic communities in prisons represent a sensitive political integration: between society's need both to punish crime and also to understand and treat the causes of it in offenders. HMP Grendon opened as a therapeutic community in 1962 and has continued working since, being the only prison in the country that is run as a therapy-based institution, with five treatment wings. It is a medium security prison with 250 inmates, who all have more than 18 months of their sentences left to serve, and of whom about 40% are serving life sentences. It has an active research department and has produced evidence of reduced reconviction rates (Marshall 1997). There are also prison TCs in the Max Glatt Centre at Wormwood Scrubs and HMP Gartree. A new therapeutic community prison is due to open in Staffordshire in late 2001, and the commissioning of other TC facilities in the prison and probation service is under consideration by the Home Office. Difficulties in maintaining openness and collaboration in such settings, and conflicts arising out of the potentially competing demands of therapy and security – in running TC programmes in prisons – have been studied (Rawlings 1998).

Other therapeutic communities

'Concept TCs' use a psychosocial environment which is different from 'democratic TCs' for the rehabilitation of people with alcohol and drug problems. Their development took place in USA, independent of the British developments, and they now exist throughout the world (Kennard 1998). They are also known as 'behavioural' or 'programmatic' TCs, and the work is now backed up by a rigorous evidence base (see Rawlings and Yates, in press). One notable feature of their practice is the prominent use of ex-addicts in the treatment programmes. Therapeutically, these units integrate a strict behavioural programme with an atheoretical model of peer-pressure and containment by group dynamic forces.

Early attempts to integrate a TC approach into acute settings for those with active psychotic conditions did not survive, or develop to any great extent, although the underlying principles and elements of the approach were widely adopted (Clark 1999).

Contemporary research base

Researching the therapeutic community, especially in terms of its therapeutic processes, is potentially problematic. The researchers themselves will exert an influence on the environment which is their field of study. To minimize this distortion requires an integration of the researcher into the therapeutic community as a whole, albeit their retaining a clearly defined participant-observer status. For a fuller discussion of this see Morant and Warren (2001).

The systematic international review

The highest level of rigour, or '*type I evidence*', as defined in the National Service Framework for Mental Health (Department of Health 1999) is 'at least one good systematic review, including at least one RCT [randomized, controlled trial]'.

A systematic international review was commissioned by the Department of Health in 1998 and published by the Centre for Reviews and Dissemination in 1999. Its title is *Therapeutic community effectiveness: a systematic international review of therapeutic community treatment for people with personality disorders and mentally disordered offenders.*

In addition to the research literature, the reviewers targeted the 'grey' literature, by writing to known TCs, writers, and workers in the field, asking for any published and unpublished research they had and for information about their principles, organization, and practices. The work was conducted in accordance with the guidelines from the Centre for Reviews and Dissemination, using protocols for searching and criteria for describing relevance and quality of identified research. Systematic meta-analysis was only possible for part of the results, since much of the literature was not numerically comparable. They began with 8160 papers, and reduced them to 294 broadly covering the relevant area. 181 TCs named in 38 countries. There were 113 items on outcome studies in a range of settings. Of those 113, 52 were controlled: 10 RCTs, 10 cross-institutional, and 32 other controlled.

A meta-analysis was set up for those 52 with controls, but 23 were excluded because outcome criteria were unclear, raw numbers were not reported, or original sample before attrition was not clearly specified. Odds ratios and 95% confidence intervals were calculated for the remaining 29. Then odds ratios were combined into subsections and overall. The meta-analysis showed strong evidence for effectiveness: across all 29 acceptable studies, the summary odds ratio is 0.57 with an upper 95% confidence interval of 0.61. Other groupings – like all the RCTs, and the three different subgroupings of TCs,

Table 10.1 Results of meta-analysis

Grouping	Odds ratio	95% confidence interval
All studies ($n = 29$)	0.567	0.542–0.614
RCTs only ($n = 8$)	0.464	0.392–0.548
Democratic TCs ($n = 21$)	0.695	0.631–0.769
Secure unit TCs ($n = 22$)	0.544	0.498–0.596
Concept TCs ($n = 8$)	0.318	0.271–0.374

all show strong results with upper confidence intervals well below 1.0. This shows that no one subset of studies was strongly affecting the overall summary result.

Considerable efforts were made to try to avoid publication bias from negative results not being submitted or published – but little grey literature was found. Odds ratios were plotted against sample size in a 'funnel plot'. The lower the sample size, the higher should be the odds ratio reported, giving a funnel-shaped scattergram. The expectation is that a scattergram would reveal blank spots caused by unpublished findings or 'lost' studies. The funnel plot for this meta-analysis does not suggest that this is the case.

The systematic review went on to make several recommendations: for more studies, in different types of TC; for ways of reducing dropout; for a cross-institutional design of British TCs; and for doing another meta-analysis, of concept TCs. One of the RCTs reported ran into major problems with attrition and contamination between the two limbs and a cross-institutional design was suggested as a more promising methodology for future studies, although a more complex methodology and less definitive in results.

The cross-institutional multi-centre study

As a result of this recommendation, a cross-institutional study started in late 1999, addressing four research questions in a 23-centre UK project:

♦ What are the general social backgrounds and psychiatric problems of the patients in this sample of TCs and how do they vary between non-secure, prison, and special hospital wards?

♦ What are the distinctive elements of the TC treatment process in this sample of communities?

♦ How do these treatment elements and their interrelationships with the physical and programme context vary between non-secure, prison, and special hospital wards?

♦ How are elements of the TC treatment process and context related to good outcome for personality disorders?

The methodology is based on multi-level modelling, common in analysis of educational research data – where numerous factors are analysed, for example at the level of individual pupil, class, school, and county.

In the TC study, natural variations in process and outcome over the 23 communities are measured, and the resulting variation in key variables is used to build up a path analytic causal model of the interaction between the constituent parts of the process, and hence their indirect or direct effects on the outcome of treatment. There is also a qualitative element: to refine understanding of the treatment elements, which will be carried out at three representative TCs. It will use both ethnographic observation and semi-structured interviews. The focus will be on the 'career pathway' by which residents and staff make their way through the TC and the different kinds of social reality constructed by residents and staff.

The study will bring together numerous staff from different backgrounds and sectors, using a common protocol for data collection. This will require considerable integration between services and disciplines which normally have little contact with each other. The common analysis of data from such disparate sources will also be an integrative process.

Cost-offset research

A Henderson Hospital study (Dolan *et al.* 1996; Menzies and Clarke 1993) examined a cohort of 29 admissions, of whom 24 were followed up 1 year after treatment. Service usage was assessed for psychiatric inpatient, day-patient, outpatient, and periods of imprisonment. The average cost of treatment at Henderson was £25#461 per patient. Total psychiatric and prison costs for the year before treatment were £335#196, and £31#390 for the year after treatment. This was calculated as an average cost-offset of £12#658 per patient per year, which if maintained would mean the Henderson treatment would pay for itself in just over 2 years.

A more recent study at Francis Dixon Lodge in Leicester (Davies *et al.* 1999) looked at 52 consecutive admissions, and examined histories of inpatient admissions for 3 years before and 3 years after admission to the TC. Psychiatric bed use dropped from 74 to 7.2 days per year for the patients referred from outside the district, and from 36 to 12.1 days per year for those locally based. This represents an average cost offset of £8571 over 3 years following treatment.

A Cassel Hospital cost-offset study (Chiesa *et al.* 1996) compared 26 consecutive admissions to 26 in a post-treatment group. Although, for that and other reasons, it was methodologically less exacting, they estimated a cost offset of £7423 per patient.

The development and use of modified TCs, including outreach elements and treatment in day units, has been proposed. For patients not requiring residential treatment there would be obvious cost benefits and other clinical advantages, provided the

Table 10.2 Comparison of cost-offset studies

	Unit		
	Cassel	FDL	Henderson
Number of patients: pre (post)	26 (26 of 52)	12 (12) out of area (ECR) 40 (35) local	29 (25)
Mean OBDs/yr before admission	31	74 ECR 36 local	71
Mean OBDs/yr after admission	0.2	7.2 ECR 12.1 local	7.5
Diagnosed borderline/emotionally unstable Cost offset	£7423	87% £8571	74% £12#658

ECR = extra contractual referrals, OBD = occupied bed days

treatment was proved to be effective. Similar day programmes have good evidence of effectiveness (Bateman and Fonagy 1999, 2000; Karterud 1998; Piper *et al.* 1993).

Training, skills maintenance, and quality assurance

Training for those working in TCs

Most practitioners working in mental health service TCs have a professional background in nursing, psychiatry, psychology, occupational therapy, or social work. Some are employed as 'social therapists'. The latter tend to be junior staff, often spending an elective period of time before going on to further professional training. For example, it could be viewed as worthwhile experience for psychology graduates before proceeding to clinical psychology training. Some TC workers, including some social therapists, have recognized psychotherapy qualifications, and some TCs require this from their staff. This is particularly the case in day units, where the therapy timetable is more concentrated and only allows a limited time for activities which are not specifically designated as psychotherapy.

Most TCs have some form of in-service educational programme and comprehensive systems for clinical supervision. Many staff in British and Italian TCs have attended brief experiential courses run by the Association of Therapeutic Communities, where a transient 3-day residential community is established for staff to be 'patients'. These have a simple programme of twice-daily community meetings, small groups, and various living–learning activities, as determined by the participants. The experience they have is determined solely by consensus, which is often difficult to achieve. These workshops, together with supervised clinical work in approved communities, theoretical learning, and appropriate personal development, go together to make up an informal portfolio of training experience. This is an integrative model of training in so much as it offers a shared experience of community living for those from different backgrounds and seniority. Although participants often find it rewarding, there are difficulties. For example, senior staff are often uncomfortable 'letting their hair down' in the company of those who are more junior, although this is less problematic if they were hitherto strangers. Also, therapists who are trained in analytic approaches often find the non-opaque way of working uncomfortable; for example, cooking with one's group conductor. There is also a high level of 'rough and tumble' in therapeutic communities – whether for therapy or training – and this can be disorientating for therapists who are used to clear boundaries around weekly outpatient therapy sessions. Everything that happens, from the interactions in the kitchen to negotiation of sleeping arrangements, is available for scrutiny and exploration. Much of the therapeutic leverage of the model is in the subsequent examination of these discomforts.

For many professionals, on-going training is via an apprenticeship model. Training is thereby integrated with clinical work. This integration is effected via the use of pre-groups and after-groups; staff meetings immediately before, and immediately following, the various therapy and activity groups. In pre-groups, relevant clinical and group dynamic aspects are rehearsed prior to the group activity in question. This then influences the mode of co-therapist functioning, all group activity being led by co-therapists rather than a single therapist. After-groups are strategically placed to review what went on during the group, particularly with reference to any goals identified in the pre-group. Also in the after-group there are opportunities to debrief if there have been disturbing or other untoward matters, and to develop an open exchange of views, particularly in relation to the co-therapists' counter-transferences. It is also possible to begin to identify the effects of interpersonal splitting deriving from the interaction with clients. A common example is where some staff feel sympathetic to a resident's material discussed in a community meeting, and others are irritated, bored, or feel negative about it. Discussion of this difference often leads to a new level of understanding about how the resident feels and behaves.

Training opportunities for others in TCs

Therapeutic communities are also a valuable training resource for a wide range of professionals, where a knowledge of small group and large group processes, psychoanalytic ideas, psychotherapy techniques, systems theory, institutional dynamics, user empowerment, crisis management (non-physical and non-chemical), social therapy, or milieu therapy can significantly enhance services. Indeed, they are an ideal place for unimodal trainings to be tried out, balanced, and compared with each other. This is an environment where the differences can be continually monitored and used to enrich the practice of all those participating. For example, simple techniques such as writing contracts are not done as part of many therapies but, in TC groups, practitioners can observe how they work, when they are appropriate, and what effect they have. This can help practitioners develop the flexibility and breadth and that is a hallmark of a mature clinician.

Most TCs welcome day visitors and trainees on longer placements, as staff and members themselves gain benefit by having to explain how they work (without jargon or complex psychological language) and from regularly responding to questions, criticism, and scrutiny from those outside. TC placements are highly valued by trainees doing a general or specialized mental health training, and the relevance of this for dynamic psychotherapy training of specialist registrars has been described by Norton and Fainman 1994.

Conclusions

The essence of an effective therapeutic community is integration both internally and externally. Internally, this is of its constituent treatment elements, psychotherapy and sociotherapy. Externally it involves integration with services, systems, and structures which relate to it in various ways, including training, supervision, clinical governance, and referral networks.

Internally, the treatment elements may derive from a single theory or single professional group. Typically, however, TCs embrace more than one explanatory model and staff teams are multidisciplinary. With such complexity comes the need to pursue integration to guarantee a coordination and harmonization of therapeutic goals. A therapeutic community may be usefully construed as both a modality and method.

Often the TC's clientele has been marginalized or never enjoyed a settled or secure position in society or attachment within the family. As a result many reach adulthood with unintegrated personalities and a sense of social and interpersonal dislocation. For them the TC represents an externally provided set of stabilizing and integrating influences. Through regularly encountering such structuring of time and place an intrapsychic integration (or individualization) of the person can sometimes be achieved. For this to be successful some support before and early on during treatment is required to make the successful transition from the set of external systems into the TC, whether it is a residential or day facility.

Making an attachment to an unfamiliar environment which demands a high level of commitment, but which offers consequent rich rewards of real belonging, asks much of neophyte members. They are frequently puzzled by the explicit expectation to reveal healthy personal, interpersonal, and social functioning. Many resort to former means of self-destructive and maladjusted coping as a defence. There is support, however, for full integration, a sign of acceptance of TC mores.

For those who complete their therapeutic course in a TC, something of the structured environment is internalized. But this is accompanied by a great sense of impending loss close to discharge – the more integrated the personality, the more powerful the conscious experience of the loss. Re-integration into wider society, or perhaps integration for the first time, represents a painful rebirthing process for which external support is often required. For this to occur, attention has to be paid to the complex set of supraordinate systems in which the system of the TC is situated. Placed as they are currently, TCs fulfil an integrative function for a variety of marginalized and alienated sections of society.

Chapter 11

Supportive psychotherapy as an integrative psychotherapy

Susie Van Marle and Jeremy Holmes

Definitions and meanings

Supportive psychotherapy is not easy to define. The Oxford Dictionary's definition of the term 'support' involves 13 phrases, of which several are relevant to supportive therapy; for example, 'to be actively interested in, to endure, tolerate, give strength to and to encourage'. It is important to make a distinction between

+ The supportive component of clinical management, whether medical or psychiatric.
+ The supportive components of all psychotherapies.
+ Supportive psychotherapy as a specific model of treatment.

All three require reliability, consistency, and attentiveness of the practitioner and a well-established therapeutic alliance. The latter has been shown to be the best predictor of good outcome in psychotherapy (Orlinsky and Howard 1986).

The crucial role of support in clinical management is rarely emphasized or defined. In depression of all degrees of severity, reassurance, warmth, encouragement, and engendering a sense of hope can be beneficial for patients (Wilkinson *et al.* 1999) and assist drug compliance. Psychiatrists have begun to examine and value the informal psychotherapeutic content of their contact with patients (Andrews 1993).

Support, directiveness, and expressiveness are found in all psychotherapies in different proportions (Holmes 1996a). Therapies rarely exist in pure culture. Supportive elements are often emphasized when therapeutic models are applied to patients with severe, complex, long-standing difficulties. For example the goodbye letter in cognitive analytic therapy (Ryle 1990) (see Chapter 6) provides ongoing support to patients as it summarizes the therapeutic work, and emphasizes their courage in tackling their difficulties and their personal strengths. In dialectical behaviour therapy (see Chapter 9) Linehan (1993a) utilizes supportive techniques derived from Zen Buddhism based on self-acceptance and mindfulness of the 'present moment'. These are offered alongside cognitive–behaviour therapy to patients with self-harming behaviour to help support the patients' fragile identity. The use of live supervision and the reflecting team can support families while they are engaged in systemic therapy (see Chapter 4). The team can observe what is going on from outside the one-way screen, interject where appropriate, and join the therapeutic encounter. Many different perspectives can be kept in mind and therapists' blind spots can be dealt with by the team – if the therapist is too challenging, the team can offer a corrective supportive comment, thereby momentarily joining with the family in an alliance against the therapist – modelling healthy disagreement for the family. The various techniques of anxiety management which accompany systemic desensitization are examples of supportive components of cognitive–behaviour therapy (see Chapter 3).

Supportive psychotherapy: what is it and who is it for?

Supportive psychotherapy as a specific therapeutic modality often describes two distinct interventions (Bloch 1995). The first is the brief support that can be offered to generally healthy individuals who are suffering from an acute trauma or crisis such as a bereavement or redundancy. For this group of patients there is a great deal of overlap between supportive psychotherapy and Rogerian and other forms of brief counselling. The second is a long-term supportive therapy (LTST) offered to a group of patients with substantial, complex, chronic difficulties for whom it is either the treatment of choice or one of the preferred therapeutic options. LTST will be the focus of this chapter.

LTST has remained the poor and relatively unexplored relation alongside the more well-defined integrative psychotherapy models. LTST has been referred to as a Cinderella (Sullivan 1953), 'stuck at home during the routine psychiatric chores while the more glamorous psychotherapy sisters are away at the ball' (Holmes 1995). The 'chores' resemble the tasks of good enough parenting, where therapists need to offer themselves to vulnerable individuals at a frequency and length of session that is appropriate to the patient and sustainable for the therapist.

LTST's tendency to be defined in negative terms and to be the therapy recommended for patients unsuitable for other forms of psychotherapy has contributed to its poor image and confused identity. The current economic and evidence-based climate demands greater precision about the nature of therapies and interventions.

Rockland (1987) described psychodynamically orientated psychiatry, or 'POST', and Holmes (1992) supportive analytic therapy, or 'SAT', in an attempt to meet this challenge and improve the status of supportive therapy. Psychotherapists continue to acknowledge the limitations of 'pure' psychoanalysis for treating difficult and severely disturbed patients, and the value and comparative efficacy of supportive psychotherapy with this patient group (Kernberg 2000; Wallerstein 1986). In America supportive psychotherapy is usually described from the perspective of, and in contrast with, psychoanalysis. Thus it applies to psychoanalytic treatment which falls short of four or five times a week therapy. Rockland (1989) points to the spacing and timing for supportive psychotherapy sessions as once or twice weekly 50-minute sessions. What he calls supportive therapy would, in Britain, be more likely to be termed psychoanalytic psychotherapy (Holmes 1996c). In Britain supportive psychotherapy usually refers to therapy which is held less than once a week – fortnightly, monthly, or even every 2 months, lasting from 10 to 60 minutes and usually continuing for more than 2 years.

Some psychotherapists conceptualize dynamic and supportive psychotherapies as separate or even incompatible entities. Crown (1988) suggests that 'if it is supportive it cannot be psychotherapy; if it psychotherapy it cannot be supportive' (p. 267). Kernberg (2000) distinguishes between three different types of psychoanalytic treatment modalities: psychoanalysis, psychoanalytic psychotherapy, and supportive psychotherapy, each with their own particular aims and techniques. In contrast with this categorical classification, some favour a dimensional expressive–supportive continuum, tailored to meet the patients' needs (Gabbard 1994). This corresponds with Parry and Richardson's (NHS 1996) distinction between 'Type B' therapies, in which a variety of different psychological interventions is blended to meet a particular patient's needs, and 'Type C', or model-based therapy, in which a clearly defined method is used (see Chapter 1). In Gabbard's dimensional taxonomy, the interventions made by the therapist can be placed in seven categories along this continuum (Gabbard 1994, pp. 97–100):

♦ interpretation;
♦ confrontation;
♦ clarification;
♦ entitlement to elaborate;
♦ empathetic validation;
♦ advice and praise;
♦ affirmation.

He suggests that the majority of psychotherapeutic processes contain all of these interventions at some time during the course of treatment. Whether a therapy is classified as primarily expressive or supportive depends on which interventions predominate. Luborsky (1984) conceived of psychotherapies as a number of types ranging from supportive to expressive, with an intermediate expressive–supportive or supportive–expressive subtype.

Patients with long-standing unipolar or bipolar depression, schizophrenia, and anxiety and mood disorders related to chronic physical illness require a long-term therapeutic relationship and supportive therapy in a variety of care settings. In view of this Tyrer (1995) contests the restricted use of supportive therapy, pointing out that thousands of therapists are providing something like supportive therapy every day of the week throughout the country. This work is inherently eclectic, and draws on many different therapeutic traditions – or none! Many staff will not have any specific psychotherapeutic training. Vague, confused, and possibly unhelpful long-term relationships are not uncommon. Tyrer (1995) warns that the patients with anxious personalities are likely to rely heavily on the therapist, and sometimes doctors need to be helped to disentangle themselves from these enmeshed relationships which a 'supportive' approach may appear to sanction. Typically this occurs when patients with, for example, dependent and borderline personality disorders are taken on for long-term therapy during a crisis without a thorough assessment of their difficulties, needs, and treatment aims.

A quest for a definitive stance on LTST may not be either practical or desirable. Instead, for each patient with chronic, complex difficulties who is assessed and considered suitable for LTST, the therapeutic aims and techniques need to be outlined at the outset and revisited throughout the therapeutic encounter. Therapists from different professional trainings may use core tools and techniques but also borrow from different traditions to achieve their aims.

Indications for supportive psychotherapy

LTST is recommended for the psychological care of patients with chronic problems when there is limited chance of radical change (Rockland 1993), particularly with some patients suffering from

- ◆ psychotic illness;
- ◆ intractable personality disorders and long-standing neurotic and somatoform disorders;
- ◆ chronic physical illness.

In general it seems that the more disturbed the patient, the more important supportive therapy is likely to be. Horowitz and colleagues (Horowitz and Marmac 1984) studied the impact of supportive therapy and dynamic therapy on a group of bereaved patients. Patients with 'weak ego strength' tended to do better in supportive therapy whilst more integrated individuals fared better with a dynamic approach. Roberts (1992) considered the life narratives of patients with chronic psychosis. He found that patients with elaborate delusional systems functioned better both clinically and socially than those whose thought processes were more fragmented. He suggested that the latter group may require psychotherapeutic strategies aimed to support them rather than designed to eliminate the delusions.

Wallerstein (1986) followed up a group of severely disturbed, chiefly borderline patients, in a 25-year follow-up study in the Menninger project. Although few of the sample did particularly well, supportive therapy was, on the whole, more effective than psychoanalysis for most of these patients, and many in psychoanalysis had to be transferred to supportive therapy in the course of treatment.

Kernberg's (2000) description of supportive therapy practised by some analysts suggests a different stance, vis-à-vis psychoanalysis and psychoanalytic psychotherapy. He recommends supportive therapy as a treatment for patients with severe personality disorders who are unable to participate in psychoanalytic psychotherapy but have at least a sufficient capacity for commitment to the arrangements of ongoing treatment and an absence of severe antisocial factors.

Supportive psychotherapy seems particularly appropriate for a small group of patients who have severe long-standing psychiatric, psychological, medical, and social difficulties and whose often unrewarding use of resources is disproportionate to their numbers. Many have had severe disruption in their personality development, suffering considerable stresses in childhood and adulthood. There have often been frequent admissions to psychiatric and medical hospital beds and the patients can be frequent attenders in outpatient clinics and GP surgeries. Numerous psychotropic drugs are prescribed and they are often referred for various psychological interventions and for medical interventions, investigations, and opinions. Many have been diagnosed as suffering from borderline personality disorder, other personality disorders and/or somatization disorders. Brief therapies are often tried; sometimes with good but short-lived result. Long-term psychoanalytic therapy in this group runs the danger of provoking regression and destructive dependency and lead to 'malignant alienation' (Watts and Morgan 1994). This can lead to rejection by the staff involved and can increase the risk of self-harm and suicide. The patients are sometimes described as 'heart sink', 'black hole', or 'thick file' patients in general practice. They are difficult to manage and provoke feelings of exasperation and anxiety in their families, friends, employers, and the multiple agencies who are involved. The aim of LTST with these people, particularly if backed up by a well-communicating network of support which involves the patient's family doctor and attendance at a day centre or another community setting, is to reduce the inappropriate use of services and provide containment for the patient, their families, and the network of support.

There are other patients who are less disturbed and disturbing who can benefit from LTST. Axis 1 diagnosis is one factor but an assessment of the patient's coping strategies, maturity of defences, and psychological mindedness are equally important in deciding on LTST for a particular patient. Decisions about embarking upon supportive therapy will be made on clinical grounds based on the patient's diagnosis, personality, and the psychotherapeutic resources available.

As a form of integrated care, LTST is particularly relevant to patients with complex chronic conditions because it emphasizes healthy communication between staff in different care settings and agencies and allows for the long-term consideration of the biological, psychological, and social components of the patient's care.

The cornerstones of supportive therapy

The crucial ingredients of LTST are time, adaptability, and an implicit or explicit contract or therapeutic frame which allows the therapy to continue without the therapist feeling either trapped or disengaged. Just as parents live alongside their children and facilitate their development within a complex web of interactions, therapists providing LTST provide a real relationship and a flexible approach that can adapt to the patients' needs, over many months and years. Like the painter Howard Hodgkin, who often paints bold colourful frames around his paintings to protect and offset the emotions he is trying to convey, the therapist in LTST needs a clear boundary, and a good sense of humour if his or her work is to be successful.

Many supportive encounters with patients begin without a framework; for example, in the GP's surgery, the mental health resource centre, or inpatient unit, when someone is in crisis or suffering from acute mental illness. Professionals often lack the time, skill, and space required to complete an assessment of the patient's complex, chronic difficulties and the task can be even more demanding if the patient is not known by the GP or the psychiatric team. Staff working in primary and secondary care can find themselves within a long-term supportive relationship without the four essential preconditions of effective work:

♦ A multi-axial psychosocial and, where relevant, medical *assessment* of the patient's difficulties.

♦ A clear view of the *aims* of supportive interventions.

♦ An *integrative model* of techniques and tasks of LTST.

♦ *Support* for the therapist.

Multi-axial thinking and classification

The standard approach to medical diagnosis which aims to establish a defined condition with a specific aetiology, prognosis, and treatment is not well suited to patients with chronic complex difficulties (Turner 1998). However Tantum (1995) argues that with more disturbed and unwell patients, therapeutic errors are more likely to occur if diagnoses have not been made. Before embarking on LTST a multi-axial appraisal is essential, as a guide to therapy, and as a framework within which integrative interventions can be considered. The DSM-IV multi-axial framework modified by Hartman and Rozewien (1996) is particularly important before embarking on LTST. Each of the five categories needs to be carefully considered:

♦ diagnosis;
♦ personality and developmental factors;
♦ constitutional factors;

♦ environmental factors (both past and present);

♦ current level of functioning.

This approach to classification encourages the clinician to think about how the five axes interact with and influence each other. Personality, developmental, and environmental factors often play a crucial role in the presentation of patients with complex, chronic, psychotic and non-psychotic disorders and require careful attention, alongside the biochemical and genetic factors. Many patients have had emotional, behavioural, and educational difficulties in childhood and been subjected to different forms of abuse, neglect, and traumatic loss. Some have also had significant physical illnesses.

Multi-axial classification can serve as a useful vehicle for communication between professionals if it can be adapted to meet their different backgrounds, roles, and responsibilities – another aspect of integration. With the increasing pressure on primary care to provide mental health services, patients with complex chronic difficulties will continue to cause considerable concern to the busy GP. Turner (1998) suggests that GPs should demand better support in reviewing and managing such patients. This would include access to consultation–liaison services which would include thorough multi-faceted psycho-medico-social assessments.

Therapeutic aims

In LTST the therapeutic aims are rarely discussed. Frank's (1982) 'remoralization, remediation and rehabilitation' are core aims which continue to be relevant throughout each long-term relationship. Remoralization via ongoing emotional support can help patients reduce their symptoms and deal with some of their current life problems. Therapy is also concerned with refocusing the patient's coping skills to achieve some remediation of their symptoms. It may take months or years of rehabilitative input to address, challenge, and if possible prevent, their long-standing maladaptive behaviours and interpersonal problems.

Psychoeducation is recognized as an important goal for patients with severe psychosis but is equally important with, for example, somatization disorder, chronic dysthymia, and depression and personality disorders. Helping patients to gain some understanding of their diagnosis and difficulties, to learn to modulate and minimize the stress, and to prevent and manage the relapses are important goals of LTST. Kernberg (2000) suggests that supportive therapy provided by psychoanalysts for some patients with severe personality disorders does not aim to achieve structural intrapsychic change but to facilitate maturation of the defences and better adaption to external and internal intrapsychic needs. LTST shares these aims for a range of patients with chronic complex difficulties. For some the aims are about fostering growth, separation, and individuation, while for others they are about attempting to prevent deterioration and assist maintenance and survival.

Shared and integrated care, which is an important function of LTST, aims to provide improved patient containment with a reduction in the total health-care cost of patients who may have been heavy users of NHS resources, and a reduction in the burden of stress among the professions involved in the patients' long-term management.

The methods and techniques of supportive psychotherapy

The 'real' relationship; therapist transparency

Establishing and maintaining a real relationship or therapeutic alliance with the patient in LTST is an essential part of the framework. A passive, opaque stance is avoided and the therapist tries to provide an honest, open relationship combining warmth, empathy, and firmness.

The sessions may start with a question from the therapist: 'How's your month been?' or 'It's a tough phase for you.' Alternatively, the patient may begin: 'The month has gone past very slowly.' Therapists vary in their amount of self-disclosure and this will also vary with different patients, but it is important to consider the possible impact of these disclosures on the patient and the alliance.

Statements like 'It's difficult out there', 'Adolescence can be a pain', and 'We all need space to gather our thoughts', can convey implicit revelation but if a therapist gives details of life in their family this may lead to confusion and blurring of the boundaries.

The therapist in LTST in general is more prepared to answer questions than is usual in psychoanalytic therapy and to present themselves as a real person in the patient's life. For example, when the therapist is planning some leave this is dealt with in an open and upfront way. The possible impact of the separation is acknowledged and the therapist and patient consider how the patient might cope during a break or seek help and support from others. Although the therapist does at times become the object of misperception and projection, this is not encouraged by the transparency and the realness of the therapist, which serves to maintain the therapeutic alliance, create a sense of shared humanity, and involve the patient in the joint therapeutic work.

Holding and containing

Holding is a central function of LTST. The therapist serves as a secure container for the patients' anxieties, experiences, and feelings. By holding the patient in mind within and between the sessions, therapists can create a stabilizing structure in the patient's life. One patient with borderline personality disorder referred to the session as the place 'I sort out my monthly baggage', while another with chronic fatigue syndrome and dysthymia thought that the 2-monthly sessions became her space to tell 'the latest chapters in my life'.

Often it is the concerted action of the multidisciplinary team rather than an individual therapist which provides ongoing containment for the patient. When the patient is confused, fragmented, and acutely disturbed, the primary therapist may need to link with members of the network of support to review the understanding of the patient's difficulties and the management options. These might include extra sessions, changes in medication, home treatment, inpatient admission, and/or team case review.

The controversy about physical holding in LTST continues. Pedder (1986) argues that the need for non-sexual attachment which is underlined in attachment theory makes touching and holding less problematic than analytic theory would suggest. Some therapists may choose to shake hands with the patient at the end of the sessions, whilst others will have a different style and use words like 'Take care' to mark the separation at the end of the session, convey warmth and concern, and to hand some responsibility back to the patient in the gaps. Physical touching should always be undertaken by the therapist in full awareness of the possible meanings and implications for the patient – sexual, false reassurance, a way of diverting anger, etc. Therapy almost always demands a light touch, but touch should but not be entered into lightly.

The holding environment required for LTST relies on a consistent, reliable setting for the therapeutic encounter. A regular time and place can provide a stable structure for the work and give the patient a sense of knowing where they stand on certain days of the month. The length and spacing of sessions needs careful consideration bearing in mind the patient's mental state, the nature of their difficulties, the therapeutic aims, the network of support, and what can realistically and consistently be provided by the staff.

Transference and counter-transference

LTST demands an ongoing awareness of transference and counter-transference.

Positive transference is actively nurtured in this approach and not interpreted by the therapist, but he or she has to remain alert to strong idealized transference patterns. Sometimes the therapist accepts the idealized transference and safely contains the patient's unmanageable feelings and impulses. At other times the therapist gently confronts the patient with his/her personal limits and boundaries when, for example, there is a request for an extra session, home visits, or for support for the patient in legal proceedings.

Unhealthy destructive interactions or behaviour which occur within the therapeutic alliance and within the patient's relationship with others are frequently considered. The patient is encouraged to understand the conscious reasons for these patterns and to modify them. Kernberg (2000) refers to the reduction and the 'export' of transference (i.e. keeping it at bay within the rest of the patient's network, rather than addressing it directly in the therapy itself) as a major treatment technique in the supportive therapy provided by some analysts. Negative reactions frequently occur with some patients in

LTST. The therapist has to receive the patient's frustration, anger, distress, and disappointment when in the spaced sessions they are confronted with the absences, the limitations of therapy, and their own personal limitations and weaknesses. Mistakes and misunderstandings need to be handled with honesty and tact, with therapists owning up to their own contribution and some of their own imperfections.

Monitoring the counter-transference is essential as the risk of acting out in LTST is greater than in more formal therapies. The therapist has to consider whether to offer an extra session or ask the patient to come at the usual time, when to ask the patient to contact the GP, and when to contact the support network directly. There are also important decisions about when and how to make self-revelations. These choices are often difficult and therapists need to consider how much these decisions are influenced by their own needs and how much by those of the patient.

Specific communication tools

The background phenomena described above are informed by dynamic understanding. The integrative nature of LTST is evident from the mixture of cognitive, systemic, and sometimes psychoanalytic interventions which it deploys. The aim is always to help the patient experience understanding and validation, and find adaptive compromises and solutions to ongoing problems, conflicts, and difficulties in living. These interventions differ from standard technique only in the fact that they *are* a mixture, and the style has to be adapted to infrequent and often abbreviated sessions.

Encouragement to elaborate The therapist encourages the patient to expand on a topic he/she has brought into the session. The therapist may enquire 'So what actually happened before you stormed out?', or 'Tell me about your new boss.'

Empathic validation The therapist shows the patient that he/she is attuned to the patient's internal state. Validating comments such as 'You feel desperately alone when your daughter does not get in touch', or 'No wonder you are furious when your parents don't hear what you have to say.'

Praise/advice These interventions aim to encourage certain activities, help the patient make sense of their experiences, and manage themselves and their difficulties in a more adaptive way. Praise provides positive reinforcement for certain behaviours and actions. To a patient with a long history of altercations at work and in her school, the therapist commented 'You did really well handling your anger during that disagreement.' The patient replied 'For once I didn't get sucked in.' Advice involves the therapist giving suggestions about how the patient could act or behave.

Social interventions or creative activities may be encouraged. The therapist may say 'Have you thought about putting some of your feelings in a diary, or picking up your paint-brush again?'

Praise and advice can be useful tools but they need to be carefully and judiciously used as they can encourage unhealthy dependence and fail to nurture the patient's capacity to make decisions and find their own personal solutions.

Affirmation This intervention involves words or gestures to support a patient's comments such as 'Yes, I see what you are saying', or a nod or a smile after a patient has begun to acknowledge that angry feelings precede an episode of sulking.

Clarification and explanations Negative connotations and assumptions are clarified when they arise in LTST. The patient is encouraged to look at events and emotions that triggered or reinforced negative cognitive assumptions, and to develop a more realistic view of themselves and others. Patients sometimes describe family myths and these are clarified; for example, one patient commented 'In my family it's sissy to enjoy the arts', and another 'We never needed help from outsiders.'

LTST encourages patients to regularly clarify what is going on in key areas of their life with, for example, their parents, partners, friends, and within their support network.

Explanations, which are in some ways akin to interpretations, but are perhaps delivered in a more didactic fashion, try to explain to the patient in a straightforward way what is going on for them and why they are behaving in a certain way. To patients who regularly cut themselves or enter inappropriate sexual relationships, the therapist may point out (Higgitt and Fonagy 1992) that their behaviour may be related to their neediness, sensitivity to rejection, anger and guilt, or an attempt to master feelings of impotence and helplessness. The patient may or may not want to consider these explanations. Some initially reject them but are more ready to reconsider them when similar patterns arise during the long-term therapeutic relationship.

Confrontation Confrontation is often not classified as a supportive intervention as it challenges the patient to address something that is being avoided or minimized. The therapist suggests denied or suppressed feelings and points out how the patient's behaviour affects others or the connection between feelings and actions. Although the intervention threatens the patient's status quo, it can be experienced as supportive by the patient if it is delivered tactfully and appropriately within a strong working alliance. It is an essential tool in LTST, and a core component of therapeutic work with patients with dysfunctional interpersonal relationships who exhibit self-destructive behaviour.

Confrontation can help the patient acknowledge internal experiences and distinguish what is real from what is not real and what is inside themselves from what belongs to others.

Environmental interventions LTST aims to modulate and minimize the stress on the patient and to help him or her find new ways of coping. Environmental interventions are often utilized and encouraged, and may be initiated in the following ways:

♦ The therapist may recommend that the patient contacts friends, voluntary organizations, solicitors, GPs, and other members of their supportive network (cf. interpersonal therapy, Chapter 8).

♦ The therapist may see members of the patient's family or supportive network at the end of sessions or at an additional time. The patient is kept informed about these communications and, where appropriate, takes part in joint discussions with, for example, a partner or their CPN.

When the family member or professional involved is seen, he/she is given the opportunity to discuss his/her framing of the patient's difficulties and how he/she reacts when the patient becomes distressed, disturbed, and disturbing. The therapist acknowledges the help and support provided by family members and others and gently suggests measures which might be helpful (cf. systemic couple therapy for depression, Chapter 4). The therapist or other members of the network of support may organize a case conference to clarify the nature of the patient's difficulties, the therapeutic aims, the roles of different professionals, and the patient/staff dynamics. These may be particularly useful when there is a confusion of roles developing and the staff are finding it hard to contain the patient.

Handling defences

In LTST it is essential that the therapist carefully considers and respects the patient's defensive system which, as Vaillant (1997) suggests, assists survival by creatively rearranging the sources of conflict. He compares the defensive system to the immune system. Just as the immune system protects the body, the defences filter pain and allow self-soothing (Holmes 2001). The patient is provided with a variety of illusions which help him/her manage conflicts and cope with his/her life. The therapist attempts to nurture more adaptive combinations of impulse and defence within a supportive relationship. Rockland (1989) suggests that in supportive therapy therapists needs to 'ally' themselves with the patient's defences.

Tuning in to the patient's defensive maturation level can be particularly useful when a patient is disturbed and utilizing psychotic or immature defences like denial and projection. At these times the therapist attempts metaphorically to 'hold' the patient without assaulting the defences which have served to assist their survival. Therapists have different ways of managing these moments but the difficult phase may be acknowledged by the therapist and the 'being there' function of the therapist may be underlined. The patient may be reminded that these moments have been survived in the past. Precipitating factors like a current bereavement or a court case may be acknowledged, medication may be recommended, an extra session may be offered, or contact made with the patient's GP or psychiatrist. When the crisis is past it may be possible to try to understand this phase dynamically, and to consider other less self-destructive defences.

Learning to cope

The task of helping patients learn to cope with their complex long-standing difficulties is a core aim of LTST, requiring the instillation of hope into the patient by the therapist. The therapist conveys this hope by the mere act of offering the patient supportive sessions and giving them the experience of having someone alongside who is attempting to understand, tolerate, and contain them. The patient in LTST learns from observing and being with the therapist during the sessions, and from being coped with by the therapist when he or she contacts them between sessions, and in turn may be able to symbolize and internalize this coping function.

Holmes (1996) discusses how, in LTST, the therapists sometimes encourage 'benign projection'. The patient is told they are not to blame for their serious mental illness and that their suffering is real. This technique can be useful to some patients who suffer from severe psychosis, personality disorders, and neuroses. It may also be a useful technique in the long-term management of patients with somatization disorder. While the therapist encourages the patient to project some of their suffering onto their genes, their illness, their chemicals, and the wiring in their brain, attempts are made to help the patients live with their lives and cope with the relapses and the difficult phases in their lives.

If patients have some capacity to utilize what Vaillant (1992) describes as mature defences, for example, suppression, altruism, sublimation, anticipation, and humour, these can be reinforced in LTST as they can enhance a patient's coping strategies. Anticipation, for example, can be a useful defence for patients who have, for instance, bipolar disorder and borderline personality organization, because management is easier if the patient is tuned in to the early warning signs, the precipitating factors, and a relapse prevention plan. When humorous moments arise in LTST these can be therapeutic as they allow for expression of feelings without causing discomfort to others. Humour can make life more tolerable and help the individual face reality and be in some contact with their creative and spontaneous selves. These moments may be rare and cannot be planned for. They are more likely to occur after a strong therapeutic alliance has been established.

Psycho-education

Helping a patient make some sense of their experiences and complex psycho-social difficulties, and to manage and cope are important aims of LTST which require a psycho-educational approach. Kolb (1993) suggests that a 'large part of supportive therapy involves using small windows of opportunity to undertake therapy surreptitiously, slowly and carefully in very small manageable doses for very vulnerable patients'. The therapist has a role as a facilitating observer or educator who carefully considers what and how much the patient is ready to receive. Within LTST there is ample opportunity to help the patient and their carers consider the early warning signs and relapse prevention strategies, and to foster healthier care-seeking behaviour.

The therapist's personality and need for support

The fourth border of the therapeutic framework is the therapist's personality and the support needed for long-term supportive work. The personal characteristics required by professionals providing LTST have been touched on in the previous section. Warmth, empathy, compassion, consistency, honesty, openness, and firmness are all required within the therapeutic alliance. Holmes (1988, 1996c) suggests that LTST places a powerful burden on the therapist's narcissism as he or she has to learn to accept patients as they are, and help patients accept themselves and their reality. The therapist needs to be realistic about modest aims, the time-scale, and the frequency and length of sessions he/she can manage. The patient often expresses rage and disappointment, which as Kohut (1972) has demonstrated in his work with borderline patients, have initially to be accepted rather than challenged or interpreted. These and other feelings, like guilt, fear, and impotence are often experienced by the therapist, who then has the difficult task of sorting out and managing the boundaries between him/herself and the patient. It is essential that therapists develop some awareness of their professional and personal limitations and of the impact of their communication and behaviour on patients. Long-term contact with disturbing and disturbed patients is demanding and potential hazards should be kept in mind. An excessively supportive stance can tend to infantilize the patient and foster unhealthy, entrenched, dependent relationships which discourage the expression of negative experiences and feelings. There is always the risk of counter-transference acting out and the pattern of confusion, disputes between staff, blurred boundaries, stalemate, discharges, and re-referrals is common with many patients with chronic complex problems. Staff involved in LTST need to acknowledge their difficulties and seek help via ongoing consultation, liaison and assessment services, supervision, and support so that they can think about what is going on within their long-term therapeutic alliance. Often support is devalued within the mental health team and may be offered by the most inexperienced or least professionally qualified member (e.g. 'outreach workers') for whom opportunities for supervision and personal development may be restricted.

Clinical example

Mrs E. was a 57-year-old woman with a long history of depression and recent onset of severe panic disorder when she was referred to the psychotherapy service. In the previous year she had had two admissions to general medical wards for episodes of tachycardia, which were later found to be symptoms of panic disorder. She had a 30-year history of moderately severe rheumatoid arthritis and needed sticks to walk.

The GP found it difficult to manage her panic attacks and depression despite medication and cognitive–behavioural therapy intervention.

During an extended assessment some of the key aspects of her history were:

♦ An unsuccessful operation on her feet 18 months prior to the referral.
♦ Marital disharmony and minimal support from her husband.
♦ Early loss and separation. Her father died when she was three and she was evacuated, having to leave her mother when she was eight years old.
♦ An unempathic mother who 'always coped'.
♦ Thirty years of rheumatoid arthritis with several acute exacerbations, chronic pain, and diminished mobility and socialization.

Mrs E. was seen for four assessment sessions at monthly intervals and then for 17 supportive sessions at between 2- and 4-monthly intervals for 6 years. The aims were about

♦ minimizing her symptoms and the admissions for panic disorder;
♦ improving the quality of her life;
♦ diminishing the stress on the GP.

Her lifelong tendency to 'grin and bear it' and 'to suffer in silence' became an important focus in the early sessions and during the 6 years of therapy. Just as her mother never complained when she was left to rear 11 children with minimal finances, when she started each therapy session by the role reversal that is so typical of this sort of patient, saying 'Are you alright?' and 'How have you been?', we began to consider her assumption that others will be absent, unavailable, and fail to validate her experiences or contain her. She was helped to describe her painful and unpleasant experiences before, during, and after the operation. She discussed her fears and difficulty in expressing feelings. It was put to her that her panic disorder might be her attempt to communicate her underlying anger towards those who have failed to care and 'be there' for her, and she expressed considerable relief (a non-transference interpretation 'permitted' in LTST). She was terrified not just of dying but of not existing while in a state of panic – which seemed to relate to her mother's failure to acknowledge any weakness or difficulty – and as she became more aware of her angry feelings the attacks subsided and she was better able to cope with her own depressive phases. She began to acknowledge and express her anger, pain, and disappointment about the operation, her reduced mobility, the years of depression, rheumatoid arthritis, her unhappy marriage, and her minimal social life. She also stopped her defensive grinning and began to consider her valuable relationships with her children and grandchildren (cf. interpersonal therapy, Chapter 8, which tends to stress the positive aspects of the social network).

Throughout the 6 years, the psychotherapist regularly liaised with the GP and the consultant rheumatologist, particularly during exacerbations of her rheumatoid arthritis and her depressive phases. Soon after the commencement of therapy, she decided to ask for a second opinion about her operation and after a few years she was awarded compensation. With the money she received she decided to sell her house and move to accommodation and a community which were better equipped for her needs. This was located in another part of the country. At the last session she expressed her concerns and sadness about leaving her network of support (note the therapist is not necessarily centre-stage in LTST) but also her pleasure in making the move while she was still fit to do so.

Theorizing supportive psychotherapy

There is no clear consensus about the theoretical basis of LTST. Most would agree that its construction requires the integration of several conceptual building blocks, including

+ attachment theory (Holmes 2001) the therapist as a secure base;
+ ego psychology's (Vaillant 1977) approach to defences;
+ a developmental model (Bergman and Mahler 1991) where a slow maturation may be observed over many years; and
+ systemic thinking, bringing the care network into the consultation as needed, together with a narrative approach (White and Epston 1990) helping patients to tell and own their story.

Unlike conceptually integrative therapies, such as cognitive analytic therapy (Chapter 6) and dialectical behaviour therapy (Chapter 9), supportive therapy is truly eclectic, drawing on a mixture of common sense, Rogerian counselling, cognitive–behavioural strategies, systemic approaches, and psychoanalysis (Crown 1988; Chapter 1). How practitioners build a theoretical basis for their supportive work will be determined by personal preferences, training and clinical experience, and exposure to different practical and theoretical models. LTST has been described as lacking a single theoretical basis, being rather like a 'a shell program' (Pinskner 1994) or umbrella framework (Chapter 1) that fits over most psychotherapies. Another image could be that of the delta, a confluence of different theoretical components that lead to the eternal sea.

An evidence base for supportive therapy?

The evaluation of LTST as practised within the NHS is essential and requires the attention of clinicians and researchers, because there are many difficulties that are not easily overcome.

It is a flexible, non-manualized form of therapy which is practised in different ways and at different levels by a wide variety of professionals. It is applied to a range of patients with chronic complex psycho-social difficulties. The lack of clear definition and the heterogeneous patient group pose enormous problems for those committed to evaluation.

The long-term nature of the work requires the financial support and the resources for the clinical work and the evaluation. There are problems of internal validity, as most patients in LTST experience important life events external to the therapeutic alliance. Many of the patients are managed by a network of professionals who provide medication and/or support. A meaningful evaluation of LTST will need to consider these factors.

Roth and Fonagy (1996) point out that the natural history of many health problems is both chronic and (in some cases) cyclic, and it is against this background that measures of improvement should be judged. They suggest that in patients with chronic complex difficulties, psychological interventions may not be 'curative' although they may improve an individual's adaptation, reduce the symptoms, and improve quality of life. These are the important aims in LTST and it may be useful to consider the following during long-term audit.

Measuring disability The measurement of the absence or presence of symptoms may have limited use in patients with chronic complex difficulties. Roth and Fonagy (1996) suggest that with patients who have chronic relapsing conditions, it may be more appropriate to judge improvement by the speed of improvement or the latency to relapse. What is needed is a much broader concept which captures the multifaceted psycho-bio-social difficulties of many of the patients seen in LTST. Measuring the patient's disability is more useful and relevant to this patient population and involves looking at, for example, a psychological dimension, coping skills, interpersonal relationships, and the patient's physical health and social circumstances, before, during, and after LTST. Monitoring a patient's quality of life is of particular relevance to patients seen in LTST.

Level of defensive maturation LTST aims to facilitate some maturation of defences and it may be useful to monitor the predominant defences utilized by the patient throughout the long-term alliance alongside the life events which they experience.

Quality of life/patient satisfaction Self-reports on quality of life and patient satisfaction of LTST can be monitored every few months.

Utilization of services Many patients seen in LTST have been high users of NHS resources prior to coming into treatment. Audit of inpatient days, GP consultations, and numbers of referrals to secondary services, alongside an estimation of the resources which are involved in the LTST, would reveal whether there has been a reduction in the total health-care cost of the patient.

Stress in the patient's network of support Some patients with complex chronic difficulties cause considerable stress to their carers and in their professional network of support. LTST aims to reduce this stress and help the network cope better with the problems and needs of such patients. It would be useful to evaluate if these aims are achieved in LTST.

Despite the inherent difficulties in evaluating LTST, its practitioners need to develop simple practical relevant methods of auditing their therapeutic input to patients whose management often requires long-term planning. Roth and Fonagy (1996) compare the monitoring and continual contact required by many chronic patients treated in secondary and tertiary care to that required by patients with diabetes.

Conclusion

Where does LTST belong as an integrative therapy? Unlike hybrid therapies such as cognitive analytic therapy and interpersonal therapy, it does not explicitly bring together elements from other known therapies into a free-standing psychotherapeutic treatment. LTST is a pycho-social therapy which combines dynamic, systemic, cognitive–behavioural, and psycho-educational elements. There is also considerable overlap between different integrative therapies. Gabbard (1994, p. 231) refers to interpersonal therapy (Chapter 8) as dynamically informed supportive therapy. Some of the tools and techniques used in LTST are similar to those outlined in psychodynamic interpersonal therapy (Chapter 7), and although Guthrie *et al.* (Guthrie and Moorey 1998) describe brief psychodynamic interpersonal therapy with some patients with severe psychiatric illness, they also refer to long-term individual work which can continue over several years.

LTST fits well as a Type B therapy in the NHS classification (NHS 1996), tailored to the specific needs and aptitudes of patients with chronic complex difficulties and reliant on the therapist's capacity to integrate different elements of technique or theory in their work.

LTST can also be conceptualized as a form of chronic disease management or integrated care for some patients with chronic complex difficulties.

As suggested, evaluations are needed to show whether there are clinical benefits and cost savings and to compare these outcomes with those derived from more intensive and model-based interventions.

LTST challenges Hunter's (2000) concern that 'the NHS has largely failed to exploit its innate strength and to perform as a whole system' – a thoroughly integrative aspiration – as it nurtures relationships, healthy communication, and collaborative care. Within mental health it challenges therapists to set aside rivalry and exclusiveness, to search for common factors, and to adapt their methods to the needs of the severely ill patients who form the bulk of mental health practice in the public sector – aims which also embody the overall spirit of this book.

References

Ablon, J. S. and Jones, E. E. (1998) How expert clinicians' prototypes of an ideal treatment correlate with outcome in psychodynamic and cognitive behavioural therapy. *Psychotherapy Research*, 8, 71–83.

Ablon, J. S. and Jones, E. E. (1999) Psychotherapy process in the National Institute of Mental Health Treatment of Depression Collaborative Research Program. *Journal of Consulting and Clinical Psychology*, 67 (1), 64–75.

Ackerman, N. W. (1966) *Treating the troubled family*. New York: Basic Books.

Agazarian, Y. (1998) *Systems-centered therapy for groups*. New York: Guilford Press.

Aitken, R. (1982) *Taking the path of Zen*. San Francisco: North Point Press.

Albeniz, A. and Holmes, J. (1996) Psychotherapy integration: its implications for psychiatry. *British Journal of Psychiatry*, 169, 563–570.

Andersen, T. (1987) The reflecting team. *Family Process*, 26, 415–428.

Anderson, C. and Sawin, D. B. (1983) Enhancing responsiveness in mother–infant interaction. *Infant Behavior and Development*, 6, 361–368.

Anderson, H. and Goolishian, H. A. W. (1986) Problem determined systems: toward transformation in family therapy. *Journal of Strategic and Family Therapy*, 4, 1–13.

Andrews, G. (1993) The essential psychotherapies. *British Journal of Psychiatry*, 162, 447–451.

Arkowitz, H. (1989) The role of theory in psychotherapy integration. *Journal of Integrative and Eclectic Psychotherapy*, 8, 8–16.

Arkowitz, H. (1992) *Integrative theories of therapy*. Washington, DC: American Psychological Association.

Asen, E. (1997) From Milan to Milan: true tales about the structural Milan approach. *Human Systems*, 8, 39–42.

Asen, E. (1999) *The limits of technique in family therapy*. London: Whurr.

Asen, K. E. (1995) *Family therapy for everyone: how to get the best out of living together*. London: BBC Books.

Asen, K. E. and Tomson, P. (1992) *Family solutions in family practice*. Lancaster: Quay.

Asen, K. E., Stein, R., Stevens, A., *et al*. (1981) A day unit for families. *Journal Family Therapy*, 4, 345–358.

Aveline, M. (2001) 'Innovative contemporary psychotherapies' (editorial). *Advances in Psychiatric Treatment*, 7, 241–242.

Barkham, M. and Hobson, R. F. (1990) Exploratory therapy in two-plus-one sessions. A single case study. *British Journal of Psychotherapy*, 6, 89–100.

Barkham, M., Guthrie, E., Hardy, G., *et al*. (in press) *Psychodynamic interpersonal therapy*. London: Sage.

Barley, W. D., Buie, S. E., Peterson, E. W., *et al*. (1993) The development of an inpatient cognitive-behavioural treatment programme for borderline personality disorder. *Journal of Personality Disorders*, 7, 232–241.

Basseches, M. (1984) *Dialectical thinking and adult development*. Northvale, New Jersey: Ablex.

Bateman, A. (1997) Borderline personality disorder and psychotherapeutic psychiatry: an integrative approach. *British Journal of Psychotherapy*, 13 (4), 489–498.

Bateman, A. and Fonagy, P. (1999) The effectiveness of partial hospitalization in the treatment of borderline personality disorder – a randomised controlled trial. *American Journal of Psychiatry*, 156, 1563–1569.

Bateman, A. W. and Fonagy, P. (2000) Effectiveness of psychotherapeutic treatment of personality disorder. *British Journal of Psychiatry*, 177, 138–143.

Bateman, A. W. and Fonagy, P. (2001) Treatment of borderline personality disorder with psychoanalytically oriented partial hospitalisation: an 18-month follow-up. *American Journal of Psychiatry*, 158, 36–42.

Bateman, A. and Holmes, J. (2001) Psychotherapy training for general psychiatrists. *Psychiatric Bulletin*, 25, 124–125.

Bateson, G. (1972) *Steps to an ecology of the mind*: Chandler.

Bateson, G., Jackson, D., Haley, J., *et al.* (1956) Toward a theory of schizophrenia. *Behavioural Science*, 1, 251–264.

Beck, A. T. (1976) *Cognitive therapy and the emotional disorders*. New York: International Universities Press.

Beck, A. T. and Emery, G. (1985) *Anxiety disorders and phobias: a cognitive perspective*. New York: Basic Books.

Beck, A. T. and Freeman, A. (1990) *Cognitive therapy of personality disorders*. New York: Guilford Press.

Beck, A. T., Ward, C. H., Mendelson, M., *et al.* (1961) An inventory for measuring depression. *Archives of General Psychiatry*, 4, 561–571.

Beck, A. T., Rush, A. J., Shaw, B. F., *et al.* (1979) *Cognitive therapy of depression*. New York: Guilford Press.

Beitman, B. D. (1992) *Integration through fundamental similarities and useful differences among the schools*. New York: Basic Books.

Bennett, D. and Parry, G. (1996) The accuracy of reformulation in cognitive analytic therapy: a validation study. *Psychotherapy Research*, 8, 84–103.

Berger, M. (1993) *Use of video in group psychotherapy* (3rd edition).

Bergin, A. E. and Garfield, S. L. eds. (1994) *Handbook of psychotherapy and behaviour change*. Chichester: Wiley.

Bergman, A. and Mahler, M. (1991) The third subphase: rapprochement in the psychological birth of the human infant. London: Maresfield Library.

Beutler, L. E. (1991) Have all won and must all have prizes? Revisiting Luborsky *et al.*'s verdict. *Journal of Consulting and Clinical Psychology*, 59, 226–232.

Bibring, E. (1953) The mechanism of depression. In *Affective disorders* (ed. P. Greenacre), pp. 13–48. New York: International Universities Press.

Bion, W. R. (1961) *Experiences in groups*. London: Tavistock.

Blagys, M. D. and Hilsenroth, M. (2000) Distinctive features of short-term psychodynamic-interpersonal psychotherapy: a review of the comparative psychotherapy process literature. *Clinical Psychology: Science and Practice*, 7, 167–188.

Blatt, S. J., Stayner, D. A., Auerbach, J. S., and Behrends, R. S. (1996) Change in object and self-representations in long-term, intensive, inpatient treatment of seriously disturbed adolescents and young adults. *Psychiatry*, 59, 82–107.

Blatt, S. J., Auerbach, J. S., and Levy, K. N. (1997) Mental representations in personality development, psychopathology, and the therapeutic process. *Review of General Psychology*, 1, 351–374.

Bloch, S. (1995) *Supportive psychotherapy*. Oxford: Oxford University Press.

Bloor, M., McKenagy, N., and Fonkert, D. (1988) *The historical development of therapeutic community approaches. Chapter one of one foot in Eden*. London: Routledge.

Bordin, E. S. (1979) The generalizability of the psychoanalytic concept of the working alliance. *Psychotherapy: Theory, Research, and Practice*, 16, 252–260.

Boscolo, L., Cecchin, G., Hoffman, L., *et al.* (1987) *Milan systemic family therapy: theoretical and practical aspects*. New York: Harper and Row.

Bosley, C. M., Fosbury, J., Parry, D. T., *et al.* (1992) Psychological aspects of patient compliance in asthma. *European Respiratory Journal*, 5.

Bourdon, K. H., Boyd, J. H., and Rae, D. S., *et al.* (1988) Gender differences in phobias: results of the ECA community survey. *Journal of Anxiety Disorders*, 2, 227–241.

Bowlby, J. (1969) *Attachment and loss. Vol. 1: Attachment*. London: Hogarth Press and the Institute of Psycho-Analysis.

Boyd-Franklin, N. (1989) *Black families in therapy: a multisystems approach*. New York: Guilford Press.

Braverman, A. (1989) *Mud and water: a collection of talks by the Zen master Bassui*. San Francisco: North Point Press.

Brockman, B., Poynton, A., Ryle, A., *et al.* (1987) Effectiveness of time-limited therapy carried out by trainees: comparison of two methods. *British Journal of Psychiatry*, 151, 602–609.

Brody, A. L., Saxena, S., Stoessel, P., *et al.* (in press) Regional brain metabolic changes in patients with major depression treated with either paroxetine or interpersonal therapy: preliminary findings.

Brown, D. (1992) *Assessment and selection for groups*. London: Routledge.

Brown, G. W. and Harris, T. O. (1978) *Social origins of depression: a study of psychiatric disorders in women*. London: Tavistock.

Brown, P. M. (1999) *The conversational model*. In Essentials of psychotherapy. Stein, S., Haigh, R., Stein, J. (eds.) Oxford: Butterworth-Heineman

Burns, D. D. Nolen-Hoeksama, S. (1992) Therapeutic empathy and recovery from depression in cognitive-behavioural therapy: a structural equation model. *Journal of Consulting and Clinical Psychology*, 60, 441–449.

Burns, T. (2000) The legacy of therapeutic community practice in modern community mental health services. *Therapeutic Communities*, 21 (3), 165–174.

Caine, T. M., Wijesinghe, D. B. A., and Winter, D. A. (1981) *Personal styles in neurosis: implications for small group psychotherapy and behaviour therapy*. London: Routledge and Kegan Paul.

Casement, P. (1985) *On learning from the patient*. London: Tavistock.

Castonguay, L., Goldfried, M., Wiser, S., *et al.* (1996a) Predicting the effect of cognitive therapy for depression: a study of unique and common factors. *Journal of Consulting and Clinical Psychology*, 64, 497–504.

Castonguay L. G., Goldfried, M. R., Wiser, S., *et al.* (1996b) Predicting the effect of cognitive therapy for depression: a study of unique and common factors. *Journal of Consulting and Clinical Psychology*, 64, 497–504.

Cecchin, G., Lane, G., and Ray, W. A. (1992) *Irreverence: a strategy for therapists' survival*. London: Karnac Books.

Champion, L. A. (2000) *Depression* (2nd edn). Hove: Psychology Press.

Chiesa, M., Iccoponi, E., and Morris, M. (1996) Changes in healthy service utilization by patients with severe borderline personality disorder before and after inpatient psychosocial treatment. *British Journal of Psychotherapy*, 12 (4), 501–512.

Chomsky, N. (1968) *Language and mind*. New York: Harcourt, Brace and World.

Clark, D. (1999) *Social psychiatry: the therapeutic community approach*. London: Jessica Kingsley.

Clarkin, J. F. and Kendall, P. C. (1992) Comorbidity and treatment planning: summary and future directions. *Journal of Consulting and Clinical Psychology*, 60 (6), 904–908.

Clarkin, J. F., Kernberg, O. F. and Yeomans, F. (1999) *Transference-focused psychotherapy for borderline personality disorder patients*. New York, NY: Guilford Press.

Cooklin, A., Miller, A., and McHugh, B. (1983) An institution for change: developing a family day unit. *Family Process*, 22, 453–468.

Cooper, D. (1970) *Psychiatry and anti-psychiatry*. London: Paladin.

Crits- Christoph P., Connelly, M. B., Shappell, S., *et al.* (1999) Interpersonal narratives in Cognitive and Interpersonall Psychotherapies. *Psychotherapy Research*, 9, 22–35.

Crown, S. (1988) Supportive psychotherapy: a contradiction in terms? *British Journal of Psychiatry*, 152, 266–269.

Dare, C. (1992) Change the family, change the child? *Archives of Disease in Childhood*, 67, 643–648.

Dare, C. (1998) Psychoanalysis and family systems: the old, old story? *Journal of Family Therapy*, 20, 165–176.

Dare, C. and Eisler, I. (2000) A multi-family group day treatment programme for adolescent eating disorder. *European Eating Disorders Review*, 8, 4–18.

Davenport, S., Hobson, R. F., and Margison, F. (2000) Treatment development in psychodynamic-interpersonal psychotherapy (Hobson's 'conversational model') for chronic treatment resistant schizophrenia: two single case studies. *British Journal of Psychotherapy*, **16**, 287–302.

Dawson, D. (1988) Treatment of the borderline patient: relationship management. *Canadian Journal of Psychiatry*, **33**, 370–374.

Dawson, N. and McHugh, B. (1986) Application of a family systems approach in an education unit. *Maladjustment and Therapeutic Education*, **4**, 48–54.

Dawson, N. and McHugh, B. (1994) *Parents and children: participants in change*. London: Routledge.

Department of Health (1996) *NHS psychotherapy services in England. Review of strategic policy*. London: HMSO.

Department of Health (1999) *National service framework for mental health*. London: HMSO.

Department of Health (2000) *National service framework for mental health*. London: HMSO.

Department of Health (2001) *Treatment choice in psychological therapies and counselling*. London: HMSO.

Derlega, V. J. and Berg, J. H. (1987) *Self-disclosure: theory, research and therapy*. New York: Plenum Press.

DeRubeis, R. J. and Feeley, M. (1990) Determinants of change in cognitive therapy for depression. *Cognitive Therapy and Research*, **14**, 469–482.

DeRubeis, R. J., Hollon, S. D., Evans, M. D., *et al.* (1982) Can psychotherapies for depression be discriminated? A systematic investigation of cognitive therapy and interpersonal therapy. *Journal of Consulting and Clinical Psychology*, **50**, 744–756.

De Shazer, S. (1982) *Patterns of brief therapy: an ecosystemic approach*. New York: Guilford Press.

Dickinson, A. (1987) *Animal conditioning and learning theory*. New York: Plenum Press.

Dolan, B., Warren, F., Menzies, D., *et al.* (1996) Cost-offset following specialist treatment of severe personality disorders. *Psychiatric Bulletin*, **20**, 413–417.

Dollard, J. and Miller, N. E. (1950) *Personality and psychotherapy*. New York: McGraw-Hill.

Dowling, E. and Osborne, E. (1985) *The family and the school: a joint systems approach to problems with children*. London: Routledge and Kegan Paul.

Edelson, M. (1970) *Sociotherapy and psychotherapy*. Chicago: University of Chicago Press.

Elkin, I., Shea, M. T., Watkins, J. T., *et al.* (1989) National Institute of Mental Health Treatment of Depression Collaborative Research Program: general effectiveness of treatment. *Archives of General Psychiatry*, **46**, 971–982.

Elliott, R., Hill, C. E., Stiles, W. B., *et al.* (1987) Primary therapist response modes: comparison of six rating systems. *Journal of Consulting and Clinical Psychology*, **55**, 218–223.

Elliott, R., Shapiro, D. A., Firth-Cozens, J., *et al.* (1994) Comprehensive process analysis of insight events in cognitive-behavioural and psychodynamic-interpersonal psychotherapies. *Journal of Counselling Psychology*, **41**, 449–463.

Ellis, A. (1962) *Reason and emotion in psychotherapy*. New York: Lyle Stuart.

Ellis, A. (1987) *Handbook of rational-emotive therapy*. New York: Springer.

Ellis, A. (1993) Group rational-emotive and cognitive behavioural therapy. *International Journal of Group Psychotherapy*, **43**, 63–80.

Endicott, J., Spitzer, R., Heiss, J., *et al.* (1976) The global assessment scale. A procedure for measuring overall severity of psychiatric disturbance. *Archives of General Psychiatry*, **33**, 766–771.

Epstein, S. (1994) Integration of the cognitive and the psychodynamic unconscious. *American Psychologist*, **49**, 709–724.

Eysenck, H. J. (1952) The effects of psychotherapy: an evaluation. *Journal of Consulting Psychology*, **16**, 319–324.

Fennell, M. J. V. and Teasdale, J. D. (1987) Cognitive therapy for depression: individual differences and the process of change. *Cognitive Therapy and Research*, **11**, 253–271.

Ferenczi, S. (1922) The further development of an active therapy in psychoanalysis. In *Further contributions to the theory and technique of psychoanalysis*, pp. 198–216. London: Karnac Books, 1980.

Fonagy, P. (1991) Thinking about thinking: some clinical and theoretical considerations in the treatment of a borderline patient. *International Journal of Psycho-Analysis*, **72**, 1–18.

Fonagy, P. and Target, M. (1997) Attachment and reflective function: their role in self-organization. *Development and Psychopathology*, 9, 679–700.

Fonagy, P., Kachele, H., Krause, R., *et al.* (1999) *An open door review of outcome studies in psychoanalysis*. London: International Psychoanalytical Association.

Fosbury, J. A. (1994) *Cognitive analytic therapy with poorly controlled type I diabetic patients*. Paper presented at the European Association for the Study of Diabetes, 27 September to 1 October, Dusseldorf, Germany.

Foucalt, M. (1975) *The Birth of the Clinic*. Brighton: Harvester.

Foulkes, S. H. (1946) On group analysis. *International Journal of Psychoanalysis*, 27, 46–51.

Foulkes, S. H. (1975) *Group analytic psychotherapy*. London: Gordon and Breach.

Frank, E., Kupfer, D. J., Wagner, E. F., *et al.* (1991) Efficacy of interpersonal therapy as a maintenance treatment of recurrent depression. *Archives of General Psychiatry*, 48, 1053–1059.

Frank, J. D. (1973) *Persuasion and healing* (2nd edition). Baltimore: Johns Hopkins University Press.

Frank, J. D. (1982) *Therapeutic components shared by all psychotherapies*. Washington, DC: American Psychological Association.

Frank, J. D. (1988) Specific and non-specific factors in psychotherapy. *Current Opinion in Psychiatry*, 1, 289–292.

Freud, S. (1912) The dynamics of transference. In *Standard edition of the complete psychological works of Sigmund Freud*, Vol. 12. London: Hogarth.

Freud, S. (1919) Lines of advance in psycho-analytic therapy. In *Standard edition of the complete psychological works of Sigmund Freud*, Vol. 17, pp. 157–168. London: Hogarth.

Frieswyk, S. H., Allen, J. G., Colson, D. B., Coyne, L., Gabbard, G. O., Horwitz, L., and Newsom, G. (1986) Therapeutic alliance: its place as a process and outcome variable in dynamic psychotherapy research. *Journal of Consulting and Clinical Psychology*, 54, 32–38.

Gabbard, G. O. (ed.) (1994) *Psychodynamic psychiatry in clinical practice: the DSM-IV edition*. Washington: American Psychiatric Press.

Garfield, S. (1994) Eclecticism and integration in psychotherapy: developments and issues. *Clinical Psychology: Science and Practice*, 1, 123–127.

Garfield, S. (1998) Some comments on empirically supported treatments. *Journal of Consulting and Clinical Psychology*, 66, 121–125.

Garfield, S. and Bergin, A. (1986) *Handbook of psychotherapy and behavior change: an empirical analysis*. New York: Wiley.

Gaston, L. (1990) The concept of the alliance and its role in psychotherapy: theoretical and empirical considerations. *Psychotherapy*, 27, 143–153.

Gaston, L., Thompson, L., Gallagher, D., *et al.* (1998) Alliance, technique, and their interactions in predicting outcome of behavioural, cognitive, and brief dynamic therapy. *Psychotherapy Research*, 8, 190–209.

Goldberg, D. P., Hobson, R. F., Maguire, G. P., *et al.* (1984) The clarification and assessment of a method of psychotherapy. *British Journal of Psychiatry*, 114, 567–575.

Goldfried, M. R. (1995) *From cognitive-behavior therapy to psychotherapy integration*. New York: Springer.

Goldfried, M. R., Raue, P. J., and Castonguay, L. G. (1998) The therapeutic focus in significant sessions of master therapists: a comparison of cognitive-behavioural and psychodynamic-interpersonal interventions. *Journal of Consulting and Clinical Psychology*, 66 (5), 803–810.

Goldfried, M. R. and Wolfe, B. (1998) Toward a more clinically valid approach to therapy research. *Journal of Consulting and Clinical Psychology*, 66, 143–150.

Goldner, V., Penn, P., Sheinberg, M., *et al.* (1990) Love and violence: gender paradoxes in volatile attachments. *Family Process*, 29, 343–364.

Goldsamt, L. A., Goldfried, M. R., Hayes, A. M., and Kerr, S. (1992) Beck, Meichenbaum, and Strupp: a comparison of three therapists on the dimension of therapist feedback. *Psychotherapy*, 29, 167–176.

Gunderson, J. G., Frank, A. F., Ronningstam, E. F., *et al.* (1989) Early discontinuance of borderline patients from psychotherapy. *Journal of Nervous and Mental Disease*, 177, 38–42.

Guthrie, E. (1999) Psychodynamic interpersonal therapy. *Advances in Psychiatric Treatment*, 5, 135–145.

Guthrie, E. and Moorey, J. (1998) Brief psychodynamic interpersonal therapy for patients with severe psychiatric illness which is unresponsive to treatment. *British Journal of Psychotherapy*, 15, 155–166.

Guthrie, E., Moorey, J., Margison, F., *et al.* (1999) Cost-effectiveness of brief psychodynamic-interpersonal therapy in high utilizers of psychiatric services. *Archives of General Psychiatry*, 56, 519–526.

Haigh, R. (1999) 'The quintessence of a therapeutic environment – five essential qualities'. London: Jessica Kingsley.

Haley, J. (1963) *Strategies of psychotherapy*. New York: Gruner and Stratton.

Hamilton, M. (1960) A rating scale for depression. *Journal of Neurology, Neurosurgery and Psychiatry*, 23, 56–62.

Hamilton, V. (1996) *The analyst's preconscious*. Hillsdale, NJ: Analytic Press.

Hardy, G. E., Barkham, M., Shapiro, D. A., *et al.* (1995) Credibility and outcome of cognitive-behavioural and psychodynamic-interpersonal psychotherapy. *British Journal of Clinical Psychology*, 34, 555–569.

Harrison, T. (1999) *Bion, Rickman, Foulkes, and the Northfield Experiments*. London: Jessica Kingsley.

Hartman, D. and Rozewein, L. (1996) The psychiatric consultation reconsidered. *Psychiatric Bulletin*, 20, 580–583.

Hayes, A. M., Castonguay, L. G., and Goldfried, M. R. (1996) The effectiveness of targeting the vulnerability factors of depression in cognitive therapy. *Journal of Consulting and Clinical Psychology*, 64, 623–627.

Hayes, S. C. (1982) The role of the individual case in the production and consumption of clinical knowledge. In *Handbook of research methods in clinical psychology* (ed. P. C. Kendall and J. N. Butcher). New York: Wiley.

Henry, W. P., Schacht, T. E., and Strupp, H. H. (1986) Structural analysis of social behaviour: application to a study of interpersonal process in differential psychotherapeutic outcome. *Journal of Consulting and Clinical Psychology*, 54, 27–31.

Herink, R. (1980) *The psychotherapy handbook*. New York: Meridian.

Higgitt, A. and Fonagy, P. (1992) Psychotherapy in borderline and narcissistic personality disorder. *British Journal of Psychiatry*, 161, 23–24.

Hinshelwood, R. D. (1988) Psychotherapy in an in-patient setting. *Current Opinions in Psychiatry*, 1, 304–308.

Hinshelwood, R. D. (1997) *Therapy or Coercion?* London: Karnac.

Hobson, R. F. (1974) Loneliness. *Journal of Analytical Psychology*, 19, 71–89.

Hobson, R. F. (1985) *Forms of feeling: the heart of psychotherapy*. New York: Basic Books.

Holmes, J. (1988) Supportive analytic psychotherapy: an account of two cases. *British Journal of Psychiatry*, 152, 824–829.

Holmes, J. (1992) *Between art and science: essays in psychotherapy and psychiatry*. London: Routledge.

Holmes, J. (1993) *John Bowlby and attachment theory*. London: Routledge.

Holmes, J. (1995) Supportive psychotherapy: the search for positive meanings. *British Journal of Psychiatry*, 167, 437–445.

Holmes, J. (1996a) *Attachment, autonomy, intimacy*. Hillsdale, NJ: Jason Aronson.

Holmes, J. (1996b) Psychotherapy and memory – an attachment perspective. *British Journal of Psychotherapy*, 13 (2), 204–218.

Holmes, J. (2001) *The search for the secure base: psychotherapy and attachment theory*. London: Routledge.

Holmes, J. and Lindley, R. (1991) *The values of psychotherapy*. Oxford: Oxford University Press.

Holyoak, K. J., Koh, K., and Nisbett, R. E. (1989) A theory of conditioning: inductive learning within rule-based default hierarchies. *Psychological Review*, 96, 315–340.

Horowitz, M. and Marmac, C. (1984) Brief psychotherapy of bereavement reactions: the relationship of process to outcome. *Archives of General Psychiatry*, 41, 438–448.

Horvath, A. O. and Symonds, B. D. (1991) Relation between working alliance and outcome in psychotherapy: a meta-analysis. *Journal of Consulting and Clinical Psychology*, **38**, 139–149.

Hunter, D. (2000) Disease management: has it a future? *British Medical Journal*, **320**, 530.

Imber, S. D., Pilkonis, P. A., Sotsky, S. M., *et al.* (1990) Mode-specific effects among three treatments for depression. *Journal of Consulting and Clinical Psychology*, **58**, 352–359.

Jacobson, N. S. and Gortner, E. T. (2000) Can depression be de-medicalised in the 21st century: scientific revolutions, counter-revolutions and the magnetic field of normal science. *Behaviour Research and Therapy*, **38**, 103–117.

James, W. (1962) *Psychology: briefer course*. London: Collier.

Jenkins, H. and Asen, K. E. (1992) Family therapy without the family: a framework for systemic practice. *Journal of Family Therapy*, **14**, 1–14.

Jensen, J. P., Bergin, A. E., and Greaves, D. W. (1990) The meaning of eclecticism: new survey and analysis of components. *Professional Psychology: Research and Practice*, **21**, 124–130.

Johnson, D. R. (1997) An existential model of group therapy for chronic mental conditions. *International Journal of Group Psychotherapy*, **47**, 227–250.

Jones, E. (1993) *Family systems therapy: developments in the Milan-systematic therapies*. Chichester: John Wiley.

Jones, E. and Asen, E. (2000) *Systemic couple therapy and depression*. London and New York: Karnac Books.

Jones, E. E. and Pulos, S. M. (1993) Comparing the process in psychodynamic and cognitive-behavioral therapies. *Journal of Consulting and Clinical Psychology*, **61**, 306–316.

Jones, M. (1968) *Social psychiatry in practise*. Harmondsworth: Pelican Books.

Karterud, S. *et al.* (1998) The Norwegian network of psychotherapeutic day hospitals. *Therapeutic Communities*, **19**, 15–28.

Kay, J. (2001) *Integrated treatment: an overview*. Washington, DC: American Psychiatric Publishing.

Kennard, D. (1998) *Introduction to therapeutic communities*. London: Jessica Kingsley.

Kernberg, O. F. (1975) *Borderline conditions and pathological narcissism*. New York: Jason Aronson.

Kernberg, O. (2000) Psychoanalysis, psychoanalytic psychotherapy and supportive psychotherapy: contemporary controversies. *International Journal of Psychoanalysis*, **81**, 853–879.

Kernberg, O. F., Selzer, M. A., Koenigsberg, H. W., *et al.* (1989) *Psychodynamic psychotherapy of borderline patients*. New York: Basic Books.

Klein, D. K. and Ross, D. C. (1993) Reanalysis of the National Institute of Mental Health Treatment of Depression Collaborative Trial. *Neuropsychopharmacology*, **8** (3), 241–251.

Klerman, G. K. (1979) *The psychobiology of affective states: the legacy of Adolf Meyer*. Baltimore: Johns Hopkins University Press.

Klerman, G. L., Weissman, M. M., Rounsaville, B. J., *et al.* (1984) *Interpersonal psychotherapy of depression*. New York: Basic Books.

Knowles, J. (1995) *How I assess for group psychotherapy*. London: Routledge.

Kohut, H. (1972) Thoughts on narcissism and narcissistic rage. *Psychoanalytic Study of the Child*, **27**, 360–400.

Kohut, H. (1977) *The Restoration of the Self*. New York: International Universities Press.

Kolb, J. (1993) In a review of supportive psychotherapy by Rockland L, 1986–1992. *Hospital and Community Psychiatry*, **44**, 1053–1060.

Koons, C. R., Robins, C. J., Bishop, G. K., *et al.* (1998) *Efficacy of dialectical behavior therapy with borderline women veterans: a randomized controlled trial*. Paper presented at a meeting of the Association for the Advancement of Behaviour Therapy, Washington, DC.

Krause, I. B. and Miller, A. (1995) *Culture and family therapy*. London: Routledge.

Krupnick, J. L., Sotsky, S. M., Simmons, S., *et al.* (1996) The role of the therapeutic alliance in psychotherapy and pharmacotherapy outcome: findings in the NIMH Collaborative Research Programme. *Journal of Consulting and Clinical Psychology*, **64**, 532–539.

Kuipers, L., Leff, J., and Lam, D. (1992) *Family work for schizophrenia: a practical guide*. London: Gaskell.

Laing, R. D. and Esterson, A. (1964) *Sanity, madness and the family*. London: Tavistock.

Lambert, M. J. and Bergin, A. E. (1994) The effectiveness of psychotherapy. In *Handbook of psychotherapy and behavior change* (ed. A. E. Bergin and S. L. Garfield), pp. 143–189. New York: Wiley.

Lang, P. and McAdam, E. (1997) Narrative-ating: future dreams in present living. *Human Systems: The Journal of Systemic Consultation and Management*, 8 (1), 3–12.

Laqueur, H. P., La Burt, H. A., and Morong, E. (1964) Multiple family therapy: further developments. *International Journal of Social Psychiatry*, 10, 69–80.

Lees, J., Manning, N., and Rawlings, B. (1999) *Therapeutic community effectiveness. A systematic international review of therapeutic community treatment for people with personality disorders and mentally disordered offenders.* NHS Centre for Reviews and Dissemination: University of York (CRD Report 17).

Leff, J., Kuipers, L., Berkowitz, R., et al. (1982) A controlled trial of social intervention in the families of schizophrenia patients. *British Journal of Psychiatry*, 141, 121–134.

Leff, J., Vearnals, S., Brewin, C., et al. (2000) The London depression intervention trial: an RCT of antidepressants versus couple therapy in the treatment and maintenance of depressed people with a partner: clinical outcomes and costs. *British Journal of Psychiatry*, 177, 95–100.

Leiman, M. (1992) The concept of sign in the work of Vygotsky, Winnicott and Bakhtin: further integration of object relations theory and activity theory. *British Journal of Medical Psychology*, 65, 209–221.

Leiman, M. (1994) Projective identification as early joint action sequences: A Vygotskian addendum to the procedural sequence object relations model. *British Journal of Medical Psychology*, 67, 97–106.

Leiman, M. (1997) *Early identification of problematic experiences by dialogical sequence analysis.* Paper presented at the International Meeting of the Society for Psychotherapy Research, Geilo, Norway.

Levins, R. and Lewontin, R. (1985) *The dialectical biologist.* Cambridge, MA: Harvard University Press.

Lewinsohn, P. (1974) *A behavioral approach to depression.* New York: Winston-Wiley.

Linehan, M. M. (1987) Dialectical behavioural therapy: a cognitive behavioural approach to parasuicide. *Journal of Personality Disorders*, 1, 328–333.

Linehan, M. M. (1993a) *Cognitive-behavioural treatment of borderline personality disorder.* New York: Guilford Press.

Linehan, M. M. (1993b) *The skills training manual for treating borderline personality disorder.* New York: Guilford Press.

Linehan, M. M. (1997a) *Validation and psychotherapy.* Washington, DC: American Psychological Association.

Linehan, M. M. (1997b) Self-verification and drug abusers: implications for treatment. *Psychological Scientist*, 8, 181–184.

Linehan, M. (2000) The empirical basis of dialectical behaviour therapy: development of new treatments versus evaluation of existing treatments. *Clinical Psychology: science and practice*, 7, 113–119.

Linehan, M. M. and Egan, K. (1983) *Asserting yourself.* London: Multimedia Publication.

Linehan, M. M., Armstrong, H. E., Suarez, A., et al. (1991) Cognitive-behavioural treatment of chronically parasuicidal borderline patients. *Archives of General Psychiatry*, 48, 1060–1064.

Linehan, M. M., Heard, H. L., and Armstrong, H. E. (1993) Naturalistic follow-up of a behavioral treatment for chronically parasuicidal borderline patients. *Archives of General Psychiatry*, 50, 971–974.

Linehan, M. M., Tutek, D. A., Heard, H. L., et al. (1994) Interpersonal outcome of cognitive behavioural treatment for chronically suicidal borderline patients. *American Journal of Psychiatry*, 151, 1771–1776.

Linehan, M. M., Schmidt, H., Dimeff, L. A., et al. (1999) Dialectical behavior therapy for patients with borderline personality disorder and drug dependence. *American Journal on Addictions*, 8, 279–292.

Luborsky, L. (1984) *Principles of psychoanalytic psychotherapy: a manual for supportive-expressive (SE) treatment.* New York: Basic Books.

Luborsky, L., Singer, B., and Luborsky, L. (1975) Comparative studies of psychotherapies: is it true that 'everybody has won and all must have prizes'? *Archives of General Psychiatry*, 37, 471–481.

Luborsky, L., Woody, G. E., McLellan, A. T., *et al.* (1982) Can independent judges recognise different psychotherapies? An experience with manual-guided therapies. *Journal of Consulting and Clinical Psychology*, 50, 49–62.

Luborsky, L., McLellan, A. T., Woody, G. E., *et al.* (1985) Therapists success and its determinants. *Archives of General Psychiatry*, 42, 602–611.

Luborsky, L., Crits-Christoph, P., Mintz, J., *et al.* (1988) *Who will benefit from psychotherapy? Predicting therapeutic outcomes.* New York: Basic Books.

Luborsky, L., McLellan, A. T., Diguer, L., *et al.* (1997) The psychotherapist matters: comparison of outcomes across 22 therapists and 7 patient samples. *Clinical Psychology: Science and Practice*, 4, 53–65.

Maguire, G. P., Goldberg, D. P., Hobson, R. F., *et al.* (1984) Evaluating the teaching of a method of psychotherapy. *British Journal of Psychiatry*, 144, 575–580.

Mahoney, M. J. (1993) Diversity and the dynamics of development in psychotherapy integration. *Journal of Psychotherapy Integration*, 3, 1–14.

Main, T. F. (1946) The hospital as a therapeutic institution. *Bulletin Menninger Clinic*, 10, 66–68.

Main, T. F. (1983) *The concept of the therapeutic community: its variations and vicissitudes.* London: Routledge and Kegan Paul.

Malan, D. H., Balfour, F. H. G., Hood, V. G., and Shooter, A. M. N. (1976) Group psychotherapy: a long term follow-up study. *Archives of General Psychiatry*, 33, 1303–1314.

Mallinckrodt, B. (2000) Attachment, social competencies, social support, and interpersonal process in psychotherapy. *Psychotherapy Research*, 10, 239–266.

Manning, N. (1989) *The therapeutic community movement: charisma and routinisation.* London and New York: Routledge and Kegan Paul.

Maple, N. and Simpson, I. (1995) *CAT in groups.* Chichester: Wiley.

Margison, F. (1991) *Learning to listen: teaching and supervising basic psychotherapeutic skills.* London: Churchill Livingstone.

Margison, F. (1999) Psychotherapy: advances in training methods. *Advances in Psychiatric Treatment*, 5, 329–337.

Margison, F. (2000) Editorial cognitive analytic therapy: a case study in treatment development. *British Journal of Medical Psychology*, 73, 145–149.

Margison, F. and Moss, S. (1994) Teaching psychotherapy skills to inexperienced psychiatry trainees using the conversational model. *Psychotherapy Research*, 4, 141–148.

Margison, F., Barkham, M., Evans, C. E., *et al.* (2000) Measurement and psychotherapy: evidence based practice and practice based evidence. *British Journal of Psychiatry*, 177, 123–130.

Marmar, C. R., Gaston, L., Gallagher, D., *et al.* (1989) Alliance and outcome in late-life depression. *Journal of Nervous and Mental Disease*, 177, 464–472.

Marshall, P. (1997) A reconviction study of HMP Grendon therapeutic community. *Home Office Research and Statistics: Research Findings Number 53.*

Martin, D. J., Garske, J. P. and Katherine Davis, M. (2000) Relation of the therapeutic alliance with outcome and other variables: a meta-analytic review. *Journal of Consulting and Clinical Psychology*, 68, 438–450.

Martin, J. and Margison, F. (2000) *The conversational model.* London: Sage.

Martin, S. and Martin, E. (1999) *Spectrographic analyses pre and post interpersonal psychotherapy.* Paper presented at the Current practice in interpersonal psychotherapy, Annual meeting of the American Psychiatric Association, Washington, DC.

Marziali. E, N., T., Munroe-Blum, H., and Dawson, D. (1989) Manual and training materials for relationship management psychotherapy. *Unpublished manuscript.*

Mason, B. (1993) Towards positions of safe uncertainty. *Human Systems*, 4, 189–200.

Maturana, H. and Varela, F. J. (1980) *Autopoesis and cognition: the realization of the living.* Dordrecht: D. Reidel.

May, G. G. (1982) *Will and spirit.* San Francisco: Harper and Row.

Meares, R. (1993) The metaphor of play: disruption and restoration in the borderline experience. Northvale, NJ: Jason Aronson.

Meares, R. and Hobson, R. F. (1977) The persecutory therapist. *British Journal of Medical Psychology*, 50, 349–359.

Meares, R., Stevenson, J., and Comerford, A. (1999) Psychotherapy with borderline patients: a comparison between treated and untreated cohorts. *Australian and New Zealand Journal of Psychiatry*, 33, 467–472.

Meichenbaum, D. and Turk, D. (1987) *Facilitating treatment adherence: a practitioner's guidebook*. New York: Plenum Press.

Menzies, R. G. and Clarke, J. C. (1993) A comparison of in vivo and vicarious exposure in the treatment of childhood water phobia. *Behaviour Research and Therapy*, 31, 9–15.

Miller, A. and Thomas, L. (1994) Introducing ideas about racism and culture into family therapy training. *Context*, 20, 25–29.

Miller, A.L., Rathus, J.H., Linehan, M.M., Wetzler, S. and Leigh, E. (1997) Dialectical behavior therapy adapted for suicidal adolescents. *Journal of Practical Psychiatry and Behavioral Health*, 3, 78–86.

Millon, T. (1991) Classification in psychopathology: rationale, alternatives, and standards. *Journal of Abnormal Psychology*, 100, 245–261.

Minuchin, S. (1974) *Families and family therapy*. London: Tavistock.

Minuchin, S. and Fishman, H. C. (1981) *Family therapy techniques*. Cambridge, MA: Harvard University Press.

Minuchin, S., Montalvo, B., Guerney, B. G., *et al.* (1967) *Families of the slums*. New York: Basic Books.

Minuchin, S., Rosmon, B., and Baker, L. (1978) *Psychosomatic families: anorexia nervosa in context*. Cambridge, MA: Harvard University Press.

Morant, N. W. F. and Warren, F. (2001) Outsiders on the inside: researchers in therapeutic communities. London: Jessica Kingsley.

Myers, J. K., Weissman, M. M., Tischler, G. L., *et al.* (1984) Six-month prevalence of psychiatric disorders in three communities. *Archives of General Psychiatry*, 41, 959–967.

Newell, A. (1990) *Unified theories of cognition*. Cambridge, MA: Harvard University Press.

NHS (1996) *NHS psychotherapy services in England: review of strategic policy*. Department of Health: Wetherby.

Nitsun, M. (1996) *The anti-group*. London: Routledge.

Norcross, J. C. and Goldfried, M. R. (eds.) (1992) *Handbook of psychotherapy integration*. New York: Basic Books.

Norton, K. (1992) A culture of enquiry – its preservation or loss. *Therapeutic Communities*, 13 (1), 3–25.

Norton, K. R. W. (1999) *Joining and leaving*. Vol. . London: Jessica Kingsley.

Norton, K. and Fainman, D. (1994) Applications of the TC concept: dynamic psychotherapy training. *Therapeutic Communities*, 15 (2), 99–105.

Norton, K. R. W. and McGauley, G. (1997) *Counselling difficult clients*. London: Sage.

Orlinsky, D. and Howard, K. (1986) *Process and outcome in psychotherapy*. Chichester: Wiley.

Ormont, L. (1990) The craft of bridging. *International Journal of Group Psychotherapy*, 40, 3–17.

Ormont, L. (1999) Progressive emotional communication: criteria for a well-functioning group. *Group Analysis*, 32, 139–150.

Pearce, J. M. (1997) *Animal learning and cognition: an introduction*. Hove: Psychology Press.

Pearce, W. B. and Cronen, V. E. (1980) *Communication, action and meaning*. New York: Praeger.

Pedder, J. (1986) *Attachment and a new beginning*. London: Free Association.

Perris, C. and McGorry, P. D. (eds.) (1998) *Cognitive psychotherapy of psychotic and personality disorders: handbook of theory and practice*. Chichester: Wiley.

Perry, J. C., Banon, E., and Ianni, F. (1999) Effectiveness of psychotherapy for personality disorder. *American Journal of Psychiatry*, 156 (9), 1312–1321.

Pines, M. (1998) *Psychic development and the group analytic situation*. (Vol. 19). London: Routledge.

Pines, M. (1999) Forgotten pioneers of therapeutic communities. *Therapeutic Communities*, 20, 23–42.

Pinskner, H. (1994) The role of theory in teaching supportive psychotherapy. *American Journal of Psychotherapy*, 48, 530–542.

Piper, W. E., Debanne, E. G., Bienvenu, J. P., *et al.* (1986) Relationships between the object focus of therapist interventions and outcome in short-term individual psychotherapy. *Archives of General Psychiatry*, 48, 946–953.

Piper, W. E., Azim, H. F. A., Joyce, A. S., *et al.* (1991) Transference interpretations, therapeutic alliance, and outcome in short-term individual psychotherapy. *British Journal of Medical Psychology*, 59, 1–11.

Piper, W. E., Rosie, J. S., Azim, H. F. A., *et al.* (1993) A randomised trial of psychiatric day treatment for patients with affective and personality disorders. *Hospital and Community Psychiatry*, 44, 757–763.

Power, M. J. (1987) *Cognitive theories of depression*. New York: Plenum Press.

Power, M. J. (1989) Cognitive therapy: an outline of theory, practice and problems. *British Journal of Psychotherapy*, 5, 544–556.

Power, M. J. (1991) Cognitive science and behavioural psychotherapy: where behaviour was, there shall cognition be? *Behavioural Psychotherapy*, 19, 20–41.

Power, M. J. and Brewin, C. R. (1991) From Freud to cognitive science: a contemporary account of the unconscious. *British Journal of Clinical Psychology*, 30, 281–310.

Power, M. J. and Brewin, C. R. (1997) *The transformation of meaning in psychological therapies*. Chichester: Wiley.

Power, M. J. and Champion, L. A. (1986) Cognitive approaches to depression: a theoretical critique. *British Journal of Clinical Psychology*, 25, 201–212.

Power, M. J. and Champion, L. A. (2000) *Models of psychological problems* (2nd edn). Hove: Psychology Press.

Power, M. J. and Dalgleish, T. D. (1997) *Cognition and emotion: from order to disorder*. Hove: Psychology Press.

Power, M. J., Champion, L. A., and Aris, S. J. (1988) The development of a measure of social support: the significant others (SOS) scale. *British Journal of Clinical Psychology*, 27, 349–358.

Pretzer, J. L. and Beck, A. T. (1996) A cognitive theory of personality disorder. In *Major theories of personality disorder* (ed Clarkin, J. F. and Lenzweger, M. F.), pp. 36–105. New York: Guilford Press.

Prochaska, J. O. and DiClemente, C. C. (1992) *The transtheoretical approach*. New York: Basic Books.

Rachman, S. (1997) *The evolution of cognitive behaviour therapy*. Oxford: Oxford University Press.

Rawlings, B. (1998) The therapeutic community in the prison: problems in maintaining therapeutic integrity. *Therapeutic Communities*, 19 (4), 281–294.

Rawlings, B. and Yates, R. (in press) *Therapeutic communities for the treatment of drug users*. London: Jessica Kingsley.

Roberts, G. (1992) The origins of delusion. *British Journal of Psychiatry*, 161, 298–308.

Robinson, L. A., Berman, J. S., and Neimeyer, R. A. (1990) Psychotherapy for the treatment of depression: a comprehensive review of controlled outcome research. *Psychological Bulletin*, 108, 30–49.

Rockland, L. H. (1987) A supportive approach: psychodynamically oriented supportive therapy – treatment of borderline patients who self-mutilate. *Journal of Personality Disorders*, 1, 350–353.

Rockland, L. (1989) *Supportive psychotherapy: a psychodynamic approach*. New York: Basic Books.

Rogers, C. R. (1957) The necessary and sufficient conditions of therapeutic personality change. *Journal of Consulting Psychology*, 21, 95–103.

Rogers, C. R. (1986) *Client-centered therapy*. San Francisco: Jossey-Bass.

Rose, M. (1997) *Transforming hate into love*. London: Routledge.

Roth, A. and Fonagy, P. (1996) *What works for whom? A critical review of psychotherapy research*. New York: Guilford Press.

Russell, G. F. M., Szmukler, G., Dare, C., *et al.* (1987) An evaluation of family therapy in anorexia nervosa and bulimia nervosa. *Archives of General Psychiatry*, 44, 1047–1056.

Ryle, A. (1990) *Cognitive analytic therapy: active participation in change.* Chichester: Wiley.

Ryle, A. (1992) Critique of a Kleinian case presentation. *British Journal of Medical Psychology,* 65, 309–317.

Ryle, A. (1993) Addiction to the death instinct? A critical review of Joseph's paper 'Addiction to near death'. *British Journal of Psychotherapy,* 10, 88–92 (with response by Ann Scott, 93–96).

Ryle, A. (1995a) Research relating to CAT. In *Cognitive analytic therapy: developments in theory and practice* (ed. A. Ryle), pp. 175–189. Chichester: Wiley.

Ryle, A. (1995b) Defensive organizations or collusive interpretations? A further critique of Kleinian theory and practice. *British Journal of Psychotherapy,* 12 (1), 60–68.

Ryle, A. (1997) *Cognitive analytic therapy and borderline personality disorder: the model and the method.* Chichester: John Wiley.

Ryle, A. and Golynkina, K. (2000) Effectiveness of time-limited cognitive analytic therapy of borderline personality disorder: factors associated with outcome. *British Journal of Medical Psychology,* 73, 197–210.

Sackett, D. L., Rosenberg, W. M., Gray, J. A. M., *et al.* (1996) Evidence based medicine: what it is and what it isn't. *British Medical Journal,* 312, 71–72.

Safran, J. D. and Segal, Z. V. (1991) *Interpersonal processes in cognitive therapy.* New York: Basic Books.

Sandler, J. (1976) Actualisation and object relationships. *Journal of the Philadelphia Association of Psychoanalysis,* 3, 59–70.

Scholz, M. and Asen, E. (2001) Multiple family therapy with eating disordered adolescents: concepts and preliminary results. *European Eating Disorders Review,* 9, 33–42.

Schuff, H. and Asen, K. E. (1996) *The disturbed parent and the disturbed family.* Cambridge: Cambridge University Press.

Schwarzenbach, F. and Leff, J. (1995) Treatment integrity of couple, cognitive and drug therapy for depression. Unpublished manuscript. London: Institute of Psychiatry.

Scott, A. (1995) Response to Anthony Ryle. *British Journal of Psychotherapy,* 10 (1), 93–95.

Selvini Palazzoli, M., Boscolo, L., Cecchin, G., *et al.* (1978) *Paradox and counter-paradox.* New York: Jason Aronson.

Selvini Palazzoli, M., Boscolo, L., Cecchin, G., *et al.* (1980) Hypothesizing-circularity-neutrality; three guidelines for the conductor of the session. *Family Process,* 19, 3–12.

Selvini Palazzoli, M., Cirillo, S., Selvini, M., *et al.* (1989) *Family games.* London: Karnac Books.

Shapiro, D. A., Firth-Cozens, J., and Stiles, W. B. (1989) The question of therapists' differential effectiveness: a Sheffield psychotherapy project addendum. *British Journal of Psychiatry,* 154, 383–385.

Shapiro, D. A., Rees, A., Barkham, M., *et al.* (1995) Effects of treatment duration and severity of depression on the maintenance of gains after cognitive-behavioral and psychodynamic-interpersonal psychotherapy. *Journal of Consulting and Clinical Psychology,* 63, 378–387.

Shaw, B. F. and Wilson-Smith, D. (1988) *Training therapists in cognitive-behaviour therapy.* Berlin: Springer-Verlag.

Shelton, J. L. and Levy, R. L. (1981) *Behavioral assignments and treatment compliance: a handbook of clinical strategies.* Champaign, IL: Research Press.

Skynner, R. (1976) *One flesh: separate persons. Principles of family and marital therapy.* London: Constable.

Sloane, R. B., Staples, F. R., Cristol, A. H., *et al.* (1975) Short-term analytically oriented psychotherapy versus behaviour therapy. *American Journal of Psychiatry,* 132, 373–377.

Sotsky, S. M., Glass, D. R., She, M. T., *et al.* (1991) Patient predictors of response to psychotherapy and pharmacotherapy: findings in the NIMH treatment of depression collaborative research program. *American Journal of Psychiatry,* 148, 997–1008.

Spiegler, M. D. and Guevremont, D. C. (1993) *Contemporary behavior therapy* (2nd edn). Stanford: Stanford University Press.

Stanley, B., Ivanoff, A., Brodsky, B., and Oppenheim, S. (1998) *Comparison of DBT and 'treatment as usual' in suicidal and self-mutilating behaviour.* Paper presented at the Association for the advancement of Behaviour Therapy, Washington, DC.

Stevenson, J. and Meares, R. (1992) An outcome study of psychotherapy for patients with borderline personality disorder. *American Journal of Psychiatry*, 149, 358–362.

Stevenson, J. and Meares, R. (1999) Psychotherapy with borderline patients: II. A preliminary cost benefit study. *Australian and New Zealand Journal of Psychiatry*, 33, 473–477.

Stieper, D. R. and Wiener, D. N. (1959) The problem of interminability in outpatient psychotherapy. *Journal of Consulting Psychology*, 23, 237–242.

Stiles, W. (1979) Verbal response modes and psychotherapeutic technique. *Psychiatry*, 42, 49–62.

Stiles, W. B., Shapiro, D. A., and Elliott, R. (1986) Are all psychotherapies equivalent? *American Psychologist*, 41, 165–180.

Stiles, W., Shapiro, D. A., and Firth-Cozens, J. A. (1988) Verbal response mode use in contrasting psychotherapies: a within subjects comparison. *Journal of Consulting and Clinical Psychology*, 56, 727–733.

Stiles, W. B., Elliott, R., Llewelyn, S. P., *et al.* (1990) Assimilation of problematic experiences by clients in psychotherapy. *Psychotherapy*, 27, 411–420.

Stiles, W. B., Agnew-Davies, R., Hardy, G. E., *et al.* (1998) Relations of the alliance with psychotherapy outcome: findings in the second Sheffield psychotherapy project. *Journal of Consulting and Clinical Psychology*, 66, 791–802.

Stolorow, R., Brandchaft, B., and Atwood, G. (1987) *Psychoanalytic treatment: an intersubjective approach.* Hillsdale, NJ: Analytic Press.

Stone, W. N. and Klein, E. B. (1999) The waiting-list group. *International Journal of Group Psychotherapy*, 49, 417–428.

Stricker, G. and Gold, J. (1993) *Comprehensive handbook of psychotherapy integration.* New York: Plenum.

Sullivan, H. S. (1953) *The interpersonal theory of psychiatry.* New York: Norton.

Swann, W. B., Stein-Seroussi, A., and Giesler, R. B. (1992) Why people self-verify. *Journal of Personality and Social Psychology*, 62, 392–401.

Teasdale, J. (1999) *Multi-level theories of emotion.* Chichester: Wiley.

Teasdale, J. and Barnard, P. (1993) *Affect, cognition and change.* Hove: Lawrence Erlbaum Associates.

Truax, C. B. and Carkhuff, R. R. (1967) *Toward effective counselling and psychotherapy: training and practice.* Chicago: Aldine.

Turner, T. (1998) Introduction from editor. *Psychiatry Reviews*, 3 (3).

Tyrer, P. (1995) Supportive psychotherapy. *British Journal of Psychiatry*, 167, 446–447.

Vaillant, G. E. (1977) *Adaptation to life.* Boston, MA: Little Brown.

Vaillant, G. E. (1992) *Ego mechanisms of defense: a guide for clinicians and researchers.* Washington, DC: American Psychiatric Association Press.

Von Foerster, H. and Zopf, G. W. (1962) *Principles of self-organization.* New York: Pergamon.

Vygotsky, L. (1986) *Thought and language.* Cambridge, MA: MIT Press.

Wachtel, P. (1977) *Psychoanalysis and behaviour therapy: toward an integration.* New York: Basic Books.

Wachtel, P. L. and McKinney, M. K. (1992) *Cyclical psychodynamics and integrative psychodynamic therapy.* New York: Basic Books.

Waldinger, R. J. and Gunderson, J. G. (1984) Completed therapies with borderline patients. *American Journal of Psychotherapy*, 38, 190–202.

Wallerstein, R. S. (1986) *Forty-two lives in treatment: a study of psychoanalysis and psychotherapy.* New York: Guilford Press.

Wallerstein, R. (ed.) (1992) *The common ground of psychoanalysis.* Northvale, New Jersey: Jason Aronson.

Waltz, J., Addis, M., Koerner, K., *et al.* (1993) Testing the integrity of a psychotherapy protocol: assessment of adherence and competence. *Journal of Consulting and Clinical Psychology*, 61, 620–630.

Watts, D. and Morgan, G. (1994) Malignant alienation. *British Journal of Psychiatry*, 164, 11–15.

Watzlawick, P., Jackson, D., and Beavin, J. (1967) *Pragmatics of human communication.* New York: W. W. Norton.

Watzlawick, P., Weakland, J., and Fisch, R. (1974) *Change: principles of problem formation and problem resolution*. New York: W. W. Norton.

Weissman, M. M., Prusoff, B. A., DiMascio, A., *et al.* (1979) The efficacy of drugs and psychotherapy in the treatment of acute depressive episodes. *American Journal of Psychiatry*, 136, 555–558.

Weissman, M. M., Klerman, G. L., Prusoff, B. A., *et al.* (1981) Depressed outpatients: results of one year after treatment with drugs and/or interpersonal psychotherapy. *Archives of General Psychiatry*, 38, 51–55.

Weissman, M. M., Markowitz, J. C., and Klerman, G. K. (2000) *Comprehensive guide to interpersonal psychotherapy*. New York: Basic Books.

Whitaker, C. (1975) Psychotherapy of the absurd. *Family Process* 14, 1–16.

White, M. (1989) *Selected papers*. Adelaide: Dulwich Centre Publications.

White, M. (1997) *Narratives of therapists' lives*. Adelaide: Dulwich Centre Publications.

White, M. and Epston, D. (1990) *Narrative means to therapeutic ends*. New York: W. W. Norton.

Wilber, K. (1979) *No boundary*. Boulder, CO: New Science Library.

Wilflety, D. E., Frank, M. A., Welch, R., *et al.* (1998) Adapting interpersonal psychotherapy to a group format (IPT-G) for binge eating disorder. *Psychotherapy Research*, 8, 379–391.

Wilkinson, G., Moore, B., and Moore, P. (1999) *Treating people with depression*. Oxford: Radcliffe Medical Press.

Wiser, S. and Goldfried, M. R. (1996) Verbal interventions in significant psychodynamic-interpersonal and cognitive-behavioural therapy sessions. *Psychotherapy Research*, 6, 309–319.

Wolfe, B. E. and Goldfried, M. R. (1988) Research on psychotherapy integration: recommendations and conclusions from an NIMH workshop. *Journal of Consulting and Clinical Psychology*, 56, 448–451.

Yalom, I. D. (1995) *Theory and practice of group psychotherapy* (4th edn). New York: Basic Books.

Young, J. E. (1990) *Cognitive therapy for personality disorders: a schema-focused approach*. Sarasota, FL: Professional Resource Exchange.

Index

Entries are arranged in letter-by-letter alphabetical order. Page numbers in *Italics* refer to tables.